The RHS Encyclopedia of Practical Gardening

GARDEN STRUCTURES

RICHARD WILES

Editor-in-chief Christopher Brickell

MITCHELL BEAZLEY

The Royal Horticultural Society's Encyclopedia of Practical
Gardening
© Mitchell Beazley Publishers 1979, 1992

The Royal Horticultural Society's Encyclopedia of Practical
Gardening: Garden Structures
© Mitchell Beazley Publishers 1990

First published in this edition 1992

ISBN 1 85732 901 5

Edited and designed by
Mitchell Beazley Publishers
part of Reed International Books
Michelin House
81 Fulham Road
London SW3 6RB

Contents

Introduction

Gardening is about making as well as planting. This is true whether you are inheriting a virgin site or modifying an existing garden. The overall character of any garden will depend to a large extent on its basic shape, its boundaries, and various built or excavated features such as steps, rock gardens or ponds.

A truly creative gardener thus needs not only to be a horticulturist but also to learn some of the skills of a builder, carpenter, surveyor, architect, landscape architect and electrician. This may sound daunting, and many gardeners prefer to bring in professional help for such work. However, all the basic skills required for garden-making can be learned by anyone who has the necessary patience and is prepared to acquire the correct tools.

The "do-it-yourself" approach is invariably less expensive than having a job tackled professionally, and there is a great deal of satisfaction to be gained from constructing something oneself.

Not all gardeners will feel competent to tackle the larger-scale jobs described in this book. The intention, however, is that you should take as little, or as much, from these pages as you wish. Having read through a complete section to determine how complex a job is, you may decide to leave part, or most, of the work to a professional. But even if you do delegate most of the job, a clear understanding of how a structure is put together can be invaluable in your role as planner and coordinator.

Garden Structures illustrates the kinds of materials available in garden construction, and includes detailed information on the standard sizes, typical quantities and optional qualities that can be obtained from local suppliers. The step-by-step instructions and illustrations are designed to make even complex-sounding tasks as straightforward as possible.

Where relevant, shortcuts are suggested, including the use of special tools and equipment which may make a job less labour-intensive.

Selecting materials 1

Making a garden usually involves a great deal more than organizing the planting and laying the lawn. All gardens must have basic structural elements—walls, fences, paths and so on—in order to link, separate or screen various areas of the plot. This hard framework will be composed of different materials put together to create a particular effect. The result must be satisfactory in both visual and practical terms.

The materials used in garden construction vary enormously in cost, durability, maintenance requirements and aesthetic appeal. To make the best of your garden it is important that you choose the materials bearing all these factors in mind.

Buying timber

Timber is one of the most popular materials used in gardens, and is suitable for numerous kinds of structure. It is cut from many varieties of trees, but for practical purposes can be divided into two main groups: hardwoods and softwoods. These terms can be misleading, as they are not necessarily an accurate guide to actual hardness of the wood, but in general terms softwoods are usually softer than hardwoods.

Softwoods are derived from coniferous, or cone-bearing, trees, which include pine, redwood, fir and larch. Hardwoods come from broad-leaved trees such as beech, mahogany, teak and oak.

Softwood Economical to buy and easy to saw, plane and sand, softwoods will also hold screws well. Nails, however, can cause the wood to split along the grain.

Sold in a vast range of lengths and sections (see chart, right), softwoods are available in two forms: "sawn" or "planed" ("prepared"). The sawn type is less expensive than the planed type and is generally used where a smooth, fine appearance is unnecessary. Sawn wood is suitable for most of the timber construction work mentioned in this book.

Planed timber, often known by the abbreviation PAR (which means "planed all round"), is sold in nominal planed sizes. The actual size may be about $\frac{7}{8}$in (3mm) less all round. Obviously, when something that demands precise measurements is being made, such as mortise-and-tenon joints, it is essential to take the actual dimensions of the timber rather than working on the nominal size.

Timber is usually obtainable in metric lengths, although some suppliers confusingly offer it in units of 300mm, which is often referred to as a "metric foot". This, however, actually measures $11\frac{3}{4}$in. So beware when ordering: 6 metric feet of timber might measure only 5ft $10\frac{1}{2}$in. If the timber you want is available only in units of metric feet, you will have to order 7 metric feet to obtain a 6ft length, and there will thus be some waste.

Hardwood Less common and usually much more costly than softwoods, hardwoods are not normally used for general garden construction. They are used for garden furniture, where their natural beauty enhances the appearance of a table or seat. Unlike softwoods, planed hardwoods are sold in their actual rather than nominal sizes.

Preserving timber

Most timber will succumb to rot or insect attack unless properly treated with a suitable preservative. One exception is western red cedar, a softwood which naturally weathers well, assuming a mellow silvery-grey tone with time.

When ordering softwood for outdoor use, it is best to ask for "vacuum-treated", "pressure-impregnated", or "tanalized" timber, which has been injected with a preservative fluid against fungal decay and insect attack. However, pre-treated timber is more costly than untreated timber, and you may prefer to buy the latter and treat it yourself. Preservative can be brushed on, sprayed on or—the most effective method—you can soak the timber in a makeshift bath of preservative.

Types of preservative

Creosote is the traditional preservative for softwood, although it is the one with the shortest lifespan: the timber must be treated every two years to ensure good protection. Based on oil and tar, creosote has a strong and distinctive smell and will stain the wood a dark tone. Unfortunately, creosote may cause damage to plants—particularly when it is freshly applied. If fences have been treated with creosote, climbers or other plants should not be grown in the vicinity until the toxic effects have worn off, which is frequently not for several months. It is also impractical to treat fences with creosote on a regular basis if climbers are trained against it. Solvent-based preservatives are a better choice in terms of protective quality and longevity. They are produced in a number of popular wood shades and as a clear finish. Unlike creosote, most of these fluids can be over-painted.

Avoiding timber defects

All timber should have been "seasoned" in order to reduce its sap and moisture content. This makes it easier to work with and gives it greater resistance to rot, but it also often introduces certain defects which could mar your work. Select your timber carefully to avoid the following common faults, which are largely associated with too rapid or uneven drying processes.

Knots Knots can present real problems when you are working with wood: if the knots ooze resin you will not only find the timber difficult to saw but also the sticky resin is likely to bleed through any subsequent paint finish you apply. Applying a shellac knotting compound will, however, seal "live" knots against oozing. Dry, loose knots often fall out, leaving a hole in the timber.

Warps Hold one end of a piece of timber and peer down its length to look for bad warping across or along the grain, and reject any badly misaligned timber.

Shakes Look out for splits along the grain, or between the annular rings of the timber, which could become worse and—in serious cases—even cause the timber to fall apart, especially when nails are driven in to the timber, close to a flaw.

Surface checking A covering of fine cracks need not be a serious fault; very fine ones can be planed away or filled before painting—but reject timber with wider cracks.

Bricks and blocks

For walls, barbecues, planters, flights of steps and other solid structures in the garden, bricks and blocks are widely used. Durable in damp conditions, masonry structures also have strength and stability, enabling them to support loadings from other constructions—the timber roof of a pergola, for example. Strength is not only inherent in the density of the brick or block: the bonding arrangement in which the individual units are laid provides rigidity as well as a decorative face for the structure.

A guide to sawn and planed timber sizes

thickness (mm)	12.5	16	19	25	32	38	50	75	100	125	150	175	200	225	300
12.5	*			*		*	*	*	*		*				
16		*		*		*	*								
19			*	*		*	*	*	*		*	*		*	*
25				*		*	*	*	*	*	*	*	*	*	*
32					*		*	*	*		*	*		*	*
38						*	*	*	*		*			*	*
50							*	*	*		*	°	°	*	°
75								*	*		*	°	°	*	
100									*				°	*	*

Key

* = sawn or planed

° = sawn only

Selecting materials 2

Bricks Nowadays made in standard metric sizes which correspond roughly to the old imperial sizes, modern bricks measure 225 × 112.5 × 75mm ($8\frac{7}{8}$ × $4\frac{3}{8}$ × 3in). The measurements are nominal and allow for the mortar joints: the actual size of a brick is $\frac{3}{8}$in (10mm) less all round. This makes calculation of the height of a wall or structure much easier: if the mortar joint allowance were not part of the brick's nominal dimension you would have to allow for each mortar joint independently.

Bricks are commonly made of clay that is fire-burnt to invest them with their strength and durability. Moulded concrete bricks, or other types made from calcium silicate, are also available. Clay bricks are produced in two main qualities: "ordinary" for general use and "special" for use in exposed sites. Calcium silicate bricks are graded from Class Two (the weakest) to Class Seven (the strongest). Dense, hard engineering bricks are essential for use in damp conditions, or below ground level. Impervious to water, they are produced in Classes A or B, which refer to strength and water resistance. Class A are stronger, and class B more water-resistant.

Bricks are also described by their colour and place of origin, although choice in this respect does not influence their use in the garden—merely their aesthetic appearance. If possible, choose bricks of a colouring that matches, complements or blends with local brick types. Choose "facing" bricks, which have attractive face textures, where appearance is important. Choose the cheaper "commons" where a good-looking face is not a vital consideration.

Blocks Some walling blocks resemble natural stone and offer a softer, more natural appearance than bricks. They are moulded from concrete and may have natural stone aggregate added for a more authentic appearance and texture. Various colours are available usually mimicking local stone colours: buff tones, greens, yellows, reds and greys are popular. Only one long face and one end face are usually textured, by being either "split" (having the appearance of split stone) or "pitched" (artificially chipped to give rougher appearance). Obviously, these faces are used on the visible side of the structure.

Most blocks conform roughly to brick sizes for ease of laying and matching to areas of brickwork. However, some blocks are modular in format, comprising a moulded facing which resembles several smaller blocks laid in an overlapping bond. These larger units enable a wall to be constructed more rapidly than using individual units.

Breezeblocks Where the building requirements are purely structural—for example, if you are going to render or clad a structure with timber, and the appearance of the blockwork itself is immaterial—large, grey breezeblocks may be needed instead of bricks. Moulded from concrete in various densities, breezeblocks measure 6 to 9in high × 18, 24 or $24\frac{1}{2}$in long × $2\frac{1}{2}$in thick (150 to 225mm high × 450, 600 or 620mm long × 60mm thick). The purpose and size of the structure, and the type and condition of the ground, will determine the density of the breezeblocks used.

Pierced screen blocks Moulded from concrete, usually white, screen blocks are used to construct screening walls which have minimal inherent strength. The blocks, pierced with various geometric patterns, measure about 12 × 12 × 4in (300 × 300 × 100mm), and are laid in "stack bond"—one on top of the other, without overlapping joins—between slotted "pilaster" blocks. The hollow-centred pilaster blocks form supporting piers at intervals along a screen wall, and are usually reinforced with iron bars and the cavities filled with mortar.

Natural stone
Bought from a quarry or large garden centre, natural stone can be used to construct features such as a traditional dry-stone wall (see page 72) or rock garden (see page 150).

Used for building walls, natural stone is both heavy and expensive—and it requires some skill to use it successfully. It is usually laid without mortar, relying on the weight of the stones and the way they are laid to create a rigid, long-lasting structure. A manufactured type of "dry-stone walling block" is available from some suppliers. This offers an easier way to create a country-style wall: the blocks are lighter and fairly regular in form, but are still laid without mortar.

More irregularly-shaped stones and boulders should be used to build a rock garden or create natural-looking rocky outcrops.

Concrete

Cast concrete is versatile and economical. It can be used as a means of forming a base for a garden structure, or as a surface in its own right. It consists of a mixture of Portland cement, the aggregates sharp sand and stones (known as "ballast" when combined), and water. Chemical reaction results in the cement and water forming a paste, which binds the aggregates together into a dense material which, before it starts to harden, can be moulded and shaped.

For small jobs, simply buy pre-bagged dry mixes of concrete, which contain all the ingredients, properly proportioned and ready for mixing with water. You can buy pre-mixed bags containing between $5\frac{1}{2}$lb (2.5kg) and 1cwt (50kg) of concrete.

For large jobs, it is more economical to buy the ingredients separately in bulk and mix them yourself. You can mix by hand, or use a hired motorized mixing machine. However, for a job such as casting a driveway or large patio slab, which will require over 4 cubic yards (3 cubic metres) of concrete, it is best to buy ready-mixed concrete. Ready-mix is delivered to your house by mixer lorry and—given suitable access—it is possible to have the load dumped directly onto the prepared foundations (see pages 8-17). With such a large amount of wet concrete, speed in spreading and compacting the mix is essential before hardening (curing) commences, so some assistance will be needed.

Different jobs demand different concrete mixes, the different mixes being determined by the ratio of ingredients (by volume). There are three commonly used mixes, as described on page 10.

Surface materials

There is an enormous range of materials that can be used to form the surface of a path or patio, or the treads of a flight of garden steps.
Paving slabs Made of moulded concrete, paving slabs are ideal for laying in large areas where a decorative appearance is required. The range of sizes, shapes, colours and face-textures is considerable, and the slabs can be mixed and matched successfully with most other paving materials.

There are basically two types of concrete slab. "Cast" slabs are about 2in (50mm) thick and intended for light to medium use; "hydraulically pressed" slabs are only $1\frac{1}{2}$in (38mm) thick, lighter in weight but much stronger and better suited to a surface, such as a drive, which will have to support the weight of a car.

The most popular size for square slabs is 18 × 18in (450 × 450mm) although both smaller and larger versions are made. Rectangular half-slabs are also available, as are hexagonal slabs which range in size from about 9in (225mm) square to about 27 × 18in (675 × 450mm). Circular slabs of similar diameters are also available.

Broken slabs, used as crazy paving, offer the durability of a paved surface with a random appearance that suits a more informal setting.
Pavers On a smaller scale, paving blocks or bricks moulded from concrete or clay, with patterned or textured top surfaces, will produce a highly decorative finish for a path or patio, especially when they are laid in a complex pattern of curves, angles and geometric shapes.

Sizes correspond roughly to those of traditional bricks—8 × 4 × $2\frac{1}{2}$in (200 × 100 × 65mm). There are also shaped versions which can be laid in an "interlocking" design without the need to bed them in mortar; these are easy to lay.
Gravel and stones Although not really suitable for use on a large scale, cobblestones are excellent as small features that complement areas of other paving materials. Bedded in mortar on prepared foundations, they create a heavily textured surface.

Gravel can be used as an attractive drive or path surface, or as a decorative infill for other areas. For a drive or path, a layer of "pea" gravel should be raked over a sub-base of hardcore (broken bricks and concrete).

Gravel gardens can be features in their own right. The surface of the soil is sprinkled with a 25mm (1in) layer of fine stones. Not only does this create an attractive surface but it also discourages weeds.

Types of foundations

Foundations are necessary for any structure that you build in the garden, in order to support and spread its load to firm ground. Whether you are constructing a solid footing on which to build a brick boundary wall, or laying the base for a garden outbuilding, the basic principles are similar.

Strip foundations

Small structures such as brick planters and masonry garden walls must be built on strip foundations. These consist of a trench filled with a layer of compacted hardcore (which comprises broken stones or bricks) topped with fresh concrete.

The foundation is built wider than the wall, so that the weight of the wall is spread out at an angle of 45 degrees ("the angle of dispersion") from its base into the foundation and on into the subsoil. To gauge the correct width of foundation for a given wall width you should, as a rule of thumb, allow two times the width of the masonry.

The depth of the concrete foundation depends on the height and thickness of the wall and on the condition of the soil, but in general it should be half as deep as it is wide, and project beyond the ends of the wall by half the width of the masonry. For example, a wall over six courses of bricks high would require a trench about 16in (400mm) deep.

Brick foundations

There may be no need to build concrete foundations if your wall or other structure is less than about six courses of bricks high and less than about 20ft (6m) long. A foundation strip consisting of bricks laid crosswise on a well-compacted subsoil base topped with a thin layer of sand will probably be sufficient. The bricks are grouted with a "slurry" comprising a creamy mixture of cement and water.

Foundations for steps

Garden steps built into a bank (see page 50) will require a cast concrete footing at the base of the flight, beneath the first riser (the vertical part of the step), to prevent the structure from slipping downwards. The treads (the part on which you walk) should be laid on well-compacted hardcore, while the intermediate risers can be built either directly on the back of the tread below, or else on a base of compacted hardcore behind each tread.

For freestanding garden steps (see page 54), which lead, say, up to a raised area of lawn from a lower level, it is acceptable to put down concrete strip foundations to support the outer walls of the structure, with the inner area filled with compacted hardcore.

Paving foundations

Paving slabs, block pavers and other paving materials must be laid on a surface that is firm, flat and stable. In many cases a base of well-compacted subsoil is sufficient for laying paving, but where the soil is soft it will be necessary to add a layer of compacted hardcore to prevent the paving from sinking.

Hardcore contains many hollows, even after consolidation by garden roller, which are filled by spreading a "blinding" layer of sand or a "lean" concrete mix (ie 1 part cement : 3 parts sand) over the surface and levelling it with the back of a garden rake. (Always remember to clean tools thoroughly after dealing with wet concrete. It is very difficult to remove traces once the concrete has had a chance to dry.)

Paving slabs or other small-scale pavers can be laid directly on the blinding layer using mortar, although some block pavers can be laid loose on a prepared sand bed without mortar.

Cast slab (raft) foundations

Whereas a small, lightweight garden shed or solid fuel bunker can be erected on a foundation of paving slabs on a hardcore base, larger structures such as a garage or a summerhouse must be built on a firmer base. A slab (or raft) foundation consists of a cast concrete surface laid over the prepared base.

Slab foundations are also used in drive- or path-laying, where no above-ground structure is involved but the top of the cast concrete forms the top surface of the drive or path, or creates a suitable base for another surfacing material.

The slab is formed by erecting a timber framework or "formwork" at the perimeter of the site, fixed to stakes driven into the

SOIL CONDITIONS

For the foundation to provide adequate support for the structure, the concrete must be laid on firm subsoil. This lies beneath the softer topsoil, the depth of which varies from area to area, but which could be anything between 4 and 12in (100 and 300mm). What this means is that you have to dig down to the subsoil before you start to dig out enough for the depth of the concrete itself, which is another 3 to 6in (75 to 150mm).

Types of subsoil also vary in their load-bearing capacities: for example, chalky soils can support more weight than clay soils, but sandy soils support less weight. Basically, the weaker the subsoil the wider you must make the foundation slab. If you are unsure about the prevailing soil conditions in your area, consult your local authority's Building Control Department.

The climate plays an important part in determining how deep to place your foundation. Shrinkage and swelling of the earth due to prolonged dry spells or periods of rain can cause sufficient ground movement to crack the foundation concrete. For this reason you have to lay the foundation below the point at which it can be affected by these conditions.

Once you have dug the trench you can either lay the minimum thickness of concrete required for the size of structure you are building, and be prepared to lay extra courses of bricks to reach ground level, or else fill the trench to ground level and save on the number of bricks you use.

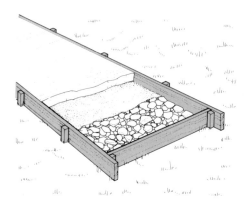

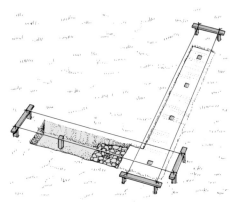

Slab foundations comprise a layer of hardcore to firm up the soil base, a blinding layer of sand to fill voids in the hardcore, and fresh concrete moulded and levelled in timber formwork fixed to stakes at the perimeter of the slab.

Strip foundations comprise a trench containing well-rammed hardcore topped with a blinding layer of sand and fresh concrete levelled to guide depth pegs in the base; trench-fill versions, used where the topsoil is very deep, are filled to ground level with concrete.

ground (see pages 14-15). The wet concrete is poured onto the prepared base, compacted and levelled to the top of the formwork, which is removed after the mix has hardened or "cured".

Correct compaction and curing of the concrete slab are essential if the slab is to be strong enough for its intended purpose (if it is a driveway it might have to support the weight of a car or a caravan) and to withstand the extremes of weather to which it will be exposed.

Concrete

Choosing a concrete mix

It is vital that you mix the concrete ingredients—sand, cement and aggregates—in the correct proportion to give the most suitable strength of mix for the job. There are basically three mixes:

A: general purpose for surface slabs and bases where you need a minimum thickness of 3 to 4in (75 to 100mm).

B: light duty for garden paths and bases less than 3in (75mm) thick.

C: bedding, a weaker mix used for garden wall foundations and bedding in slabs.

What to order

When ordering the ingredients to make up 35 cubic feet (1 cubic metre) of the three different concrete mixes described above, consult this chart:

Mix	Cement: number of 110lb (50kg) bags	Sharp sand plus aggregate	OR	All-in aggregate
A	× 6	17⅔cu ft (0.5cu m) + 26½cu ft (0.75cu m)		35⅓cu ft (1cu m)
B	× 8	17⅔cu ft (0.5cu m) + 26½cu ft (0.75cu m)		35⅓cu ft (1cu m)
C	× 4	17⅔cu ft (0.5cu m) + 26½cu ft (0.75cu m)		45cu ft (1.25cu m)

What to mix

Concrete mixes are made up by volume, and it is convenient to use a bucket as your measure. For the concrete mixes previously listed, mix the following, remembering that each mix requires about half a bucket of water (although this does depend on how damp the sand is).

Mix A
1 bucket cement
2½ buckets sharp sand
4 buckets washed aggregate

OR
1 bucket cement
5 buckets all-in aggregate

Mix B
1 bucket cement
2 buckets sharp sand
3 buckets washed aggregate

OR
1 bucket cement
3¼ buckets all-in aggregate

Mix C
1 bucket cement
3 buckets sharp sand
6 buckets washed aggregate

OR
1 bucket cement
8 buckets all-in aggregate

Making a strip foundation

1 Fix profile boards at each end of the proposed trench, with nails attached to the cross-pieces to mark the trench width.

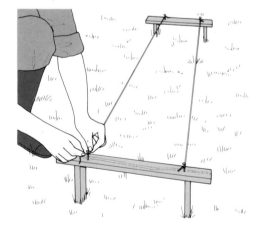

2 Attach stringlines to the width markers, linking both sets of profile boards at each end of the proposed trench.

Strip foundations 1

LAYING STRIP FOUNDATIONS

Strip foundations set in a trench are used as footings for garden walls and small structures. First mark out the position of the trench on the ground.

Setting up "profile" boards

Profile boards are used to set out the position of the foundation trench on the ground. Hammer pairs of 24in (600mm) long pegs of 2 × 1in (50 × 25mm) rough-sawn softwood into the ground at each end of the proposed foundation and nail cross-pieces on top.

Hammer nails partially into each cross-piece to correspond with the width of the trench and link the cross-pieces with string stretched between the nails. Transfer the positions of the strings to the ground by scoring a line in the earth with a spade, or by carefully sprinkling sand along the lines as a guide.

Remove the strings but leave the profile boards in place as a guide to bricklaying later.

Marking out corners

If the wall or structure incorporates corners, you will need to mark out a trench to suit. Set up stringlines and profile boards at right angles to the first set, checking that the intersecting lines are set at 90 degrees by holding a builder's square (see page 15) in the angle.

Digging the trench

First remove the topsoil and set aside for possible re-use elsewhere in the garden. Dig the trench to the correct depth. Lever out any large stones carefully, possibly retaining them for use in a rock garden (see page 150).

Keep the base of the trench consistently deep and the walls vertical. If the soil is very friable (of a crumbly consistency) you might have to shore it up temporarily with plywood shuttering and timber props until the concrete is added.

Hammer 1in (25mm) sq wooden pegs into the base of the trench so that they protrude by the depth of the concrete (plus the depth of any hardcore) needed for the foundations.

Place a straight-edged plank and spirit level across the tops of the pegs and adjust them so that they are horizontal, hammering them down or raising them accordingly.

Where the soil is soft, shovel hardcore into the trench and ram it down using a sledgehammer or a stout length of timber (if using timber, wear thick gardening gloves to protect your hands from splinters).

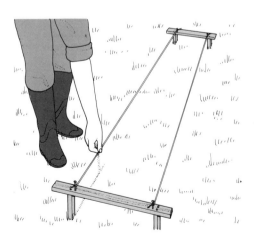

3 Sprinkle sand along the strings to transfer the width marks to the ground, then remove the strings. Leave the profile boards in place.

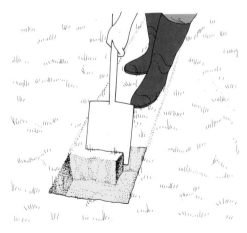

4 Dig out the trench to the required depth, making sure that you keep the base flat and the sides upright.

Strip foundations 2

Dealing with drainpipes

If the trench crosses underground drainage pipes, carefully dig away the soil around the obstruction and down to the depth you require for your foundation, then cast the concrete at each side. Surround the pipe with gravel to protect it from damage, then bridge it with a double thickness of paving slabs laid across the concrete foundation.

Mixing the concrete

For simple strip foundations it is not too laborious to mix the concrete by hand. Mix up sufficient concrete on a hard, flat surface near the foundations—an existing concrete surface will do, or a panel of hardboard.

Mix the sand and aggregate, then tip the cement over the aggregate and form into a crater. Add half the water by bucket, then collapse the sides of the heap and turn it over several times. Run your spade across the mix in steps to test the consistency: when mixed correctly the ridges should be firm and lump-free.

If you hire a motorized mixing machine, follow the mixing instructions on page 16. Set the machine on a firm, flat surface and wedge the wheels. Familiarize yourself with the oper-

ating instructions—be sure to use a reputable hire company that supplies such information. Never put your hands or a shovel into the drum while it is turning; wear goggles.

Tipping in the concrete

Before adding the concrete, soak the trench with water and allow it to drain away. This prevents the soil sucking too much moisture from the mix too rapidly, which could cause the concrete to crack. Shovel the concrete into the trench. Slice into the mix several times with your spade in order to dispel air bubbles.

Compact the concrete by tamping the surface with the edge of a length of stout timber in a chopping motion so that it is level with the top of the depth guide pegs. Place a spirit level on top of the plank to check that the concrete is horizontal. Leave the pegs in the concrete.

Allow the concrete to set. If it dries out too quickly, it is liable to crack. During hot weather cover the concrete with old sacking dampened with water. You should not lay concrete during very cold weather, but if there is any likelihood of a snap frost, cover the concrete with blanket loft insulation, lay

5 Drive in pegs so that they protrude by the depth of concrete needed. Check the pegs are level.

6 Soak the trench with water, then add hardcore where the ground is fairly soft and ram down well with a sledgehammer.

MAKING STEPPED FOUNDATIONS

On sloping or uneven ground a stepped foundation trench is needed. You will need to measure the vertical height of the slope in order to determine how many steps the foundations should comprise. Stick a length of cane in the ground at the base of the slope and a timber peg at the top. Stretch a length of string between the two. Set the string horizontal with a spirit level, then measure the length of the cane from the ground to the string. Divide this length by the depth of an ordinary brick (or a multiple thereof) to give the number of levels your sloping foundation will need.

Dig out the lower level first, levelling it with the aid of timber pegs driven into the centre and a spirit level spanning across the tops. Dig out the next level, taking

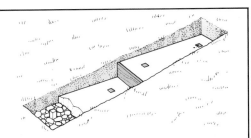

care not to collapse it by treading on it; work from the side if possible.

When casting the fresh concrete, start with the lower step, laying the mix on well-rammed hardcore. Use timber pegs driven into the base as a guide to the depth of concrete needed.

Fix a length of board at the front of the second (and subsequent) steps to retain the concrete for the level above it. Secure the board with wooden stakes driven into the ground at the side of the board.

a sheet of heavy-gauge polythene over this and weight it down at the edges with bricks.

Do not walk on the concrete surface for about 48 hours: otherwise curing may not be complete. You can start to build on the foundation after two days, but take care not to crumble the vulnerable edges. Leave the formwork in place for one week.

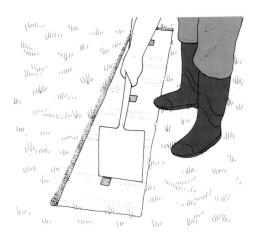

7 Pour in the concrete and work in by slicing into the mix with a spade. This dispels air bubbles which could weaken the foundations.

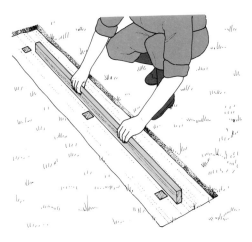

8 Compact the concrete by tamping with a straight-edged length of timber and level it to the tops of the guide pegs.

Slab foundations 1

Making slab foundations
Slab or raft foundations are necessary to support larger garden structures, and as a surface for paths and drives. Timber formwork is used to mould and contain the wet concrete until it has set hard. Set up stringlines stretched between wooden pegs at the perimeter of the proposed foundations, then dig out the topsoil until you reach firm subsoil. Compact the subsoil by trampling over the surface with your boots, or run a garden roller across the site.

Constructing formwork
When selecting timber for formwork, choose reasonably straight-edged lengths that are free from serious warps. Old floorboards about $\frac{1}{2}$ or $\frac{3}{4}$in (12 or 20mm) thick are ideal as formwork.

Drive pointed timber stakes into the ground just outside the stringlines using a club hammer. Space stakes at each corner and then about 4ft (1.2m) apart along the stringlines. Place a straight-edged plank with a spirit level on top across the stakes and set them level.

Constructing formwork

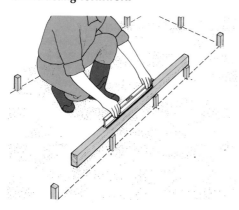

1 Drive pointed stakes into the perimeter of the proposed foundation and set horizontal.

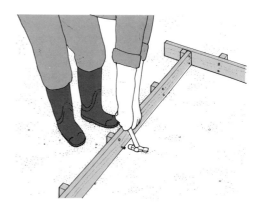

2 Nail formwork to the stakes, butted end-to-face at the corners.

4 Add the hardcore to the foundation and compact thoroughly using a garden roller.

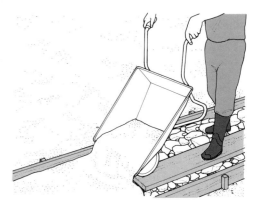

5 Tip the concrete from a mixing machine or barrow directly onto the foundations.

Remove the stringlines, then nail the form-work planks to the inner face of the stakes. Butt up the boards end-to-face at the corners to make it easier to knock the formwork apart when the concrete has set.

On long foundations—for example, if you are making a path—you might have to butt-join formwork planks end-to-end: secure both planks by nailing to extra stakes.

Incorporating a drainage fall
Large slabs should be laid with a slight slope

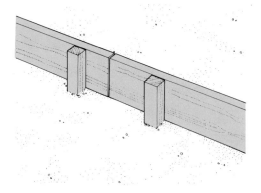

3 On long slabs butt-join formwork boards end-to-end and support with extra stakes.

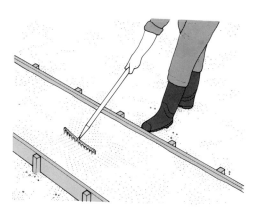

6 Rake out the concrete so that it is level and just protruding above the formwork.

MAKING A BUILDER'S SQUARE

Use a builder's square to check the corners of your formwork. You can make one from three lengths of straight-edged 2 × 1in (50 × 25mm) timber, screwed together to form a triangle in the ratio 3:4:5. A convenient size has sides measuring 24, 32 and 40in (about 600, 800 and 1,000mm) long. Use the builder's square to check the corners of the stringlines during setting out, and then the formwork, before you nail it to the stakes.

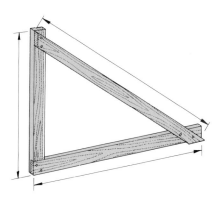

Make a builder's square from three lengths of softwood in the ratio 3:4:5.

Use the builder's square to check the formwork is set at 90 degrees.

Slab foundations 2

to one side in order to drain off surface rainwater rapidly. The slope must be consistent. An easy way to set the slope is by spanning across the formwork with a spirit level on a long plank. Place a small offcut of wood—called a "shim"—underneath the end of the plank at the proposed lower side of the slab. Adjust the depth of this formwork plank so that the spirit level registers horizontal: the slab will therefore slope by the thickness of the "shim" which should be about 1in (25mm).

Adding the hardcore
You may need to add hardcore to the foundation base to give a suitably firm surface. Although the depth of hardcore depends on how soft the soil is and how thick the concrete slab will be (which should be determined by its intended use), in general you should allow about the same depth of hardcore as the depth of the concrete.

Buy hardcore (from a builder's merchant or demolition site) made only from broken bricks and concrete; do not use plaster pieces as they disintegrate and may cause the foundations to subside. Tip barrowloads of hardcore into the foundations and spread it out as evenly as possible. Consolidate the hardcore by running over the surface with a garden roller, or ram down well with a sledgehammer. Add more hardcore pieces to fill voids in the surface.

Top the hardcore with a layer of sand to fill any holes which would otherwise be wasteful of concrete. Rake out the sand as flat as possible and finish off by drawing the back of the rake across the surface.

Mixing the concrete
Mix up the concrete, ideally using a motorized mixing machine (which you can readily hire) close to the foundations: you can then simply pour the mix directly onto the prepared base.

When mixing concrete by petrol-driven or electric machine, add half the aggregate by bucket to the revolving drum, followed by half the water by hosepipe (fitted with an isolating nozzle for convenient control of the flow). Tip in the remaining ingredients and operate the mixer until the concrete has reached the correct consistency which is

when the concrete falls cleanly off the mixer blades and holds its shape.

Pouring the concrete
If you have to wheel the mix to the foundations by barrow, set up a walkway of planks extending over the formwork and into the centre of the foundation to avoid damaging any adjoining lawn or flower bed. You will need a heavy-duty barrow, as a lightweight type will not be able to cope with the heavy load of the wet concrete.

Use a garden rake to spread the concrete over the entire surface, so that it stands just proud of the formwork boards. Slice a spade into the mix at the sides several times to work the concrete well into place.

Compacting the concrete
Place a stout timber beam across the slab, resting on the formwork at the edges, and, with the help of an assistant, work along the slab with a chopping motion. This compacts the concrete and helps to dispel the air bubbles which could cause weakness and cracking.

Work back along the slab, this time drawing the tamping beam back and forth with a sawing motion. This action levels the concrete to the tops of the formwork planks and tends to highlight any hollows in the surface. Fill these straight away with fresh concrete, then compact and level once more.

When the concrete has been well compacted, tap the sides of the formwork boards with a hammer to help settle the mix.

Finishing and curing
The rough texture left by the tamping beam is an ideal surface for building on, with a good "key" for mortar. But if you want a smoother finish—say, if the slab itself forms the finished surface—use a steel trowel or wooden float (a tool with a handle attached to a square wooden surface) with a circular motion to produce a finer texture. Alternatively, simply draw the bristles of a stiff broom across the surface to give a ridged, non-slip finish.

Cover the slab with heavy-gauge polythene held down at the edges by bricks. If a cold spell threatens, you can insulate the slab by spreading a layer of sand over the polythene.

Although you can remove the formwork after about 24 hours, you should not start to build on, or walk over, the concrete for about four days to ensure complete curing. When you come to remove the formwork, simply tap the protruding corner pieces apart with a hammer. With the formwork removed, fill around the slab with soil so that it is level with the surrounding ground.

Adding reinforcement

Where your concrete slab will double as the surface for a drive, it is worth while considering adding reinforcement, particularly if you have more than one vehicle, or own a caravan. This is also a good safeguard where the soil is fairly soft or unstable, whether the surface will receive heavy treatment or not.

Reinforcement can be in the form of galvanized steel mesh, available from builder's merchants in rolls. A length with a 4 × 4in (100 × 100mm) mesh, made from $\frac{1}{4}$in (6mm) diameter wire, is suitable for this purpose. Lay the mesh on the hardcore prior to casting the fresh mix.

Casting the concrete

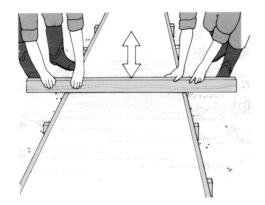

1 Compact the concrete using a stout timber beam with a chopping motion.

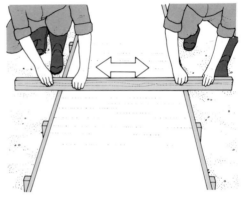

2 Level the concrete using the beam with a sawing motion as you work along the slab.

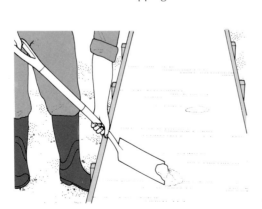

3 Fill in hollows which appear after the levelling using fresh concrete, then re-level.

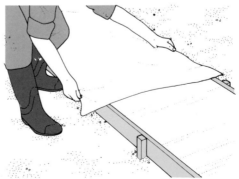

4 Cover the slab with heavy-gauge polythene and leave to cure for about four days.

Paths 1

SETTING OUT CURVES

A path winding down the garden can be difficult to set out unless you make a scale plan of its size and route on squared paper. This will enable you to estimate the materials you will need and help you transfer the shape accurately to the site.

Using stringlines Stretch a stringline along the site for the longest edge of the path area, and another at right angles for the width of the path area. Measure along the stringlines at right angles to them in increments that are relative to your scale plan to give you the correct positions for fixing marker pegs. Stretch more stringlines from marker peg to marker peg to translate the shape drawn on your plan to the actual site. If pegs and stringlines must be removed to excavate the path, put them back after digging to serve as a guide for the formwork, which will provide a support for the concrete while it sets.

Curving wooden formwork For a cast concrete path which incorporates curves you will need to construct timber form-work that follows the shape. Softwood planks, about 1in (25mm) thick, are most

suitable, but slightly thinner planks, used with more stakes, will do. They must be as wide as the desired depth of concrete. Make a number of partial saw cuts (up to half the thickness of the wood) across the breadth of the formwork planks at about 5in (125mm) intervals so that you are able to bend the timber as necessary to the shape of the path. Drive in more stakes than are needed for a straight foundation in order to support the planks adequately without their springing straight. Nail the stakes to the outer face of the formwork planks. For gradual curves the saw cuts should be on the outside of the formwork, but for tight bends the timber is less likely to snap if the saw cuts are on the inside of the curve.

Hiring road forms On a particularly long path, buying timber formwork can be costly. Consider hiring metal road forms, which comprise flat metal lengths with attached stakes: flexible and rigid types are available for curved or straight paths respectively. The forms are, of course, removed once the concrete has fully set.

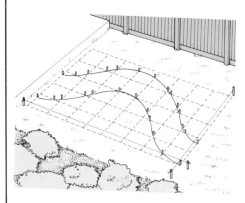

Measure along the outer strings to points that correspond with the scale plan and drive stakes into the ground. Run stringlines from stake to stake to mark out the curved path.

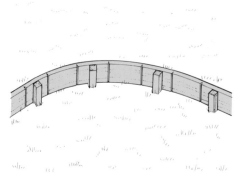

Form curves in formwork by making saw cuts across the planks at intervals, then bend the timber and secure to stakes. Cast the concrete within the formwork and remove when set.

Planning a path

The first stage in making a path, whatever your choice of material as the surface, is planning the route it will take through the garden. The first rule in planning is that any path must lead somewhere, whether it is to a garden shed or ornament, or simply from one area of the plot to another.

Straight or angular paths will tend to segment the garden and give a formal appearance, whereas by incorporating curves you can produce a more natural effect. You should take into account the profile of the ground itself, both for the appearance of the path and for practical considerations: for example, a path sloping towards the house or other outbuilding will create a direct route for heavy rainwater to flow to the house walls rather than soaking into the ground as it would normally.

Draw a scale sketch plan and a side elevation of the garden to help you plan out the route of the path and any obstacles you might encounter. Consider also that looking at a curved path drawn from above on paper is quite misleading: in reality the curve will foreshorten. For an impression of what the path will actually look like, lower your eye to the level of the paper and look along the drawn curve.

Setting out the path

Whether you are intending to cast a solid concrete path or lay individual pavers, you must mark out the route on the ground, using strings stretched between pegs (or use a long hosepipe to help plot the course of a curved path).

Decide what use the path will be put to: if it is to be used for access with a wheelbarrow, be sure to allow enough width for passage. Two people walking side by side will require about 3ft (915mm) width for comfort.

Choosing paving materials

Your choice of paving materials depends on appearance and durability. The options are basically cast concrete, preformed concrete paving slabs, bricks, moulded paving blocks, gravel or asphalt. Natural stone, for example York paving, is attractive but comparatively expensive. Concrete is plain, dull and utilitarian but ideal for a heavy-duty path, or for areas of the garden where appearance is not an important consideration.

Paving slabs are tough and durable and available in a range of colours—usually reds, greens, greys, yellows and buff tones—and various shapes and surface finishes. Square and rectangular slabs are the most commonly available type, although you can also buy hexagonal or circular types. The most popular size of slab is about 18in (460mm) square. Slabs suitable for path-laying are usually about 2in (50mm) thick. Finishes vary: the slabs may have a smooth, non-slip surface, be riven with the appearance of split stone or textured with an exposed aggregate surface, or be patterned to give the appearance of bricks, tiles or cobblestones.

Crazy paving is made from broken concrete or stone slabs, and sold in many different sizes, shapes and colours by the square yard. It may look highly decorative but is not really a practical consideration if the path is to receive heavy traffic from garden equipment.

Bricks of many types, new or secondhand, are suitable for use as a path surface, and can be laid in decorative patterns or simple brick bonding arrangements. Do not use the more porous bricks, which are susceptible to damage by frost. Engineering brick is the hardest and, consequently, the best performer against damp. There is a wide range of bricks available, from white to brown, and including yellows and reds. Bear in mind comfort (for walking) and drainage before selecting a textured finish.

Concrete paving blocks—which are about the same size as bricks, and sometimes decoratively shaped—are laid in interlocking pattern on a sand bed. Finished to resemble old bricks, they come in the same colour ranges, often textured to simulate real brick.

Gravel can be used for paths provided there is some means of edge restraint—a kerb of bricks on end, for example—to prevent it from spreading to adjoining surfaces. It should also be laid on a concrete base to avoid sinking problems. Lay a 2in (50mm) thick sub-base of coarse gravel mixed with sand topped with a 1in (25mm) thick layer of fine pea gravel, then roll the surface to compact it thoroughly.

Paths 2

Cold cure asphalt—coloured red or black—is sold prepacked in sacks for direct application to a prepared base and, although really intended as a resurfacing material, can be successfully used for a new pathway. Apply the asphalt to a hardcore base, rake level, then roll flat and compact. As an alternative finish you can embed stone chippings in the surface.

Cobblestones can be set in a 2in (50mm) deep layer of dry concrete mix that has been poured into a prepared shallow trench. Pack the stones tightly; tamp them level. Sprinkle the path with water, to activate the concrete and to clean the cobbles.

Wooden paths are well suited to rural areas—and are a practical solution if a mature tree has been felled in your garden. Dig down 8in (200mm); level and compress a gravel and sand mix to a depth of 2in (50mm). Use 6in (150mm) deep sections of logs, cut whole from the trunk and thicker branches. Lightly sand down any sharp edges on the upper surface and arrange the logs on the base material, grain upwards. Pay attention to the size, shape and colour of logs in your design. Work them firmly into the gravel and sand, then pour more of the mixture between the logs. Using a broom, sweep the infill across the path, until it is flush with the top of the logs. Hammer down any logs that stick out of the gravel.

Low-lying plants can further enhance such a path; remove some of the sand and gravel mixture and replace it with the appropriate quantity and type of soil. After planting, water in the plants.

Preparing the sub-base

Most paths which are to receive normal loading from people and wheelbarrows can be simply laid on a firm, level base formed by the earth itself, without the need for a firmer sub-base. Set up stringlines and pegs to mark out the shape and route of the path, then remove vegetable matter, stones and topsoil or remove turf as necessary within the guidelines.

Where the path joins a lawn, plan to set the paving about $\frac{3}{4}$in (20mm) below the surrounding level so that you can mow the grass without damaging the mower blades.

Ram down the exposed subsoil with a stout timber post, or compact thoroughly with a garden roller. For a long path it is best to work in easily manageable bays rather than digging out the foundations for the entire run in one go. Check that the base is level using a spirit level on a long timber plank (or your tamping post laid on its side). Where the path

Laying the foundations

1 Dig out the topsoil within the stringlines, which are set 2in (50mm) wider than the finished path. Retain any turfs for re-use elsewhere.

2 Compact the base using a stout timber post, sledgehammer or garden roller. If using a post, wear thick gloves to protect your hands.

follows the undulations of the ground, check that the base undulates consistently with ground level.

Allow a drainage crossfall to one side of the path using a shim of timber to set the slope (see page 16). Tip barrowloads of sand onto the sub-base and spread it 2 to 3in (50 to 75mm) thick using a straight-edged length of plank the width of the path.

Edge restraints
It is not necessary on fairly narrow paths to incorporate edge restraints to prevent the surface materials from creeping, although of course if you are casting a concrete slab you will have to construct timber formwork in the same way as described for making raft foundations (see pages 14–15).

However, you might want to include some form of decorative edging purely for appearance. A number of garden centres stock preformed edging, for example in a classic Victorian rope design, or a plainer kerbstone style. The edging is simply set, without mortar, in a slim trench at the sides of the paving.

Adding the hardcore
Where it is necessary to support loads heavier than normal traffic, or alternatively, where the soil is soft, you should lay a sub-base of compacted hardcore.

Tip a layer of about 3in (75mm) of hardcore into the sub-base and ram this down well using a sledgehammer or a garden roller, then top with a 1 or 2in (25 or 50mm) thick blinding layer of sand, raked level.

The base is now ready for laying the paving material, whether you have chosen fresh concrete, precast slabs, bricks or crazy paving or a combination of these.

Expansion joints for concrete paths
Temperature variations cause concrete to expand and contract, and unless this is controlled a cast concrete path will crack at weak or vulnerable areas.

Divide the path into bays about 6ft (1.8m) long by inserting a permanent expansion joint consisting of a length of preservative-treated softwood about $\frac{1}{2}$in (12mm) thick between the outer formwork planks.

To be fully effective the joints must be set at 90 degrees to the edges of the path, even when the path is curved.

Support the expansion joint on dabs of fresh concrete, with its top edge flush with the top of the formwork. Pour in the concrete as previously described, then carefully tamp from each side of the expansion joint to avoid dislodging it.

3 Add hardcore to the base and ram this down well with a sledgehammer or compact with a roller to a thickness of about 3in (75mm).

4 Blind the surface with a layer of sand spread about 2in (50mm) thick with a garden rake as a means of filling large hollows in the hardcore.

Paths: loose-laying

Paving slabs can be laid on a sand bed without mortar where there is likely to be minimal pedestrian use. The bed should be about 2in (50mm) thick: you will need to buy 0.5 cubic metre of sand for every 20sq metres of path (or 1.7 cubic feet for every 215sq feet). Where the path will be used for heavy gardening equipment or bicycles, it is preferable to lay the slabs on mortar dabs, as for a patio (see page 30).

For either method, prepare the base as previously described for foundations (see page 6) and spread the sand over the surface.

Using a datum peg

It is important that the path is consistently level over its surface, so it is usual to set each slab according to a common reference point such as a "datum" peg driven into the ground at the start of the path. The top of this datum peg should be set at the level required for the finished path, which may be relative to an adjoining surface or a wall.

Moving paving slabs

Paving slabs can be quite heavy to carry so it is often best to "walk" them along the ground, taking care not to damage the corners. If you have to lift them, make sure you get a firm grip on the sides and bend your knees, not your back.

Placing the slabs

Lift the first slab into position on the sand bed, placing one edge against the adjoining surface and lowering the other end onto the sand. Wiggle the slab slightly to bed it on the sand. Place one end of a long spirit level on the slab and rest the other on top of the datum peg. If the slab is not lying flat, tap with the handle of a club hammer to bed it down properly.

If the slab is too low, lift it and trowel more sand underneath the low part, then replace it and tap level. Check that the slab is level in both directions and adjust the level if necessary.

Place the second slab alongside the first one, align their edges, then tap the second slab gently with the club hammer to bed it firmly in the sand. Adjust if necessary in order to maintain the correct level in both directions.

Forming joints between slabs

Butt the edges of the slabs up against each other or, for wider joints, insert pieces of hardboard between them. However, avoid making the joints wider than about $\frac{1}{2}$in (12mm), or you will have trouble creating—and maintaining—a level surface, as the slabs will tend to sink at the corners when they are walked upon.

Loose-laying paving slabs

1 Lay the first slab on the sand bed and set level with the top of the datum peg, checking with a spirit level.

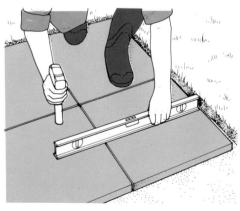

2 Level the slabs by tapping with the handle of a club hammer: adjust the sand level under slabs that are too high or low.

CUTTING PAVING SLABS

When you are laying paving slabs you will probably need to cut some slabs to fit around corners or at the end of the path—it is unlikely that whole slabs will fit exactly throughout the path. Where you have used a staggered design you will have to cut slabs to fit at the edges.

Hydraulic stone splitters are available for hire to make short work of cutting slabs accurately, but there is no reason why you cannot simply cut the slabs with a club hammer and bolster chisel.

Measure the width of the gap you have to fill and transfer the measurement to the slab. Scribe along the slab using a bolster chisel held against a straight-edged length of timber. With the slab resting on a firm, flat surface such as a lawn, chop along the groove carefully using the club hammer and bolster chisel, then rest the slab on the straight-edged timber, aligned with the groove. Tap the slab sharply with the handle of the club hammer to break it cleanly along the scored line. Fit the cut slab with the slightly rough cut edge to the outside of the path where it will not be too noticeable.

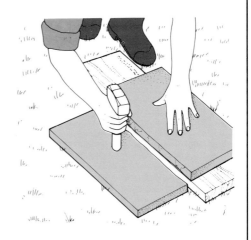

Score the slab with a bolster chisel, then place over a length of timber on a firm flat surface and break along the score line by tapping firmly with a club hammer.

3 Fill the joints with a mixture of soil and cement, brushed in to fill the gaps; water in using a watering can and rose.

Continuing the path

A basic path will probably be only two slabs wide. Lay the slabs for the second row in the same way, and level them to the first ones, checking with the spirit level. Place the level diagonally across the slabs to check that they are horizontal in all directions.

Finishing the joints

Once all the slabs have been laid on the sand bed you can fill the joints. Mix some sand and dry cement in the proportions 1:3 in a bucket or wheelbarrow and brush into the gaps between slabs until they are filled.

Either leave the joints as they are, or sprinkle water over the surface with a watering can fitted with a fine rose: this hardens the cement mixture enough to prevent the slabs from moving too much.

Crazy paving

Laying crazy paving
Crazy paving comprises pieces of broken paving slabs laid to produce a complex, decoratively patterned surface. However, despite the apparently random effect of the paving, the pieces must be laid in a strict formula both for a symmetrical appearance and for strength.

The sides of the path are formed by a row of fairly large slab pieces which have at least one straight edge, placed outermost. Similar-sized pieces with irregular edges are positioned along the centre of the path (or evenly spaced within a large area such as a patio). Smaller irregular pieces are used to fill in the spaces between the larger slabs.

Preparing the site
Crazy paving is obtainable from larger garden centres, building contractors or your local council, in a choice of colours—reds, greens, greys and buff tones—and a variety of thicknesses. Make sure you are given a good mixture of shapes, sizes and colours (unless you specify all one colour), and have them dumped as close as possible to the site. Alternatively, use natural stone, with its seams and marbling. Stratified rock is ideal as it splits when quarried.

Stack the slabs, grouped by colour, shape and size, alongside the run of the path so that it is easy to select the types you require as you are laying them.

Prepare the base by digging out the topsoil. If the subsoil is not firm, dig this out too and replace with 3 to 4in (75 to 100mm) hardcore. Top with about 2in (50mm) of sand, raked and levelled.

Laying the perimeter pieces
Begin by placing a stringline at the required level. Place the perimeter pieces of crazy paving along the edges of the path, level with the stringlines, to check that they fit correctly. Mix some mortar on a nearby hard surface or board, then lay the first stone on dabs of mortar, trowelled onto the sand bed. Press the slab down on the mortar dabs with a wiggling motion to bed it firmly, then lay the neighbouring pieces. Place a spirit level across the slabs to check that they are level (or sloping consistently on a sloping site).

Laying the central slabs
Dry-lay the larger slabs of irregular shape along the centre of the path, then return to the starting point, lift them one at a time, remove or add sand as necessary to give a level finish, and re-lay on four or five dabs of mortar trowelled onto the base.

Check that the central slabs are set level with the perimeter slabs using the spirit level. Place a stout length of timber across the entire path and tap this with a club hammer in order to level the slabs consistently: it is otherwise quite difficult to set each slab level with its neighbour.

Placing the small infill slabs
Fill in between with the small irregular pieces, bedded on single dabs of mortar. It is often easier to "butter" the back of the smallest pieces of crazy paving with mortar, scraping it off the trowel and furrowing the surface with the blade to aid adhesion.

Use the timber and club hammer, as described above, to tap the slabs level with the surrounding ones.

Pointing the joints
The gaps between the crazy paving slabs must be filled with a fairly wet mortar mix to hold each slab in place. The pointing should also be bevelled to drain surface water from the path.

Laying crazy paving

1 Bed the straight-edged slabs on dabs of mortar at the sides of the path.

Mixed paths

Mixing materials
The materials and methods outlined so far can be combined to great effect. But show restraint in the number of surfaces you mix, and do not be over-ambitious in the design; paths seldom work in the elaborate designs that can sometimes be effective for patios.

Paving slabs are available in a range of colours, but these should not be used to make paths that are multicoloured mosaics. Usually it is best to create a more subtle effect, which does not draw too much attention to itself. It is often better to rely on contrasts of texture rather than contrast of colour.

Economic factors may be a consideration. For example, combining brick with less expensive gravel or concrete is a good compromise.

Possible combinations of materials that work for paths include wooden logs set in gravel or cobbles, or cobbles punctuated with textured concrete.

Bear in mind that mixing materials can complicate maintenance. For example, wooden surfaces will need to be wire-brushed in winter to prevent them from becoming too slippery, whereas surrounding hard surfaces can be left unattended.

Where a brick path laid lengthwise in stretcher bond meets a lawn, an unusual treatment would be to fan out the individual lines of the bond, to make a transition area where the grass and the bricks alternate.

The "pace" of a path
The arrangement of paving units in a path can subtly affect the speed at which we walk. A uniform grain along the path—for example, that created by bricks laid lengthwise in stretcher bond—can seem to hurry us on, whereas a less directional pattern will encourage a slower pace. The treatment may be chosen to suit the purpose of the path—a "slow" path where there is plenty to admire, a "faster" path where the aim is simply to provide access to another part of the garden.

Stepping-stone paths
A path does not have to be a continuous run of concrete, bricks or slabs. Setting individual preformed slabs, irregularly shaped crazy paving stones, or even sawn log rounds, in a lawn or broad planting bed as a row of light-duty stepping-stones is quite straightforward.

Simply place the slab or log round on the surface and mark around it with a spade or lawn edger. Remove the turf or topsoil and dig out enough for about 1in (25mm) of sand plus the thickness of the slab or log. Allow for the slab or log to be sunk beneath the surface of a lawn by about $\frac{3}{4}$in (20mm) to enable mowing without damaging the blades. Place the stepping stone in the hole and tap with the handle of a club hammer to bed it firmly. It can be effective to continue stepping-stones from a lawn across a pond.

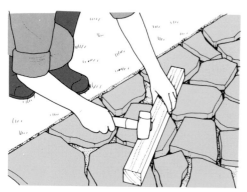

2 Lay the larger central slabs and smaller infill pieces in the remaining gaps and tap level using a club hammer and a length of stout timber.

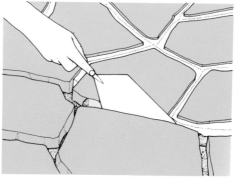

3 Point the joints between the crazy paving slabs with mortar, bevelled to drain water.

Patios: preparation 1

Planning a patio

A patio should be built where it will receive the most sunshine, although it is also desirable to site it close to some shade for very hot days. Alternatively, you can create your own shady area by constructing a pergola or awning over part of the patio.

Patio size As a rough guide to the scale of a patio, you should allow sufficient space to accommodate garden furniture for four people in addition to permitting passage through to the garden. The minimum practical size for this is about 40sq ft (3.7sq m).

Drainage The large area of the patio will prevent rainwater from soaking into the ground as normal, so you should take into account where the excess water will go. The entire patio must slope slightly—about 1in in 6ft (25mm in 1.8m)—towards the garden or flower bed, but not towards the house walls, or you could create a damp problem. If the ground naturally slopes towards the house you will have to incorporate a drainage channel at the end of the patio to divert the rainwater sideways to a suitable drainage point.

Existing drain runs It is likely that your patio will cover existing drain runs and possibly inspection chambers. You will either have to build up the walls of an inspection chamber to set the manhole cover at the new surface level, or else cover the existing manhole cover with a loose-laid paving slab for access in case of a blockage.

Surface materials A patio can be constructed from the same materials used for paths, including bricks, blocks, slabs, cast concrete—and even timber (see page 38).

Marking out the base

It is essential that you set out the base correctly to ensure the surface has a firm, flat foundation that will not collapse.

Use stringlines and pegs to mark the perimeter of the patio. Most patios adjoin the house and must be constructed so that the level is not higher than the damp-proof course (DPC) of the house walls.

Datum pegs A "datum" peg—made from 1in (25mm) sq softwood with a pointed end—is used to set the top level of the patio.

Setting the prime datum peg

Drive in the "prime datum peg" so that its top is at the height required for the patio. This must be at least 6in (150mm) below the level of a DPC to prevent rainwater splashing from the patio surface onto the house wall above the DPC.

Setting out the base

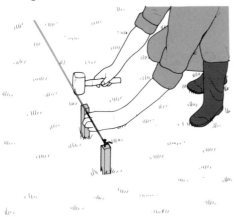

1 Stretch stringlines between pegs driven in at the perimeter of the patio, indicating the corners with more pegs set at the ultimate level of the patio.

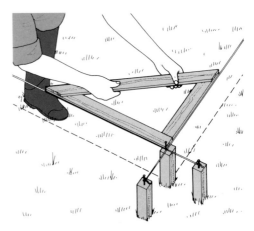

2 Check the corners with a builder's square to ensure that the stringlines are set at right angles. Adjust as necessary.

In the top of the peg hammer a nail to which you can attach the stringline. Position a second datum peg at the other side of the proposed patio, and set it at the same level as the prime datum by spanning across the two pegs with a spirit level on top of a long straight-edged plank of wood. Or use a water level—a garden hose pipe, with transparent plastic tubing in either end, filled with water which is visible through the plastic. The water level will remain constant; align the water line at one end of the pipe with the top of the prime datum peg and use the other end to fix the next peg. For a wide patio you might need to drive in an intermediate datum peg. Fix a nail in these pegs.

Attaching the stringlines

Attach stringlines—ideally, coloured nylon twine—to the datum pegs.

Stretch the lines out from the house wall at each side and drive in pegs about 12in (300mm) beyond the area of the patio so you will have ample space to work. Fix another stringline between two more pegs to mark the outer edge of the patio. Indicate the corners of the patio by driving in more pegs.

Check that the corners are set at 90 degrees using a builder's square (see page 15).

Fixing intermediate pegs

It is vital that the foundations of the patio are perfectly flat. Drive in more pegs around the perimeter of the patio at intervals of about 5ft (1.5m). Place a plank and spirit level on the prime datum peg and the adjacent perimeter peg and level the latter. Move on from the second peg to the subsequent perimeter pegs, levelling in the same way.

When the perimeter pegs have been set accurately, drive in more pegs at 5ft (1.5m) intervals over the entire surface of the base, levelling them to the outer pegs with the plank and spirit level. The top of each peg will be at the desired level of the patio.

Excavating the base

Dig out the topsoil (see Foundations, page 9, for details) using a spade and a pick-axe for hard ground, then add 3 to 4in (75 to 100mm) of hardcore and ram this down well, using a garden roller or, preferably, a hired motorized plate compactor. This tool has a vibrating plate underneath, which will compact the hardcore thoroughly. Add a 2in (50mm) blinding layer of sand and vibrate this too, taking care not to dislodge the datum pegs fixed across the surface. The datum pegs should now protrude above the layer of sand by the

3 Level the pegs by spanning across the tops from a prime datum peg with a spirit level and plank. Tap down or raise the pegs as necessary.

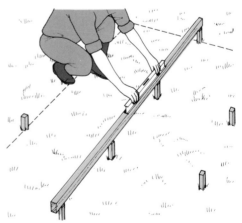

4 Level the entire base by driving intermediate pegs at 5ft (1.5m) intervals across the surface and levelling them to the perimeter pegs.

Patios: preparation 2

thickness of the patio surface; if, for example, you are using bricks, this will be $2\frac{1}{2}$in (760mm).

Edge restraints and formwork

If you are casting a concrete slab, fix formwork to the inside faces of the perimeter pegs, aligning the top edge of the planks with the tops of the pegs.

For other paving, some form of permanent edge restraint is desirable to stop the patio from creeping.

Where the patio abuts the wall of the house you can use the wall itself as a means of restraining the paving material, but you will still need to support the outer edges. There are various alternatives.

Precast concrete kerbstones are available from garden centres and builders' merchants. The kerbs usually have a bevelled top edge and may incorporate a moulded pattern for decorative effect. Dig a trench just outside the perimeter of the patio and bed the stones upright in 2in (50mm) concrete, with their top edge level with the datum pegs.

Brick edging looks particularly attractive with a brick or block paved surface. Again dig a trench and set the individual bricks (or concrete blocks) on end and side by side in 2in (50mm) of sand in a "soldier" course.

Timber edging can be used as an inconspic-

uous restraint for brick, block or slab paving. The timber must be thoroughly treated against rot with preservative. Attach the lengths to stakes driven into the ground so that their tops are level with the datum pegs, or fix to the outer datum pegs.

Dealing with sloping ground

Where the garden slopes away from the house you must build perimeter walls (see page 66) at the outer edges to create a type of "stage" on which to lay the patio.

The space within the walls can be filled with rubble and hardcore as a sub-base, then the paving laid on top as normal. Weep holes built into the perimeter walls will allow water to drain out: these can be simply unmortared vertical joints between brickwork or blockwork at intervals.

You may wish to incorporate a flight of steps within the perimeter walls for easy access to the lower part of the garden (see pages 50–53).

Spreading the sand bed

Most patio materials can be laid on a 3in (75mm) thick bed of sand, either on dabs of fresh mortar or, in the case of "flexible" concrete block pavers, simply compressed into the sand itself without mortar (the edge

5 Dig out the base to firm sub-soil using a spade or pick-axe. Take care not to dislodge the datum pegs.

6 Fill with hardcore and compact using a garden roller or motorized compacting machine. Add a blinding layer of sand and compact that too.

restraints hold the blocks rigid).

It is not easy to spread a layer of sand over a large area and at the same time maintain the levels required, so it is usual to apply it in "bays" formed by 6ft (1.8m) lengths of 2 × 1in (50 × 25mm) wooden battens laid across the blinding layer of the sub-base.

Position a batten—resting on its narrower edge—along the perimeter of the patio and another about 4ft (1.2m) away along the patio site, parallel with the first. Support the battens with heaps of sand. Check across the tops of the battens with a spirit level on a plank to ensure that they are horizontal, then tip a barrowload of sand into the bay they form. Rake out the sand so that it stands just proud.

Level the sand to the tops of the battens by drawing a straight-edged length of wood along the battens. Fill in any hollows with more sand, then level off again. When you have spread out the sand in the first bay, carefully remove the outer batten and place it about 4ft (1.2m) away from, and parallel with, the second batten, forming another bay. Fill the gap left by replacing the batten with sand and level off with a trowel or short length of straight-edged timber.

Tip sand into the second bay and level it off, then repeat the process to complete the sand bed over the entire area of the patio.

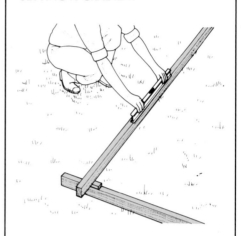

SETTING A GRADIENT

The patio surface should slope slightly to drain off rainwater. On a flat site you should set one side about 1in (25mm) lower than the other. When setting out the base use a 1in (25mm) thick piece of wood (a "shim") under the spirit level on the lower side of the base to check that the level is correct (see page 16).

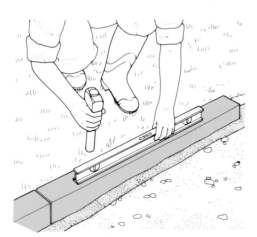

7 Set edge restraints such as precast concrete kerbstones at the perimeter of the patio to prevent the surface from spreading.

8 Add a sand bed over the sub-base onto which you can lay slabs, bricks or blocks directly. Divide the area into bays for easy spreading.

Patios: laying paving slabs

Laying paving slabs

A large area of paving slabs likely to receive considerable traffic should be bedded on mortar on a prepared sub-base, as previously described (see pages 26–9). See the box on page 33 for the correct mortar mix to use, and how to mix properly.

Start to lay the slabs in one corner of the patio and work diagonally across the surface—in this way it is easier to ensure that they are laid consistently flat.

Trowel dabs of mortar about the size of a clenched fist onto the sand bed in the position of the first corner slab. On square slabs place four dabs at the corners and one in the centre; on hexagonal slabs use the same principle of five dabs.

Lift the first slab and place its outer edge on the sand, then lower it carefully onto the mortar dabs. Tap the slab down carefully with the handle of your club hammer and place a spirit level on top to check that it is level in both directions.

Follow the stringlines carefully and the preset drainage fall should be visible when you have several slabs laid.

Position the second and subsequent slabs in the same way, checking across the tops with a spirit level. Pack out under slabs that

are too low with more mortar, or tap down slabs that are too high.

Slot $\frac{1}{2}$in (12mm) thick offcuts of wood between the slabs as consistent joint spaces, or simply butt up the slabs for finer joints.

As you work across the surface, kneel on a piece of board to distribute your weight and avoid pressing the slabs down into the still wet mortar.

Using half-slabs

If you are laying rectangular slabs, or hexagonal ones, you will need half-sizes for the perimeter. Some manufacturers produce half-size slabs, but you may have to cut others to fit, using a club hammer and bolster chisel. Measure the offcut, and score the line with the chisel along a straight-edged length of timber. Then, resting the slab on the length of timber, chop sharply with the hammer and chisel to break the slab along the line.

Lay all the whole slabs first, then cut and fit the ones for the edges.

Filling the joints

Mix dry sand and cement in the proportions 3:1 and brush this into the joints between slabs. Water in the mixture with clean water using a watering can fitted with a fine rose.

Laying paving slabs

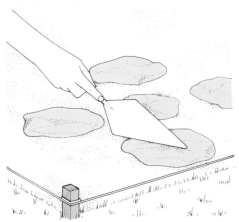

1 Apply the mortar dabs to the sub-base in the position of the first slab; trowel on five dabs, one at each corner and one centrally.

2 Lay the first slab on the mortar dabs, placing one edge first, then lowering flat. Tap level with the shaft of a club hammer.

Mixed materials

Once hardened, this filling will help keep the slabs in place and discourage weeds.

Variations
For added interest in a patio, cut in areas of different paving materials such as cobble-stones, bricks, gravel or timber—or else construct planting areas.

Creating patterns
Mixing colours By mixing different-coloured paving you can create random or formal patterns. For example, you can highlight diagonal lines across the patio with red slabs contrasted with the overall green or buff ones; or you can pick out alternate rows of slabs in another colour, working from the perimeter of the patio forming squares within squares, and finishing with a solid block of, say, four slabs at the centre.

Mixing shapes With hexagonal slabs, too, you can form interesting cut-outs by omitting units from the overall area. You may be able to mix hexagonal slabs with ordinary square or rectangular slabs of different colour.

Adding curves Some makes of slab are intended to be laid as part of a set, to make up an overall design impressed upon their faces. Other slabs are available with a segmental cut-out at one corner; these form a circular hole when four slabs are laid in conjunction.

Using bricks and timber
Brick paving Introduce areas of brick paving into a slab-laid patio to add texture and colour. For a geometric pattern lay an edging of brick pavers around each square slab. Experiment by laying the bricks flat, on edge—or even on end.

Timber Use lengths of rough-sawn preservative-treated timber in conjunction with slabs and bricks. Railway sleepers embedded in the surface can be used to break up a plain run of slabs and can form shallow planting beds.

Log inserts Log rounds, preferably of hardwood which will last better against rot, can be set within an area of missing paving slabs, and the gaps around them filled with gravel.

Aggregates for the patio
To create an attractive feature within the patio, omit a number of slabs from an area of paving and fill the gap with decorative aggregates. Many types and colours of small-scale stones are available, often pre-bagged.

Cobblestones are commonly about 2 to 3in (50 to 75mm) in size, and can be loose-

3 Lay the remaining slabs, butting the edges together or slipping spacers between each. Check the levels with a spirit level.

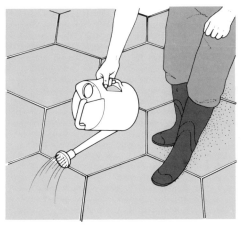

4 Fill the joints with a dry mix of 1:3 cement and sand, then water it in with clean water using a watering can with a fine rose fitted.

Patios: cobblestones

laid within your feature areas, contained by decorative edging or simply by the edges of the paving slabs. Alternatively, for a decorative area on which you can walk, bed the cobblestones in a screed of mortar, pressing them as level as possible with a stout board

and club hammer. Pebbles measure about $1\frac{1}{2}$ to 2in (40 to 50mm) and can be used in the same way as the large cobblestones.

Gravel chippings, about $\frac{1}{4}$in (6mm) in size and made of rough-edged flint, come in various colours—they are often bagged up in mixed

Laying cobblestones

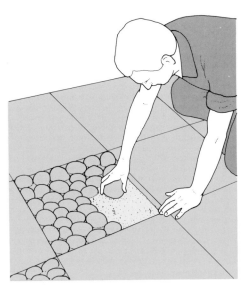

1 Cobblestones can be set in a mortar screed in feature areas within slabs or bricks. Spread out the mortar, then push in the individual cobbles about halfway, varying the colour mix.

2 Bed the cobblestones evenly by placing a straight-edged length of timber across the top (resting it on the surrounding paving slabs) to press down any high stones.

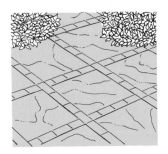

Define and soften a patio of square, riven-faced slabs with borders of bricks.

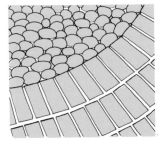

Create circular patterns with cobblestones and· bricks—for example, surrounding a tree.

Decorative areas of gravel within areas of paving slabs will avoid a plain, drab appearance.

Small-scale paving

colours—and can be scattered over planting areas to reduce evaporation from the soil, or else used to fill isolated areas where slabs have been removed. They will precisely fill any shape of hole in the patio and can be laid right up against plants without doing any harm. Marine shell, crushed, provides a fascinating infill for feature areas on the patio, especially when whole seashells are included in the area for a distinctly seaside look.

Small-scale paving

The alternative to a patio made predominantly of large-scale paving slabs is one comprising a surface of small-scale units such as bricks or concrete blocks (see pages 34-7). The benefit of these materials is that you have more freedom to create surface patterns by selecting a decorative bonding arrangement: basketweave, herringbone, caneweave, parquet or even a simple stretcher pattern are possible—and you can even lay the bricks or blocks diagonally. (See page 37 for details.) For visual relief in a large area covered with small pavers, you might still consider adding feature areas of different materials, including gravel, cobblestones—or punctuate the surface with paving slabs.

MORTAR MIXES

Mortar ingredients Mortar for slab-laying consists of cement and sharp sand mixed together with water to form a self-hardening paste. Mortar mixed in the proportions 1 part cement : 5 parts sand is adequate for laying slabs. Use buckets to proportion the ingredients accurately, tipping them on a hard, flat surface or a mixing board. **Plasticizer** Often a "plasticizer" is added to the mortar to aid the workability and flexibility of the mix. Traditionally lime was used but nowadays chemical plasticizers, which are easier to mix, are used instead. They usually come in liquid form with the amount you need to add specified on the container.

Mixing mortar

Pile the sand into a heap, form a crater in the top and pour on a bucket of cement. Turn over the sand and cement repeatedly with a shovel until a consistent colour shows that it is thoroughly mixed. Add the plasticizer to the water in accordance with the manufacturer's instructions, then form a crater in the centre of the heap and pour in half the water.

Collapse the sides of the crater inwards to mix the water with the dry mortar. Add more water as the mortar absorbs it, continually turning over the mix until you achieve a smooth but firm consistency.

Draw the spade across the mix in steps: the ridges should remain. If you add too much water you will weaken the mortar mix, but you can stiffen it again by sprinkling on handfuls of dry cement.

Ready-mixed mortar for slab-laying

When you are faced with laying one hundred or more paving slabs for a typical patio you will no doubt find the job quite strenuous. Using ordinary mortar can be tricky, especially if you constantly have to lift and re-lay slabs that have been positioned incorrectly.

Some ready-mixed paving mortars have polymer additives which are designed to enable heavy slabs to be slid into position (in a similar way to fixing ceramic wall tiles); once the mortar has set, however, the slab will be held rigidly and permanently.

Each 100lb (40kg) dry pack of ready-mixed mortar is sufficient to lay about 10 slabs that are 2ft (600mm) sq or about 14 slabs 18in (457mm) sq. The material is used with a fairly dry texture and applied in four generous dabs at the corners of the slab: the slab is lowered onto the dabs and slid into position. Once you are satisfied with the alignment of the slab you can simply tap it down to the required level with the shaft of a club hammer, compressing the mix by about 1in (25mm).

Patios: "flexible" pavers 1

Concrete paving blocks, known as "flexible" pavers because they are laid dry, without mortar, on a sand bed and can be lifted in the future if required, can be used to create an attractively patterned and textured hard surface for a patio. They are also a good choice for paths and drives, where they can support considerable loadings from vehicles.

Paver formats
Flexible pavers roughly correspond to brick sizes, although they are normally about $2\frac{1}{2}$in (60mm) thicker. Numerous colours and textures are available, often simulating regional brick types and sometimes manufactured to appear old and weather-worn.

Select a colour that will complement the house; this may restrict your choice but the end result will be more acceptable than a contrasting scheme.

Before opting for a textured finish, consider the function of the surface. An irregular finish is not ideal if you want to stand tables and chairs on the paving. A smooth finish would be better. This need not be dull; take advantage of the various colours of flexible pavers available and devise a suitable pattern.

Whether the chosen surface is smooth or textured, wet an area of one paver before you buy to check the colour change you can expect in rainy weather and to test slip-resistance. It is best to pay more for good-quality pavers that are less prone to crumbling if you should need to cut any of them.

In addition to uniform slabs, different shapes are also made, intended to interlock with neighbouring blocks to form a decorative bonding arrangement (see page 37).

Bevelled-edge In its simplest form the paver may have a bevelled top edge, which accentuates the rectangular shape of the individual block when laid.

Fishtail Another popular type is the wavy-edged "fishtail" block, often laid in a parquet design to give a characteristic rippling effect as if viewed underwater.

Angular There is also a geometric cranked rectangle block, which strictly speaking should be laid only in a diagonal stretcher bond. A bow-tie version of this creates a zig-zag pattern across the paving when laid in stretcher bond.

Patterned face Some rectangular paving blocks have a pattern impressed in their top face, such as two, four or eight smaller squares which are intended to resemble a mosaic finish, or a series of diamond shapes for a studded effect.

The shape of individual blocks will limit the patterns you can create. Some types, such

Laying flexible pavers

1 Check the position of gullies, downpipes and other obstructions in relation to the finished level of the paving blocks.

2 Place the blocks on the sand bed in your chosen pattern (here a parquet design), working from a walking board resting on the edge restraints.

as the bow-tie and cranked rectangle, can be laid successfully only in a simple stretcher bond—that is, end to end with each row staggered, usually by half the length of a block.

Other blocks, such as the fishtail, chamfered and patterned-face types, can be laid in parquet, herringbone or other weave-effect designs.

Preparing the base

Concrete paving blocks can be laid on a prepared foundation of hardcore (see page 16), 3 to 4in (75 to 100mm) in depth (or as necessary to bolster the subsoil), topped with about 2in (50mm) of sand. The edges of the paving must be lined with kerbstones, timber restraints or a row of blocks set on edge in concrete. Spread out the sand in bays, as previously described (see page 29). To allow for the compaction of the blocks lay them about $\frac{3}{8}$in (10mm) above the top of the edge restraints. Make sure that the sand bed is a block-depth less this dimension below the top of the edge restraints.

Begin laying the blocks at one corner, working systematically across and along the area. As the surface progresses across the patio, work on a board placed over the blocks in order to spread your weight.

Dealing with obstructions

Where the patio is built adjacent to the house walls there will be some obstructions to contend with, such as gullies and rainwater downpipes, which you must not cover.

Use an individual block as a gauge to check how the paving will fit against these features: it may be necessary to sink the foundation lower to avoid complicated junctions, or else create a well around the obstruction using a row of blocks on end.

There may well be manhole covers within your patio area, which you must not block permanently.

It might be necessary on your site to extend the height of the manhole walls to suit the new surface, or you may simply be able to loose-lay blocks over the manhole cover; these can be lifted in case of a blockage or overflow. Special manhole lids resembling shallow trays are available, which will accept a paving slab or row of pavers for this purpose.

Placing the blocks

Position the first block pavers against the edge restraints at one corner of the patio, following your chosen pattern. Lay only the whole blocks, leaving any cut ones for the edges until last.

To ensure the blocks are bedded down

3 Set up stringlines across the paving as a guide to laying the blocks symmetrically, especially when creating a diagonal effect.

4 Mark blocks for cutting by holding them over the space and scribing with a bolster chisel against a straight edge.

Patios: "flexible" pavers 2

sufficiently in the sand, place a stout length of timber across the surface and hit this sharply with a club hammer. Place the timber systematically in all directions to bed all the blocks level. Check with a spirit level held on top of the timber that the surface is flat. Use a shim of wood under the spirit level to set a drainage fall to one side of the patio, as described on page 29.

Work on an easily manageable area, then move your walking board further onto the surface and continue laying the blocks. It is best to work from the corner diagonally across the patio, so the finish is flat in appearance.

Setting up guide strings

Laying the hundreds of small blocks needed for a patio is not difficult but it is tricky to keep the overall bonding arrangement consistent without some guides to work to.

Stretch a string between pegs across the patio, aligned parallel with the leading edge of the section of paving you are laying. Lay the blocks up to this line, then move the line across about another 5 or 6ft (1.5 or 1.8m) and lay more blocks up to it. Should the rows of blocks wander from the true line, there is no major problem. You will have a chance to lift and re-lay them correctly before you

have progressed too far with the paving.

This method of checking the alignment of the paving blocks is most important when you are laying blocks diagonally across the surface, as shown in the diagrams below, as you have no outer guidelines—the edge restraints—to tell you whether you are laying them out of true.

Cutting block pavers

Most laying patterns used for block pavers will require you to cut some individual pieces for the edges. You can easily tackle this using a club hammer and bolster chisel: mark off the amount to be cut by scoring with a chisel against a straight edge, place the block on a firm, flat surface (say, the lawn) and strike the line sharply with the chisel and a club hammer.

If you are laying a large patio, however, cutting the many blocks necessary to fit around the perimeter would be laborious and time-consuming using a hammer and chisel. Instead, it is worth while hiring a hydraulic stone splitter. Simply mark the offcut, place the block in the jaws of the machine and operate the handle to chop the block quickly, cleanly and accurately. Whichever method of cutting you use, always wear plastic goggles to protect your eyes from flying chips; a

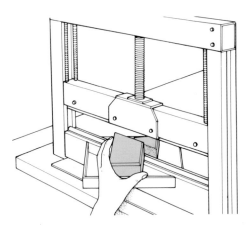

5 Cut the blocks using a hydraulic stone splitter. Place the block in the jaws, align the scribed mark and pull the handle to cut.

6 Vibrate the blocks into the sand bed using a motorized plate compacting machine fitted with a sole plate (or use a carpet to cushion).

gauze facemask will protect you from dust.

Position the cut edge of the block to the outside of the area, where it will be less noticeable.

Compacting the paved surface

Consolidating the surface of a large patio would be tiresome if you used only a block of wood and a club hammer, so it is best to hire a motorized plate compactor. Choose a machine which is fitted with a rubber bottom or "sole" plate to avoid damaging the faces of the blocks. If you cannot get hold of such a machine, you can make do with an ordinary compactor, but lay an old carpet over the blockwork and operate the compactor over this to cushion the blocks.

Spread a layer of sand over the blockwork to fill the joints between blocks, then operate the plate compactor. Run the machine across the surface: the vibrating sole plate will force the blocks well into the sand bed, and has the action of forcing sand up between the joints, making the entire area rigid and firm.

Add more sand to the surface and brush it into the joints with a stiff-bristled broom to work it well in. Follow with two or three more passes with the plate compactor (plus carpet cushion if necessary) to vibrate the sand into the joints.

7 Brush sand into the joints between blocks and vibrate the surface again using the plate compactor to form a firm, flat patio.

Laying patterns

Herringbone pattern is created by a series of zig-zagging rows of blocks laid end to side; it can be laid straight or diagonally.

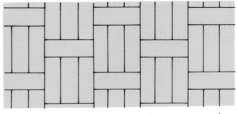

Cane-weave pattern comprises staggered rows of three blocks on end alternated with one block laid across their ends.

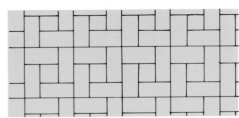

Squared design consists of whole blocks laid in a square box pattern with a cut block filling the gap in the centre.

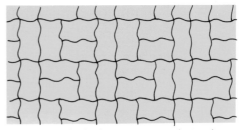

Fishtail blocks laid in a parquet design have the appearance of being underwater due to their wavy interlocking edges.

Decking 1

A raised timber deck, incorporating a pergola for shade, makes an attractive addition to the side of the house, providing space for sitting out and dining, either on built-in or freestanding furniture. The deck surface—a series of slats with small gaps between—drains quickly after rain, and is a more comfortable option than concrete slabs. The deck is built on sturdy uprights mounted on metal plates bolted to concrete foundation pads. This method of construction makes it easy to deal with sloping ground levels: the posts are cut to the required length, accommodating dips in the ground, while the deck itself is fixed horizontally to them. Integral timber steps provide access from the deck to the garden, and a balustrade runs around the front and sides.

A raised timber deck provides you with space outdoors for dozing, dining or soaking up the sun, and can be constructed using just a few specialist carpentry techniques. At its most basic the deck is simply a slatted ("duck-board") platform resting on the ground as an alternative to slabs or plain concrete. When raised on stilts, equipped with steps, rails and even an awning or pergola, it can become a traditional-style verandah. You can adapt the design shown here to your own requirements, or buy a kit of components from a specialist supplier and assemble the deck according to the instructions provided.

The basic duckboard

A basic timber slatted duckboard platform can be constructed entirely from lengths of preservative-treated sawn or planed softwood measuring about 3 × 1in (75 × 25mm) on a concrete or slab surface. Assemble the duckboard on site.

Extremely straightforward to assemble, the platform consists of lengths of timber forming the bearers, which are spaced about 30in (760mm) apart and parallel with each other. The bearers should run in the direction of the slope of the surface on which it is being laid.

Lengths of the same timber are cut to span the width of the platform and placed across the bearers at right angles to them. Set the slats about $\frac{1}{4}$ to $\frac{1}{2}$in (6 to 12mm) apart, using an offcut of wood as a spacer so that the gap is constant across its length. If the platform is up to 10ft (3m) in width, you can lay full lengths of timber across; however, for wider platforms the lengths will have to be butt-joined. Stagger the joins at each side of the platform in alternate rows so that there are no continuous break lines across the surface.

Secure the slats to the bearers by hammering in 1$\frac{1}{2}$in (35mm) long floorboard nails, two per bearer position.

The raised timber deck

A more substantial structure can be constructed along the lines of a traditional veran-dah, normally attached to the side of a house with access via a door or french window. The deck comprises a number of upright posts set on concrete pads, with an arrangement of joists fixed on top, and attached to a stout wallplate bolted to the house wall. The decking itself is fixed over the joists. By extending the length of the uprights, a side rail can be incorporated into the design; extending the uprights even further allows you to assemble a pergola or awning over the deck. Seating can be incorporated into the main structure of the deck if required.

For access onto the deck, a simple set of timber steps can be constructed. If the deck is built over an existing door, direct access to and from the house is possible—you may be able to convert an existing window into a doorway for this purpose.

Planning the structure

Decide what you are likely to use the deck for, as this helps you determine its overall size: if you intend to dine outdoors, it must be sufficiently large to accommodate a table and chairs with space for people to pass behind when serving a meal. Where the deck will be used as a sunbathing area, space must be allowed for loungers.

Consider how the deck will appear when attached to the house wall: if it is fairly nar-row—say about 10ft (3m)—and projects out from the wall about 20ft (6m), it could resem-ble a pier at the seaside. However, a deck of this width running along the wall of the house would probably appear to be in better pro-portion. A squarer deck, on the other hand, is more in keeping with a corner location, set in the angle between two walls that meet at right-angles.

Draw a scale plan of the garden on graph paper and mark in the intended position and size of the deck, plus access arrangements and other features which might influence the design. Draw a side elevation of the site to illustrate the way the ground slopes: the deck can be constructed on sloping ground by adjusting the length of the timber posts so that the deck surface is horizontal.

Set up stringlines and pegs to mark the perimeter of the proposed deck so that you can imagine the visual impact it will have on the garden and the house.

Timber requirements

Use the plans you have drawn to work out the amount of timber needed. The main

Decking 2

structural components are made from two stock sizes of timber. For the below-deck supports, use $5\frac{1}{2} \times 1\frac{1}{2}$in (138 × 38mm) timber, with 3in (75mm) square timber for the above-deck supports. The deck joists should be made from $5\frac{1}{2} \times 1\frac{1}{2}$in (138 × 38mm) softwood, supporting slats of the same size timber laid flat rather than on edge.

Setting the concrete pads
The timber posts are supported on concrete pads cast on compacted hardcore. Each pad is about 16in (400mm) square and about 6in (150mm) thick. It is not essential to make the tops of the pads level with each other, as the length of the posts can be adjusted accordingly.

Use stringlines and pegs to mark the position of each pad on the ground. Allow for the pads to be spaced about 55in (1.4m) apart (measurements should be taken from the pad centres, not their edges). Measure out from the house wall the front-to-back dimension of the deck and mark the positions of the outer pads, then measure back toward the wall to determine the location of the remaining pads.

Dig out the earth and add the hardcore as necessary at each pad position, ram this down, then add and rake smooth the blinding layer of sand (see Foundations, pages 8-9, for details). Cast the concrete in the cut-out. There is no need to set up timber formwork for the pad castings, as the sides of the cut-out will suffice.

The posts themselves are housed in metal plate sockets, which are set on each pad and secured with bolts to the wet concrete. Ensure that the sockets are aligned with each other, and square to the wall, by setting up temporary stringlines as a guide.

Treat the ground area which will be below the deck with a permanent weedkiller, then spread pea gravel over the surface.

Setting the supporting posts
The main supporting posts are made up from a combination of three 10ft (3m) lengths of $5\frac{1}{2} \times 1\frac{1}{2}$in (138 × 38mm) timber bonded together with waterproof woodworking adhesive and secured with 4in (100mm) nails for strength. Each "combination" post has a

3in (75mm) square tenon cut at the base so that it will fit into the socket of the plate fixing attached to the concrete pad. Once cut, treat the tenons with preservative, then insert them in the sockets with their broad faces to the side of the deck.

On uneven ground the posts will not all be the same length so mark the finished height on each post. If a pergola is being incorporated into the deck, rest a length of timber on top of the lowest post so that it stretches across to the adjacent post edge. Set a spirit level on top of the timber, adjust until level, then mark the second post to the same height as the first. Repeat for the other pergola posts, then remove them one by one and saw to length. A pergola roof should be about 7ft (2.1m) above the deck surface.

Fitting the deck joists
The deck joists are nailed around the supporting posts at the required height for the platform. You may also want to incorporate a split-level surface in the deck, in which case upper and lower joists will be needed.

Mark on the outer support posts the height for the underside of the joists, then measure the lengths required and cut from $5\frac{1}{2} \times 1\frac{1}{2}$in (138 × 38mm) timber. Hold the outer joists against the marked posts, set horizontal with a spirit level placed on top, then secure to the sides of the posts with 4in (100mm) nails. Use four nails per post, arranged as the corners of a square. Butt-join the return lengths of joist timber end-to-face at external corners.

Installing a wallplate
Where the deck adjoins the house wall it is necessary to attach a stout timber wallplate for the outer joists and intermediate timbers to rest on. Measure the length required and cut from $5\frac{1}{2} \times 1\frac{1}{2}$in (138 × 38mm) timber. Mark out notches $2\frac{3}{4}$in (69mm) deep and $1\frac{1}{2}$in (38mm) wide on the top edge of the wallplate, spaced $16\frac{1}{2}$in (423mm) apart, with a notch at each end to take the outer joists. Cut the notches using a saw and chisel.

Drill holes in the wallplate at 18in (450mm) intervals to take masonry bolts, hold against the wall and mark through the fixing holes. Secure the wallplate to the wall, ensuring that

Constructing a deck

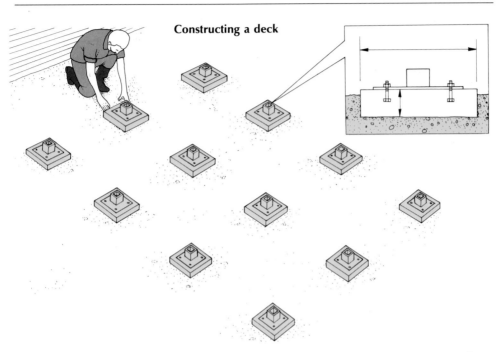

1 Concrete pads are set across the base of the proposed timber deck, and metal plate and socket fixings bolted down. The pads form the support for the deck's upright posts. Correct spacing is important. It does not matter if the ground is uneven, as the posts are cut to the correct level later, and the deck fixed horizontally.

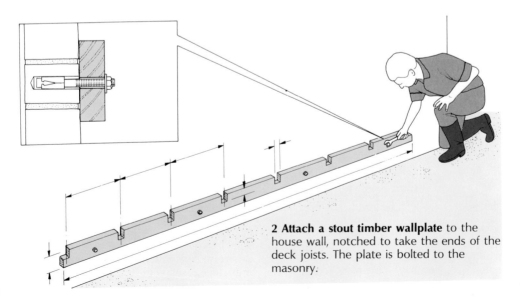

2 Attach a stout timber wallplate to the house wall, notched to take the ends of the deck joists. The plate is bolted to the masonry.

Decking 3

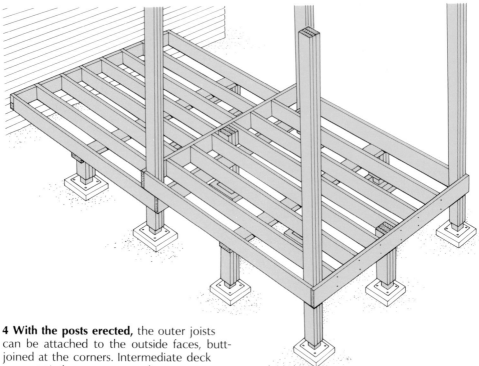

4 With the posts erected, the outer joists can be attached to the outside faces, butt-joined at the corners. Intermediate deck support timbers are propped up on shortened posts.

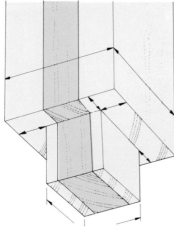

3 The main support posts are made up of three lengths of timber bonded together with glue and nails. The bottom end is then tenoned to fit into the plate sockets.

it is set perfectly horizontal, and at the correct height to coincide with the ends of the joists.

Fitting the intermediate deck supports

Intermediate deck supports are provided by lengths of $5 \times \frac{1}{2} \times 1\frac{1}{2}$in (127 × 12 × 38mm) timber laid flat under the joists and supported on the combination posts which have been cut down.

Measure the distance from the base of each intermediate post to the underside of the outer joists and deduct $1\frac{1}{2}$in (38mm). Cut the posts to this length and slot them in their sockets, supporting the deck support timber. Nail the deck support timber to the ends of the posts.

Fitting the joists

Cut the intermediate joists to length to span from the front outer joists to the wall, then cut notches to match those cut in the wallplate. The tops of the intermediate joists must be level with the top edge of the wallplate and the top edge of the outer joists.

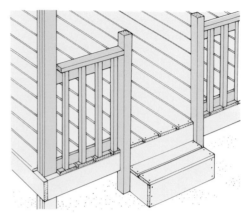

5 Cut the decking slats to length and nail to the tops of the joists, using two fixings per joist. Leave a gap of $\frac{3}{16}$in (4mm) between each slat, using a wooden spacer as a guide.

Fit the joists by setting their notched ends on the wallplate and butting the other ends against the inside face of the outer joist. Secure by driving nails through the outer joists into the end of the intermediate joists. Nail through the notched joints into the wallplate at the other end.

Laying the decking timber
When the outer framework of the deck has been erected, lay the decking surface. Cut all the lengths of timber to fit between the outer joists, then position them across the framework and secure at each joist position with 3in (75mm) round wire nails. Space each of the slats about $\frac{1}{8}$ to $3\frac{1}{6}$in (3 to 4mm) apart for ventilation and drainage of rainwater from the surface.

Incorporating rails and seating
Side rails can be built around the decking by using the main supporting posts as the corner supports. Nail lengths of 3 × 2in (75 × 50mm) timber horizontally across the posts, about

Thinner balusters fixed under a handrail make an attractive frontage to the decking, and are simply pinned on. Set them at each side of a pair of intermediate posts fixed at each side of the entrance steps.

18in (450mm) from the deck surface. Fix intermediate supporting posts of 3in (75mm) sq timber between the deck surface and the rail: these supports should be notched to accommodate the rail near the top and at the bottom to fit over the edge of the outer joists, to which they are then nailed.

Thinner balusters (the uprights making up the balustrade) of $1\frac{1}{2}$in (38mm) sq timber can be nailed underneath the rail, spaced about 2in (50mm) apart, at each side of a small flight of steps leading up the front of the deck.

Intermediate support posts can be used to form the framework of a built-in seating unit, clad with planks of thinner timber. A table with a slatted top could be constructed in the same way.

Incorporating a tree seat
If you have an attractive tree in your garden, within the proposed area of the raised decking, you will be able to incorporate this feature in the overall design of the unit.

Construct a wall around the tree from

Decking 4

bricks, concrete walling blocks, dry-stone walling blocks, or even timber, so that it protrudes through the floor of the decking by about 18in (450mm). Simple bench seating fixed to the top of the wall will provide a shady place to sit.

Foundation details

Before you start to construct the decking, build the wall around the tree. For a masonry wall you will, of course, have to create suitable foundations on which to build. A basic strip foundation around the perimeter of the proposed wall will be sufficient (see page 6), although you must be careful not to damage the roots of the tree when digging the foundation trench.

Where the roots are large, you will have to bridge the foundation trench to avoid them; make sure that this does not unduly affect the stability of the wall. If the roots are small you may be able to trim them back a little (although this will have the effect of limiting the tree's growth above ground).

Casting the foundations

Cast the concrete foundations and allow to cure properly before building the wall. The total height of the wall depends on how high the decking is above ground level, but usually you will need to lay about ten courses of bricks to give sufficient height above deck level for comfortable sitting.

Building the walls

Lay the bricks in stretcher bond, turning bricks in alternate courses to continue the return walls. When the wall is built to the correct height, neaten the mortar joints and allow to set hard for two days. If you are using blocks, the principle of construction is the same.

Making the seat

The seat itself is composed of eight lengths of 5 × 1in (75 × 25mm) softwood screwed in pairs to three cross-pieces of 2 × 1in (50 × 25mm) softwood. Arrange the pairs around the walls, abutting them end-to-face. Attach the cross-pieces to each face of the walls using metal angle brackets screwed into wallplugs.

A timber seat unit

Create a timber tree seat protruding from the raised decking using old railway sleepers stacked as for a retaining wall (see page 34). Allow about three courses of sleepers above the level of the timber decking. Connect the layers of sleepers with a metal band bent over the top and screwed through pre-drilled holes to a sleeper in each row.

Adapting the decking

Naturally, because the decking is pierced by the tree seat walling, you will have to adapt the structure accordingly. To do this, you will have to construct a timber frame around the wall, and ideally fixed to it, in order to support the ends of the decking slats.

Run the slat support joists alongside the side walls of the tree seat and attach them with expanding bolts, as used to attach the wallplate. To support the ends of the joists running up to the front and back faces of the side walls you will need to fit secondary wallplates, in exactly the same way as the main wallplate, notched to accept the ends of the joists. With a timber sleeper wall, simply screw on the joists and secondary wallplates.

Fix the decking slats to the joists, as previously described, nailing them additionally to the supporting timbers surrounding the tree seat walling.

Attractive geometrical patterns (right) can be formed by the decking. The more complex, intricate patterns may require more elaborate supports. The options available include chequerboard (top right), angled chequerboard (top left), concentric rectangles (bottom right) and herringbone (bottom left). In some situations it is preferable to opt for a simple arrangement of parallel slats, perhaps laid on a diagonal in relation to the adjacent house wall, in order to create a dynamic effect.

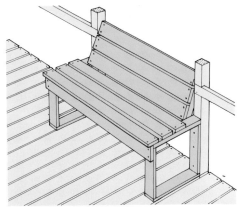

A tree seat can be supported on a brick plinth that is built on the ground and rises through a hole in the deck.

Built-in seating uses the intermediate supporting posts of the handrails as its main framework.

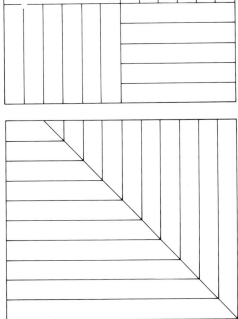

Steps: introduction

Steps give pedestrian access to the various parts of a sloping or split-level garden, while additionally providing a visual link between the separate elements—vegetable patch, lawn, planting beds, and so on. There are basically two types of steps—freestanding or cut-in—although there are many variations in the construction materials.

Cut-in steps
Cut-in steps are used where you need to negotiate a slope or a bank. The shape of the steps is cut out in the earth itself and various materials used for the treads (the parts of the steps on which you walk) and risers (the vertical parts). Cut-in steps may be formal, regular flights or meandering and informal.

Freestanding steps
Where you need access from ground level to a higher, terraced level, freestanding steps are more suitable. Built either at right angles to the retaining wall of the terrace, or parallel with it, they are usually formal in appearance.

Step formats
Sketch out the position and shape of the steps on squared paper to help you to determine how they will look and how they will fit in with the existing garden plan. Perhaps most important is to draw a side elevation of the steps, which will show you just how steep they will need to be.

You will have to take into account certain safety criteria with regard to the format. If the flight is too steep, it will be tiring to climb. Where it is too shallow there is a danger of tripping. The following dimensions are typical for comfortable, safe walking:

Risers should usually be 4 to 5in (100 to 125mm) deep, but may be up to 6 or 7in (150 or 175mm).

Treads should not be less than 12in (300mm) from front to back (sufficient to take the ball of your foot when descending without the back of your leg scraping on the step above). Consider who will use the steps: treads 24in (600mm) wide will accommodate only one person; for two people walking side by side

Basic step types

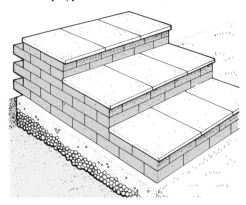 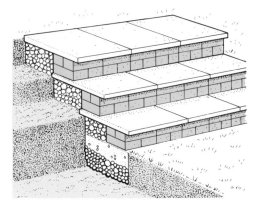

Freestanding steps are built between one flat area and another, and are "toothed into" the retaining wall to prevent the structures from parting. The perimeter walls that form the sides of the flight are built either on a raft foundation or on strip foundations under each wall.

Cut-in steps are built into a bank or slope, the shape of the flight sculpted in the ground itself, which forms the foundation. The bottom of the flight rests on a concrete strip footing. The bottom riser is built on the foundation and backfilled with hardcore, then treads are laid on top of this; subsequent risers and treads are built on the back of (or behind) the lower treads.

Cast concrete 1

make them 60in (1.5m) wide.

The nosing is the front edge of the tread, which should project beyond the riser by about 1in (25mm) to define the shape of the step with an edge of shadow.

Calculating the number of steps

To work out how many steps you will need, measure the vertical height you need to scale and divide this figure by the height of a single riser plus tread. With a terraced site just measure the height of the retaining wall. On a sloping site the job is more complicated. Drive a peg into the ground at the top of the slope and a length of cane into the ground at the base of the slope. Tie a length of string between the peg and the cane and set it horizontal using a spirit level. Measure the distance from the base of the cane to the string to give the vertical height of the slope: divide this by the depth of a riser plus tread to give the number of steps that will fit into the slope.

Safety features

Steep flights should include a handrail—about 2ft 9in (840mm) above tread height—on each side, which extends about 12in (300mm) beyond the flight, possibly linked with existing fencing or railings for a unified scheme. Alternatively you could build a wall (at handrail height) at each side of the flight.

Flights comprising more than 10 steps should be broken halfway with a landing which provides a good resting place and can also break a fall. Take this into account when calculating the number of treads required.

The treads should slope slightly towards the front—a fall of about $\frac{1}{2}$in (12mm) is adequate—so that rainwater will drain off rapidly. This is particularly important in winter, when ice would make the steps slippery and dangerous. For the same reason, choose only slab treads with non-slip textured faces.

Drainage from the steps

Although you should slope the front of the treads forward, this could cause damp problems where the flight faces a house wall. The considerable amount of water streaming down the treads must be diverted from the wall by creating a shallow cross channel at the base of the steps leading to an existing drainage inlet or gully.

On steps that run adjacent to walls it is also advisable to include drainage channels on the wall side of the flight, so that water can be taken from the surface of the treads.

Material options

The materials you choose should blend in with their context. For example, when building freestanding steps up to a terrace, use the same materials for the risers as were used for the retaining wall of the terrace; where the steps continue an existing path, use the same paving materials for the treads.

Many types of bricks, blocks, pavers, walling blocks and paving slabs are suitable for use in constructing garden steps. You can use bricks and blocks both for the risers and for the treads; face textures may be smooth, pitted or, in the case of decorative concrete blocks, resemble split stone. Slabs, although suitable only for the treads, may be smooth-faced, riven, or even geometrically patterned for an ornate appearance.

Softening the appearance of steps

A flight of steps can appear harsh and angular unless you visually soften them in some way. Colourful edging plants introduced at the sides of cut-in steps will minimize the angularity of the flight. You can even plant low-growing species against the risers: this will reduce the harsh lines of the steps and clearly mark the change of level.

On broad steps, place pots of colourful plants on the treads to create an avenue of foliage and flowers.

Casting concrete steps

A durable, if utilitarian, set of steps can be cast in concrete in situ. You can leave the concrete bare, or else cover it with other paving materials such as bricks, slabs or even quarry tiles. The steps are cast in timber formwork—known as "shuttering":

Tray shuttering One method of constructing concrete shuttering for garden steps is to make up a number of three-piece timber trays—one for each step—consisting of a pair of side boards with a front riser support fixed across. Use 8 × 1in (200 × 25mm) soft-

Steps: cast concrete 2

wood for the trays, with the front edge of the side pieces sloping inward towards the bottom to make the top front edge of each tread protrude. Alternatively, form the sides of the steps from $\frac{3}{4}$in (20mm) thick plywood, cut to the stepped shape and fixed in place with stakes and braces.

For a tray construction, set the trays in position on the prepared foundations, remembering to slope them downwards by not more than $\frac{1}{2}$in (12mm) for rainwater run-off. Support the side boards with 4 × 2in (100 × 50mm) timber stakes braced with horizontal timbers spanning the width of the flight: this is to prevent the considerable weight of the wet concrete from forcing the side boards apart. Brace the front riser supports with a diagonal length of timber staked to the ground at the base of the flight of steps, and fix wedge supports at each riser position.

Apply oil—old engine oil is suitable—to the inside faces of the shuttering to prevent the concrete from adhering to the wood. Fill most of the cavity inside the tray shuttering with hardcore, rammed down well and topped with a layer of sand to fill any large voids, leaving about 3in (75mm) depth for the layer of concrete.

Mix up the concrete, preferably using a motorized mixing machine, in the proportions 1 part cement : $2\frac{1}{2}$ parts damp sand : 4 parts coarse aggregate.

Pour in the mixed concrete and work right into the corners of the trays. Tamp the mix well down, levelling it with the top of the formwork trays. Use a steel trowel to smooth the concrete.

Reinforce the front edge of each tread on cast concrete steps by embedding a length of steel rod in the tread, spanning the width of the step.

Nail a length of wooden triangular moulding to the back top edge of each riser support shuttering to form a bevelled nosing on each tread. This will prevent the concrete from crumbling, and at the same time avoid a sharp edge which could be a danger to young children using the steps.

Leave the concrete to harden fully for about four days, then remove the shuttering. Lay your choice of facing material directly on the concrete, bedding it in mortar. The finish should be even and slip-resistant.

CAST CONCRETE STEPS

Cast concrete steps are made by constructing timber shuttering in situ, adding a hardcore backfilling, then topping with about 4in (100mm) thickness of concrete. The formwork tray must be staked and braced to prevent the concrete from forcing it apart. As an alternative to using timber formwork you can construct the side shuttering from $\frac{3}{4}$in (20mm) thick plywood.

MAKING LOG STEPS

Masonry steps can appear incongruous in an informal garden and timber steps will often be more appropriate. Cut-in steps are more suitable for this type of garden, and using sawn logs as the risers is a quick and easy way to form an attractive flight.

At each step position, drive in stout, rough-hewn stakes to align with the nosing position at each side. Place a log behind the stakes so that they support it, then backfill with hardcore. Ram down the hardcore with a sledgehammer, then top with fine gravel as the tread surface.

You can also make up a single riser from two or more slimmer logs stacked on top of each other. As an alternative to using round logs you can obtain old railway sleepers sold specifically for use in garden construction. Fix the sleepers with stakes, as for logs, to create a more formal yet still rustic flight.

Turning the flight within the bank or slope is easily done by simply fanning out the logs or sleepers.

When using timber steps, be wary of the treads becoming slippery after rainfall. There is no truly effective way to prevent this from happening, as this is the nature of the material, but keeping the steps clear of moss and lichen will lessen the risk of a slip.

MAKING CURVED STEPS

Garden steps need not always conform to a straight format. Where you have enough space, consider creating a flight composed of circular or segmental treads to scale a graceful shallow rise in the ground, perhaps leading to a formal terrace beyond.

Mark out the shape of the steps with an improvised pair of compasses made from a length of wood attached to a stake with string. Cut out the rough shape of the circular treads and cast concrete slab foundations beneath (see page 8–9). There is no need to make the foundation slab round, however; just cover the corners with soil after you have built the steps.

Use bricks or blocks laid on mortar to form the curving front edges of the treads, and fill the circles with gravel or cobblestones. You could even lay turf for a grassy flight of steps, but bear in mind that these would be very difficult to maintain and mow satisfactorily.

Circular landings

A variation on curved steps is to create circular landings, staggered and part-overlapping on a shallow slope. Use the same construction methods as for curved steps, adding compacted hardcore before the gravel.

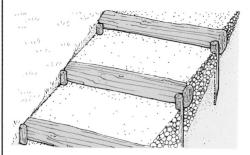

Log steps are created by supporting log risers with wooden stakes and backfilling with gravel.

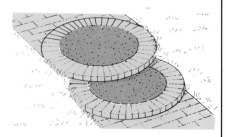

Circular steps are made from brick risers backfilled with gravel or other paving.

Steps: cut-in 1

Measuring
Measure the vertical height of the slope (see box, opposite) to determine how many steps you will need to construct.

Arranging the stringlines
Mark out the shape and size of the flight of steps on the surface of the bank using stringlines stretched between pegs driven into the ground at the sides.

First, run strings down the bank to indicate the width of the steps, then set up more strings horizontally to define the tread nosings.

Cutting out the rough shape
Working from the top of the flight, start to dig out the rough shape of the steps using a spade. Take care not to dislodge any of the stringlines. Use a stout length of timber end-on, or a sledgehammer, to compact the earth at each tread position. Although you can stand on the rough cut-outs while compacting those above, take care not to collapse them. The less you stand on the steps while they are under construction, the better, so try to compact the earth from the sides.

Defining the accurate shape
Once you have worked out the overall shape of the flight, take precise measurements and go back over the surface trimming each step accurately. Dig below and behind the nosing strings to allow for the thickness of the slab (or other) treads and brick or blockwork risers. Compact the base again if necessary.

Casting a concrete footing
On a large flight—more than, say, about 10 steps—it is advisable to cast a concrete footing in a trench at the base to support the bottom riser and prevent the entire flight from sliding down the bank. Dig the trench under the position of the bottom riser, about twice the front-to-back measurement of the riser, about 4in (100mm) wider than the step, and about 4in (100mm) deep. Ram hardcore into the base of the trench and top up to ground level with fresh concrete. Compact the concrete, level it and allow to set overnight before building on the surface.

Building the first riser
Construct the first riser on the concrete footing using your choice of blocks, bricks or

Making cut-in steps

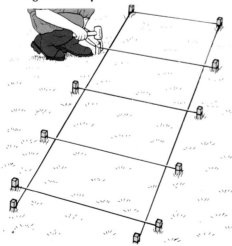

1 Set up stringlines and pegs to define the sides of the flight and the positions of the tread nosings before digging out the bank.

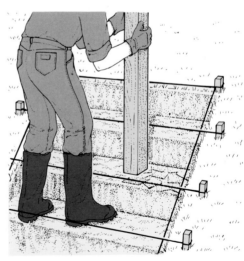

2 Cut out the rough shape of the steps using a spade, then compact the earth using a stout timber post; avoid crumbling the cut-outs.

MEASURING THE SLOPE

Work out how many steps you will need to make by measuring the vertical height of the slope. To do this, drive a peg into the top of the slope and a cane at the bottom. Connect the two with string. Set the string horizontal using a spirit level, then measure the cane from ground level to the string.

Divide the figure by the depth of a riser plus tread to give the number of steps you can fit into the slope.

If a whole number of steps is not possible, dig out the ground at the base or add earth at the top.

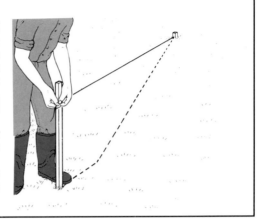

stone. Leave the stringlines in position: it is these that will give you the accurate positions for the nosings of each tread.

Whichever riser material you choose, the laying principle is the same, and follows basic bricklaying techniques. See pages 62–5 for full information on these skills, and adapt the technique for the steps.

Mix up some mortar and trowel a layer or "screed" about $\frac{3}{8}$in (10mm) thick onto the footing. Furrow the surface with your trowel to aid suction and adhesion. Place the first row of bricks or blocks on the screed and press down firmly, wiggling slightly to bed evenly. Scoop some mortar onto the trowel and scrape this off onto the end of each brick

3 Define the step shapes more accurately, according to the guide strings and the chosen size of risers and treads.

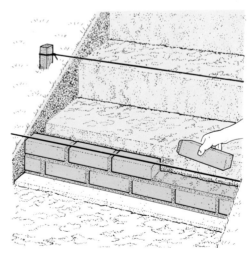

4 Lay the first riser on a concrete footing if necessary, building up two courses of bricks or blocks in a basic stretcher bond.

Steps: cut-in 2

or block to form the vertical joints. Place a spirit level along the riser to check that it is horizontal, and adjust if necessary.

When the first course of bricks or blocks is laid, trowel a further screed of mortar on top and lay the second course.

Cutting bricks or blocks

Stagger the joints between bricks or blocks by half the brick or block length in the first and second courses to form a basic stretcher bond. To maintain this bonding arrangement you will have to cut the end units in half (although in practice if the bottom edges of the risers are buried in the bank this is not necessary; indeed, leaving the bricks or blocks whole helps to anchor the risers in place).

To cut a brick or block, score a line across at the halfway mark with a bolster chisel, then place the brick or block on a firm, flat surface and strike with a club hammer and the bolster chisel.

Laying the first tread

Tip hardcore behind the riser and ram it down well—but take care not to dislodge the riser in doing so. Add more hardcore up to the base of the tread position and ram this down too. You are now ready to lay the tread.

Slab tread Lift a slab into position on the prepared base and align its top outer edge with the first stringline. If the fit seems accurate, remove the slab and trowel a screed of mortar around the perimeter of the riser. Alternatively, you can stick down the tread using five dabs of mortar (one on each corner and one in the middle) or a complete bed of mortar; the latter is best for a flight that will be put to heavy use.

Press the slab onto the mortar and wiggle it to help compress the mortar. Again, align the slab nosing with the stringline. If the step is two slabs wide, lay the second slab, leaving a small gap between the first and the second slab, to be filled later with a dry sand and cement (3:1) mix.

Place a spirit level on top of the slabs to check that they are level with each other; check also that the slabs slope not more than $\frac{1}{2}$in (12mm) towards the nosing for rainwater run-off. Tap the front edge gently but firmly with the shaft of your club hammer to give the correct slope. (Place a small shim under the down-side end of the spirit level

5 Tip hardcore behind the riser in the tread position, ram this down well, then top with sand to fill the hollows.

6 Lay the slab treads on a perimeter screed of mortar, aligning the nosings with the stringlines stretched across the flight.

"Flexible" pavers

and set the bubble to horizontal in order to set the fall.)

Small-scale treads You can use bricks or blocks as the treads, laying them on mortar in the same way as slabs. However, it is more important to set the individual pieces accurately to avoid high spots or dips that could cause people to trip. Nosings should overhang the risers in the usual way.

Use a stout length of timber on its side to level the bricks or blocks, by striking it with a club hammer. As with slab treads, ensure a slight slope towards the front for drainage.

Laying the remaining steps

The second riser can be laid on the back edge of the first tread, or immediately behind it on a base of hardcore topped with sand—decide which method you intend to use in the planning stages.

Whichever method you choose, trowel a screed of mortar beneath the riser position and lay the bricks or blocks as previously described. Backfill with hardcore as before and lay the second tread. Continue laying risers and treads in this way to complete the flight of steps.

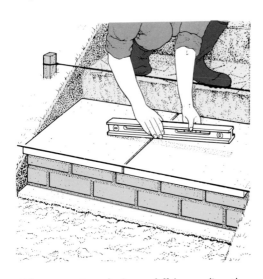

7 Incorporate a drainage fall by angling the treads slightly downwards towards the front. Use a shim to keep this angle consistent (see page 16).

Pointing the joints

To neaten the mortar joints between bricks, scrape off excess and form a half-round profile by running a length of hosepipe along the joints. Alternatively, form bevelled pointing profiles by drawing the blade of your bricklaying trowel along the joints.

Brush a dry mortar mix between the paving slab treads, or else fill the joints with wet mortar and neaten the profiles. Point the back edge of the tread where it meets the riser above.

Allow the mortar to harden for about one week before putting the steps to full use.

STEPS WITH FLEXIBLE PAVERS

Concrete block pavers can be successfully used to construct a set of garden steps, using the dry-fixing technique employed when laying pavers on a patio (see pages 34–5).

Prepare the base for the flight as previously described, adding hardcore to the prepared earth surface of the treads. Starting at the bottom of the flight, set a row of blocks on end in concrete in a narrow trench and shovel hardcore behind them. Ram this down, then top with about 2in (50mm) of sand. Place the blocks for the treads on the sand, behind the riser blocks.

Compact the blocks into the sand using a block of wood with a club hammer, set them level, then proceed to lay the second and subsequent risers and treads.

Brush sand over the surface of the blocks and work well into the joints. Tamp the surface again with the block of wood and hammer to complete the steps.

Because they are made up of many small units—the flexible pavers—you will find that in the course of time and with frequent use, parts of the steps will tend to sink slightly. Provided that settlement is not too severe (and it should not be if you have compacted the pavers properly), this should cause no problems in access. Rather, the steps will assume an aged appearance, which is usually desirable. The impression of age can be strengthened further by adding plants of low-growing, mat-like habit to the edges, and to the joins between treads and risers. Be sure, however, to keep the treads themselves clear of moss and weeds.

Steps: freestanding 1

Preparation

Freestanding steps should be constructed in the same or similar materials as the vertical terrace they are intended to climb, and ideally should be tied into the terrace as an integral feature.

Construct strip foundations to support the perimeter walls of the steps, and set up stringlines and profile boards as a guide to laying the masonry (see box below). The strings should be aligned centrally on the strip foundation, spaced apart by the width of the bricks or blocks you have chosen. See page 62–3 for full information on the bricklaying techniques needed to erect the perimeter walls and risers.

Constructing the first riser

The flight of steps is made up of a number of plinths, two courses of bricks or blocks in

---

SETTING UP PROFILE BOARDS

Profile boards used to mark out strip foundations (see page 11) can also be used to set the building lines for constructing a set of garden steps. Use a pair of profile boards and strings to mark the front edge of the U-shaped foundation trench needed for the steps. For the side walls of the steps, set up profile boards at the front end, the strings intersecting the previously fixed ones at right angles.

Stringlines At the terrace wall, you cannot fix profile boards. Instead, connect the ends of the strings to the masonry of the terrace with masonry nails driven in at the correct height and width—check for accuracy with a spirit level.

Position the stringlines to correspond with the width of the brickwork or blockwork you intend to use to construct the side walls.

Transferring guidelines Transfer the positions of the stringlines to a screed of bricklaying mortar trowelled onto the concrete strip foundation by running a spirit level, held vertically with a trowel blade held at its base, along the mortar.

1 Knock nails into the profile boards to correspond with the width of the building material and attach strings to the nails.

2 Transfer the positions of the parallel stringlines to a screed of mortar using a spirit level for accuracy and a trowel to mark the mortar.

---

depth, and each one smaller than the lower one by the front-to-back dimension of the treads. The plinths, stacked one on top of the other, with their back edges flush, form the skeleton of the steps.

Start to build the first, largest plinth on the strip foundations you have cast. Mix up some mortar in the proportions 1 part cement : 5 parts sand. Trowel a $\frac{3}{8}$in (10mm) thick screed of mortar onto the strip foundation, then transfer the position of the stringlines onto this layer.

To do this, stand a spirit level vertically alongside the string and hold the blade of a bricklaying trowel at its base. Draw the spirit level and trowel along the screed of mortar to scribe a line that lies directly below the string.

Furrow the surface of the mortar screed with the trowel to aid suction and adhesion of the masonry.

Starting at the terrace side, lay the first course of bricks or blocks for the riser, lining up the edges with the scribed line on the screed. Wiggle the brick or block as you press it down to bed it firmly and evenly, then tap with the handle of your trowel. Butter the ends of the bricks or blocks with wedges of wet mortar to form the vertical joints and press into place against the previously laid piece.

At the corner of the riser, turn a brick or block at right angles to continue the wall onto the front face. Trowel mortar on top of the first course of masonry and lay the second course in the same way, this time staggering the joints by half, stretcher fashion.

Place a spirit level along the stretcher-bonded walls to ensure they are horizontal, and adjust if necessary. If the mortar joints are not applied consistently thickly, the perimeter walls will not rise evenly. Span across both side walls with the spirit level on a long straight-edged plank to check that they, too, are aligned.

Toothing in the steps

In order that the flight of steps is permanently and rigidly attached to the terrace wall, it is necessary to bond the riser side walls into it. This is done by "toothing in"—ie chopping out alternate bricks or blocks from the terrace

and inserting alternate bricks from the new walls into the hole by half their length.

Chop out the masonry carefully using a club hammer and cold chisel. Brush dust and debris from the hole and dampen the surface to avoid the masonry sucking too much moisture from the fresh mortar, which could cause it to crack. Trowel mortar into the base of the hole, and around the end of the new brick or block. Insert the brick or block into the hole and tap to bed it down.

Backfilling the plinth

Leave the mortar to stiffen for a few hours before backfilling the plinth with hardcore. Tip in the broken bricks and rubble and ram well down. No hardcore must protrude above the level of the masonry walls.

Spread a layer of sand over the hardcore to blind the surface, filling hollows. Draw a length of wood across the walls to level and smooth the sand.

Laying the subsequent plinths

Reposition the stringlines as a guide to laying the second riser walls, stretching them between canes stuck in the ground just outside the concrete footings—at this stage the profile boards will be of no further use and can be removed.

Construct the second riser plinth on top of the first, its front edge set back by the front-to-back dimension of the tread. Tooth the masonry into the terrace wall. Backfill this plinth with hardcore, top with sand, then build the remaining plinths by the same procedure until the flight has reached the top of the terrace.

As the plinth walls rise, check frequently that they are horizontal. You can check whether the walls are bowing outwards by holding a long spirit level or length of straight-edged timber diagonally against the sides: any curvature should be corrected before the mortar starts to harden.

Check also that the mortar joints are the same thickness throughout, using a gauge rod: this is made of a length of timber marked off in brick-plus-mortar joint increments. Held vertically against the plinth walls it will show where the joints become inconsistent.

Steps: freestanding 2

Fitting the treads

When the masonry shell of the steps is finished you can add the treads. For slab treads, trowel five dabs of mortar onto the hardcore and sand base and lower the tread into place. Tap down with the shaft of a trowel, incorporating the drainage fall towards the front. Check with a spirit level that the slab is correctly aligned and adjust if necessary.

Lay the treads for the remaining plinths in the same way, then point all the mortar joints in the walls and between the slab treads. Allow the mortar to set fully for about one week before using the steps.

Completing the flight

At the top of the flight of steps you should try to continue the run of treads into the existing surface at the same level. This is quite straightforward where the steps lead up to an existing paved area, but where the steps finish at a raised lawn or planting bed it is a good idea to run a path of slabs or bricks (whichever you have used for the treads) through it to give a sense that the steps actually lead somewhere.

Steep steps should be fitted with handrails at each side, as described for cut-in steps (see page 47), while very large freestanding flights can be built with integral side walls, stepped as the flight rises, and capped with slab copings to match the treads. These should be at handrail height, about 2ft 9in (840mm).

Parallel flights

If there is insufficient space in front of the terrace wall to allow the garden steps to protrude you may be able to run the flight parallel with the terrace wall. Construction details are similar to those for a projecting flight, although in this case one side of the plinth is bonded into the brickwork of the terrace rather than into the back edge. It is also necessary to construct a back wall for the flight.

The back wall should incorporate drainage weep holes near the base to enable any water trapped inside to filter away. To form the weep holes, simply omit mortar from three or four vertical joints between bricks or blocks at the base.

Freestanding steps

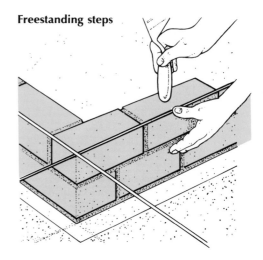

1 Lay the bricks for the first riser in two courses of stretcher bond, aligning the outer top edge with stringlines set up at the perimeter of the foundations.

4 Spread sand over the hardcore. Using a straight-edged length of wood, scrape the sand level with the top edge of the plinth risers ready to accept the treads.

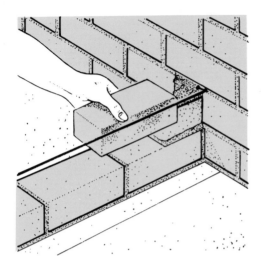

2 Tooth the risers into the terrace wall on alternate courses. Chop out a brick and insert the last riser brick into the hole by half its length, bedded on mortar.

3 Tip hardcore into the plinth and compact it thoroughly with a stout timber post or sledgehammer, taking care not to dislodge the newly laid brickwork walls.

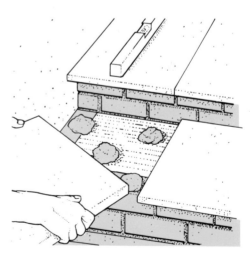

5 Lay the subsequent risers over the first plinth, using the same bonding arrangement. Check frequently that the walls are rising horizontally without bowing at the sides.

6 Bed down the treads on five dabs of fresh mortar trowelled on the hardcore and sand base. Set the slabs level across the surface but sloping forwards slightly for drainage.

Walls: materials 1

Walls are not merely decorative features. They perform numerous functions in the garden, such as defining the boundaries of your property, screening unattractive views, dulling traffic noise and providing a measure of protection against the elements.

Used within the plot they can act as demarcation for, or simply screen off, the various areas such as vegetable patch, lawn, flower-beds or patio. On a split-level site they can be employed to retain a bank of earth, forming a terrace.

BRICK BONDS

Bricks and blocks are generally laid in an overlapping bond to create a rigid structure and to spread the load to the foundations.

Half-brick walls Single thickness, half-brick walls are laid in a "running" or stretcher bond, in which the bricks are laid end to end with their long stretcher faces showing. Alternate rows are staggered by half the length of the brick.

Single-brick walls Double thickness, single-brick walls consist of parallel pairs of half-brick walls with courses of "headers" —or bricks laid across the width of the wall so their end faces are visible.

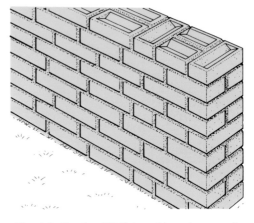

Flemish Garden Wall bond has three or five stretchers to one header per course, the headers often of contrasting colour for decorative effect.

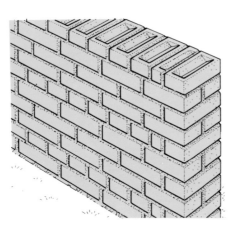

English Garden Wall bond has stretcher and header courses; three or five courses of stretchers to one of headers.

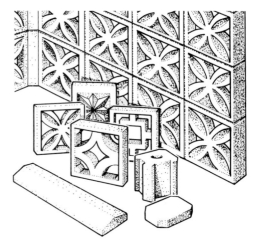

Pierced screen block walls are built in a stack bond, with no overlaps: strength is provided by piers at intervals.

Choice of materials

The materials you choose to construct your garden wall must be suitable for the purpose you want it to perform. Bear in mind colour, texture, shape and size when choosing materials so that the wall will not look incongruous in its setting. The clean lines of some types of bricks are best suited to a formal design, whereas decorative walling blocks are more rugged in appearance and evocative of an informal, natural style. Secondhand bricks or stones are usually available from builder's merchants and demolition sites, and often have a more mellow, weathered look.

Dry-stone walls are constructed without mortar, using large edging blocks with smaller infill pieces, tied by large flat stones.

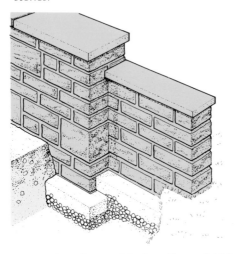

Reconstituted stone block walls are laid in the same way as bricks. Modular units span two or more courses at a time.

Bricks

Moulded from fire-burnt clay or calcium silicate, bricks are made in standard metric units measuring 225 × 112.5 × 75mm, which corresponds roughly to the old imperial size of $8\frac{7}{8} \times 4\frac{3}{8} \times 3$in. Compatibility of size is important where you intend to match a new wall with an old wall. The dimensions given for bricks are, in fact, nominal, as the actual size is $\frac{3}{8}$in (10mm) less all round to allow for the thickness of a mortar joint. Of the many types available, only three are really suitable for garden walling.

Facing bricks, also known as "stocks", have an attractive finish on the sides and ends and come in various colours with rough or smooth textures. "Faced" versions have only one or two attractive sides.

Common bricks are used where appearance is not vital, and are less costly than facing types. Commons have no special facing and are best painted or rendered. Do not use where they are likely to be subjected to heavy stress.

Engineering bricks are dense, smooth and impervious to water, and best for walls that will be exposed to dampness, or where part of the wall will be buried underground. Two classifications of engineering bricks are made—A and B—depending on their combined strength and water-resistance.

Colour and origin

Bricks are also known by a variety of names, which generally refer to their colour and texture, but often to their place of origin and the colour of the clay used in their manufacture—Flettons (from the Cambridgeshire village where they originated), Staffordshire Blues, Leicester Reds, Kentish stocks (in shades of yellow), Dorking stocks (in shades of pink) are examples.

Walls: materials 2

Special-shaped bricks

There is a variety of special-shaped bricks which are used to give a decorative effect to a plain wall, or to protect the structure from the effects of rain.

Bullnoses and bullheads are rectangular, but with one rounded end for use as a stopped end on a garden wall.

Curved bricks are curved in length for use on rounded walls or arches.

Copings come in rounded, bevelled or chamfered format, and are set at the top of a wall to finish it neatly while throwing rainwater clear. They may overhang the wall thickness to give a lip that prevents water trickling down the face of the wall.

Corner pieces are specially shaped copings that span a right-angle corner in a run of walling.

Bricks with frogs and holes

Some bricks have an indent in one face, known as the "frog", which is intended to provide a good strong bond with the mortar. Normally laid uppermost, the frog is filled with mortar during bricklaying.

Performing the same role, some bricks have not frogs but holes pierced through their middles, into which mortar is forced as the joints are formed between courses.

Decorative walling blocks

Moulded from concrete in original moulds, and often with natural stone aggregates added for a more authentic appearance and texture, decorative walling blocks—or "reconstituted" blocks—come in various single sizes and some in modular format to resemble several smaller coursed stones. The modular units are laid just like single bricks or blocks, and have the advantage of being able to achieve, in effect, several courses in one go.

The faces are generally on one long side and one short side. The blocks come in a range of greens, reds, greys, yellows and buffs.

Screen walls

Concrete walling blocks are moulded with various pierced geometric patterns, which allow air to flow through. Ideal as screen walls, these blocks are laid in stack bond—one on top of the other—so are not inherently strong. See pages 68-71 for more information on using pierced blocks.

Dry-stone walls

Natural stone blocks are laid without mortar to create a traditional dry-stone wall with its distinctive angled face, common as English field boundaries but just as successful when

Piers and corners

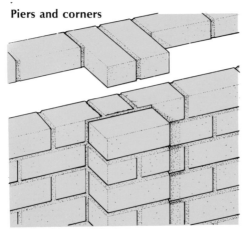

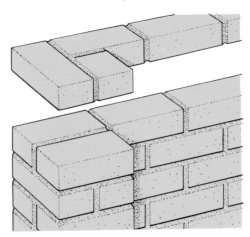

An intermediate pier in stretcher bond is formed by alternating two bricks header-on in one course with a half brick and two three-quarter bricks in the next course.

An end pier in stretcher bond is formed by turning alternate bricks header-on and filling in at the courses between with half bricks to maintain the bond.

used in the garden. See pages 72-3 for more details on construction.

Building piers

Straight walls of brickwork or blockwork more than about 3ft (915mm) high should be supported and strengthened by the addition of a column, or pier, at 6ft (1.8m) intervals, and at each end of the wall. The piers should be linked with the bonding pattern used for the wall.

Forming corners

When turning a corner in brickwork you must maintain the bonding arrangement for strength and continuity. At its most basic, on a stretcher bond wall where bricks overlap each other by half, the corner is formed by turning a brick at right angles to form the return wing of the wall, then alternating bricks at subsequent courses to maintain the pattern.

It is good building practice to build up the corners and ends of a wall first, shortening each new corner by one brick and ending in a whole brick. This process, called "racking back", gives the corners and ends a chance to become stable before the section between them is filled in, in addition to providing a means of checking the level of the structure.

A corner in a half-brick stretcher bond wall is formed by turning a brick at right angles to form the return, then alternating the bond on each course.

Special finishing bricks

Bullnose bricks are rounded at one end to give a neat curved finish to the stop-end of a garden wall of single brick thickness. They are compatible in size with standard bricks.

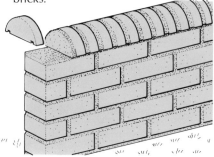

Rounded coping bricks are mortared in a row along the top of a wall, and overhang the sides slightly. Drip grooves in the underside prevent rainwater trickling onto the wall.

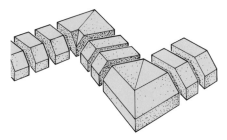

Bevelled coping and corner bricks are used on the top of a masonry wall. The corner bricks are intended to match the chamfered copings that complete the straight runs.

Walls: laying 1

Bricks and concrete blocks enable you to construct straight, curved or angular walls anything from a couple of courses to several feet in height.

However, bricklaying is not a task to be undertaken lightly, and it is essential to learn the basic skills before embarking on a full-scale project. Master the techniques described below and adapt the methods to your particular requirements.

Setting out the foundations

Accurately setting out the foundations of a wall or other masonry structure (see pages 8–17) is of prime importance if the wall is to be laid level, square and adequately supported.

For accuracy in laying the bricks, set up wooden profile boards at each end of the foundation trench, with stringlines stretched between them, spaced apart by the width of the wall—either $4\frac{1}{2}$ or 9in (110 or 230mm) depending on whether you are building a half- or single-brick wall.

Bricklaying equipment

Start by familiarizing yourself with the tools you will need for bricklaying:

A bricklayer's trowel is used to pick up, shape and apply mortar to the foundation and the bricks. The shaft of the trowel is used to tap individual bricks or blocks into place.

A spotboard is a panel of chipboard, plywood or blockboard about 2ft (600mm) square, used to hold the mortar close to the wall you are building; mount it on a portable workbench or stack of bricks so that you can easily scoop off mortar.

A hawk is a smaller board fitted with a handle, with which you can hold small quantities of mortar while laying the bricks.

A spirit level is used frequently to check that individual bricks or blocks and complete courses are horizontal; the level is also used to check that the wall does not bow outwards.

A gauge rod is used to check that the mortar joints are consistently $\frac{3}{8}$in (10mm) thick (see box on page 64).

A bolster chisel has a sharp, straight edge and is used for cutting bricks.

A club hammer is mallet-shaped and is used with a bolster chisel for cutting bricks. First,

mark the break point by holding the bolster chisel at right angles to the brick and tapping the upper end gently with the club hammer. Repeat this on all four faces. Then place the chisel on the stretcher face that will be visible

Laying bricks

1 Set up profile boards, then spread a $\frac{3}{8}$in (10mm) thick screed of mortar over the concrete strip foundation. Furrow the surface.

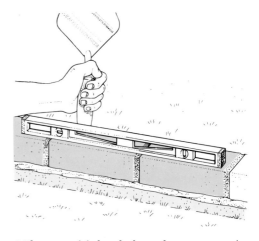

4 Place a spirit level along the course and tap the bricks horizontal using the shaft of your trowel. Pack under low bricks with more mortar.

and give a firm stroke with the hammer.
Pins and strings are used to set each brick course horizontal (see box overleaf).
Buckets are needed for proportioning the ingredients of the bricklaying mortar.

A spade is needed for mixing the mortar on a hard, flat surface (such as a large square board flat on a path or drive).
A wheelbarrow is needed to transport quantities of bricks.

2 Butter the end of the brick with mortar, by drawing the loaded trowel across the end, forming a wedge shape. Furrow the wedge.

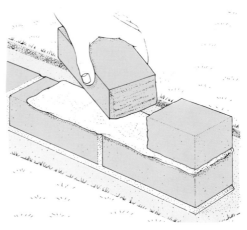

3 Lay the first bricks on the mortar screed, butting the mortared end of the second brick up to the clean end of the first-laid brick.

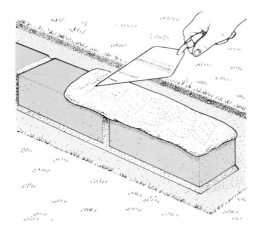

5 Trowel a screed of mortar onto the bricks of the first course, furrow the surface and position the second course on top.

6 Lay the second course as for the first, but start off the course with a brick cut in half across its width to maintain the bond.

Walls: laying 2

BUILDING LEVELS

Simply stacking bricks on top of each other is no guarantee that the wall will rise square and true, and you must be prepared to check frequently that the brick joints are the same thickness throughout, that the bricks are laid horizontally, and that the wall does not bow out at the sides or waver from a straight line.

Once you have exceeded two or three courses in height your profile boards will be redundant as a guide to laying a line and you must set up new markers to which you can lay the bricks.

Racking back Build up the corners and ends of a wall first, stepping back the brickwork by half a brick each course: this allows you to check the structure for squareness. Stretch stringlines between the ends or corners of the wall as a guide to laying the intermediate bricks accurately.

Pins and strings Bricklayer's pins and string-lines are used at each course to check that the bricks are horizontal. Push a pin into the new mortar joint at one end or corner of the wall and stretch the string along the outside edge of the new course, securing it at the opposite end of the wall with a second pin. Lay the intermediate bricks for, and raise the string and pins with, each subsequent course.

Gauge rod Make up a 3ft (915mm) long gauge rod, marked in brick-plus-mortar joint increments. Hold the rod against the corner or end of the brickwork: if the wall is rising properly the marks will be level with the top edge of each brick.

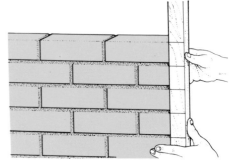

Use a gauge rod to check that the mortar joints are $\frac{3}{8}$in (10mm) thick throughout the courses.

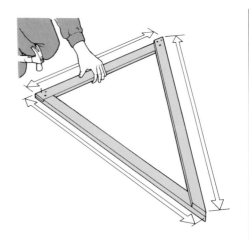

Make a builder's square from three pieces of wood in the proportions 3:4:5 and use to check right-angled corners during bricklaying (see page 15).

Basic bricklaying techniques

Mix up the mortar and tip it onto the spotboard. Scoop up two or three trowel-loads and transfer the mortar to your hawk. Practise slicing off some mortar and scooping it onto your trowel by sliding the blade underneath. Learn how to place the mortar properly: hold the trowel over the site and draw it backwards sharply, turning it over at the same time so that a sausage shape of mortar rolls off the blade.

Using this action, spread a $\frac{3}{8}$in (10mm) thick screed of mortar along the concrete strip foundation on which you are going to build the wall. Furrow the surface of the screed by drawing your trowel blade back along it in ridges: the furrows will aid the adhesion of the brick to the mortar, and form a suction

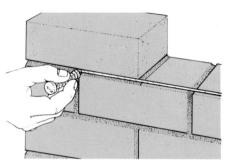

Use pins and strings to set up guidelines to which you can lay the brick courses accurately.

Build up the end and corners first, racked back, then set up stringlines and lay the intermediate brickwork to full height.

when the brick is pressed in place.

Transfer the positions of the stringlines fixed to the profile board to the screed by running a spirit level vertically along each and scribing the mortar with a trowel blade.

Laying the first course

Position the first brick on the screed of mortar, aligned with the scribed marks at each side, and flush with the proposed end of the wall. Press the brick firmly down, wiggling it to increase the suction. Some mortar will be squeezed from the sides of the brick. Scoop up the mortar from the base of the first-laid brick and use to form the vertical joint between it and the second brick.

Scrape the mortar off the trowel onto one end of the second brick, forming a wedge shape. Furrow the wedge with the trowel, then place the brick on the screed, mortared end butted up to the end of the first brick. Scoop up the excess squeezings and use to lay the third brick, and so on.

Place a spirit level on the course of bricks and check whether or not it is horizontal. Adjust the bricks in height either by lifting low ones and packing out with mortar underneath, or by tapping with the shaft of the trowel to sink them further, as necessary.

Cutting bricks

With any bonding pattern there will be some cut bricks. Cut the bricks using a club hammer and bolster chisel. Scribe across the brick with a chisel to indicate the cutting line, place the brick on a firm, flat surface and place the chisel on the line. Strike the chisel sharply with the club hammer to break the brick.

Laying subsequent courses

To form the brickwork bond you must overlap the second row of bricks with the first, so that the vertical joints do not align. For a simple stretcher bond, spread a screed of mortar along the top of the first course of bricks and start the second with a brick cut in half across its width. Continue with whole bricks, finishing the row with a half-brick.

Check the level of the course with the spirit level, then hold the level along the sides of the wall to check that it too is square.

Continue to lay subsequent brick courses to complete the wall, but take into account good building practice regarding checking levels, building to a guideline and racking back the ends and corners (see box above).

Pointing the joints

To neaten the mortar joints, press the blade of a pointing trowel against the vertical joints, bevelling the mortar to one side. Run the blade along the horizontal joints, pressing at the top to form a bevel; this will deflect rainwater from the wall.

Walls: retaining walls

Remodelling a sloping garden

A sloping garden can be laborious to work. A better option might be terraces used as planting beds, paved areas or raised lawns. Build earth-retaining walls to remodel the ground and form interesting features.

Retaining wall format

An earth-retaining wall can be constructed using the same basic building techniques described from page 62 onwards. But remember that the wall must have sufficient mass and solid enough foundations to resist the lateral pressure of earth and water.

A typical single-brick-thick earth-retaining wall up to 4ft (1.2m) high will need strip foundations the length of the wall, 20in (510mm) wide (from front to back), and 6in (150mm) thick. Set the concrete strip in a trench 20in (510mm) below soil level.

The brickwork itself should be a minimum of 9in (230mm) thick (single-brick), bonded using Flemish or English Garden Wall bond, as shown on page 58. Below ground level, use engineering bricks, which are impervious to water, with ordinary bricks above for a decorative appearance. If the wall is likely to rise above 4ft (1.2m) in height you must incorporate piers at each end, plus intermediate piers every 5 or 6ft (1.5 to 1.8m) if the wall is over 10ft (3m) long.

Adding reinforcement

Metal rods tied to a concrete casting buried in the earth bank will give further stability. At the wall end, the rod is mortared into a brick joint; at the casting end the hooked rod is encased in the concrete as an anchor.

An alternative way to stabilize the earth-retaining wall, particularly effective against sinking or slipage, is to incorporate a hooked "toe" into the bottom outer edge of the concrete strip foundation.

During the construction of the wall, you might find it necessary to shore up the earth bank temporarily. This can be achieved using a panel of chipboard held in place by wooden stakes driven into the ground.

Resisting damp

Because the retaining wall is under considerable pressure from the earth it is holding back—and because part of it is actually underground—it is necessary to make provisions against dampness.

Drainage The retained earth must drain freely from the back of the wall to prevent it from becoming waterlogged, so install plastic drainpipes extending through the thickness of the wall and sloping from back to front. Any build-up of water will naturally drain through the pipes, which should simply be mortared in as the wall is constructed. The drainpipes should be positioned just above the lower ground level.

Alternatively, you can leave "weep holes" in the ground-level course of bricks: simply leave unmortared vertical gaps between every four bricks so water can seep out.

Where the earth is particularly wet, however, it is best to lay land drainage pipes laterally in order to filter the excess water away. The unglazed ceramic or plastic pipes are bedded at the base of a trench in fine gravel. Some pipes have holes into which excess water filters, to be carried to a convenient drainage point such as a soakaway.

Damp-proof membrane As a further precaution against dampness damaging the retaining wall, it is usual to coat the back face with several coats of bitumen emulsion, which can be applied by brush.

Resisting damp

1 Insert lengths of plastic drainpipe in the retaining wall at ground level so that excess water can be channelled from the bank.

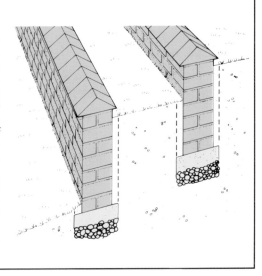

CREATING TERRACES

To create a series of terraces in steeply sloping ground it is necessary to construct earth-retaining walls, to hold back the earth you remove. Draw a plan of the garden and indicate the terraces, viewed from above. Draw a side elevation of the slope with the terraces marked. On the actual plot, use stringlines and pegs to mark out the slope with the number of terraces you want to make, then excavate and cast concrete strip footings beneath each wall position. Build the walls on the footings, then backfill with gravel, subsoil and topsoil to create the flat areas behind each wall. Incorporate drainage holes with side-discharging channels, then fit a polythene membrane behind each wall. To incorporate steps see pages 50-53.

Backfilling the wall

When the wall has been constructed and left for several days for the mortar to harden fully, backfill with earth to create the terraced effect. Tip loads of granular, porous material such as pebbles or gravel behind the retaining wall for good drainage, then add subsoil to within about 6in (150mm) of the top of the wall. Compact the gravel and the subsoil by trampling with your boots or using a garden roller, then top up with good fertile topsoil.

Leave the soil for a few weeks to settle, top up if necessary with more, then plant out, turf or pave as required.

2 Fit bevelled coping to the top of the wall—which should be just above terraced ground level—to throw rainwater clear.

3 Attach heavy-duty polythene to the back of the retaining wall as a damp-proof membrane, then backfill.

Screen walling 1

Pierced screen blocks are unlike other more conventional walling materials. Typically moulded from white concrete, they are intended for building semi-loadbearing structures such as carport roof supports, patio screens and decorative walls within the garden. However, they can be used along boundaries if they incorporate reinforcement.

Reinforcement is necessary because a wall constructed from screen blocks is not inherently strong. This is because such walls are "stack-bonded", that is the blocks are mortared one on top of the other without overlapping or staggering the vertical joints. It is clear that such a wall requires additional support to prevent collapse.

Block size and accessories

Blocks measure 12in (304mm) square × 4in (101mm) thick, and are formed in moulds that produce a pierced pattern on the face (which again weakens them). Some manufacturers also produce a solid block, moulded with a face pattern, as a contrast in an area of pierced blocks.

Pilaster blocks Screen walls need supporting with piers every 10ft (3m), and these are assembled using precast pilaster blocks which are sold with the pierced blocks. Pilasters are hollow 8in (203mm) cubes, and have channels moulded in one or two sides to take the edges of the screen blocks.

There are three types of pilaster block: one with a single slot is for use at the end of a wall; another has two slots on opposite sides for use as an intermediate pier; the third has two slots on adjacent sides, for use at a right-angled corner.

Reinforcing piers Piers constructed with pilaster blocks may themselves require support—especially if the wall is over 6ft (1.8m) high—from angle iron or steel rods set in the foundation slab on which they are built, and running up the hollow middle of each block.

A sloppy concrete mix poured into the hollow pilasters will hold the reinforcing rods rigid and strengthen the piers.

Cappings and copings To complete a screen block wall there are precast capping pieces for the tops of the piers and coping strips to run along the top of the wall. These are simply set in mortar.

Mixing materials

One benefit of screen block walls is that the size of the pierced blocks and pilasters corresponds with a whole number of bricks or decorative concrete walling blocks, enabling you to create a garden wall combining these materials. For example, it is quite straightforward to construct a low plinth wall of reconstructed walling blocks with a pitched decorative face, topped with coping slabs, then add a screen block wall on top. In the same way you can link brick walls with screen walls both to add strength to the latter and to create a highly decorative feature.

Mortar mixes

Screen blocks are best laid on a mortar mix comprising 1 part masonry cement : 5 parts builder's sand. Masonry cement has plasticizer added to make the mix more workable. Alternatively you can use a 1:1:6 mix of Portland cement, lime and builder's sand. For small walls, however, it is quite convenient to use a "pre-bagged" or "dry-mixed" bricklaying mortar to which only water is added.

Erecting a screen wall

Start constructing a screen wall by setting reinforcing angle iron or rods in the freshly

Erecting a screen wall

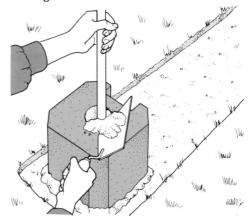

1 Slot the first pilaster block onto the reinforcing rod, bedded on mortar, then fill the hollow with a sloppy mortar mix.

cast concrete strip footings. The rod should be bent at right angles at the base to anchor it in the concrete. Mark out the positions required for the piers and set up stringlines between profile boards to indicate the width of the piers.

Stand the reinforcement rod in the wet concrete. Check with a spirit level that the rod is vertical, and support if necessary with temporary props until the concrete has set.

Building a pier
Slot the first pilaster block onto the reinforcement rod and bed it on mortar on the strip foundation. Check with a spirit level that the pilaster is level, and make sure its channel is aligned squarely with the direction the wall will take, between the stringlines attached to the profile boards.

Trowel a sloppy mortar mix into the hollow pilaster block and pack it around the reinforcement rod.

Using ordinary bricklaying mortar again, bed the second pilaster on top of the first, forming joints about $\frac{3}{8}$in (10mm) thick. Tap the block with your trowel handle to bed it firmly, then scoop off any excess mortar that squeezes out from the sides. Continue to lay pilasters until you reach the wall height.

Check that the pier is plumb by holding the spirit level against each side in turn and tapping to set it vertically.

Construct the pier at the other end of the proposed wall, plus any intermediate piers that may be necessary.

However, if you are building a low wall only about two or three blocks high you can start to build the screen wall out from a single pier, once the mortar of the first pier has hardened for a few hours—in this way you will be able to see the results of the construction evolve sooner. Build the second or intermediate pier onto the end of the screen wall. Take care to align the screen blocks correctly with stringlines.

Laying the pierced blocks
Spread a screed of mortar onto the strip foundation between the end piers, or between the end and intermediate pier. Furrow the surface of the screed. Set up stringlines to indicate the top edge of the pierced blocks.

Butter one edge of a block with mortar and furrow the surface, then fit the mortared edge into the channel in the pier. Press the block onto the screed and tap gently on the top and outer edge to bed it squarely; check with a spirit level.

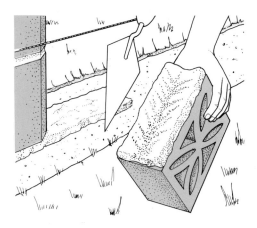

2 Erect the pier by stacking pilaster blocks on top of each other. Check they are vertical by placing a spirit level against each side.

3 Lay the pierced blocks on a mortar screed between the piers. Butter the end of the first block and insert in the pilaster channel. (Continued overleaf)

Screen walling 2

Butter the outer edge of the first block with mortar and butt the second block up to it. Continue to lay the blocks in this way to complete the course.

Take care not to smear the faces of the screen blocks or pilasters with mortar, as this would stain the white concrete. If you do happen to smear the surface, however, leave the mortar to dry and then remove it with a scraping knife.

Forming the stack bond
Trowel mortar along the first course of pierced blocks, then lay the second course, with blocks stacked one on top of the other, without overlaps between the vertical joints. Continue to build up the screen wall to the required height, checking frequently for horizontal and vertical alignment. Place your spirit level or a long straight-edged batten diagonally across the face of the wall to check for bowing, and correct if necessary.

Turning corners
Forming corners in screen wall blocks is quite straightforward. Build a pier at the corner using the pilaster blocks with channels on adjacent sides. Simply construct screens as previously described (see pages 68–9).

It is a good idea to build the second wall

in racked-back form in case you do not complete it in one day: this will ensure that the structure is rigidly bonded. If you were to stop building the wall temporarily, leaving a vertical joint the whole height of the wall, this joint would be weak after you had built the remaining section.

Fitting capping and coping
Bed pilaster cappings and block copings in mortar at the top of the wall to deflect rainwater.

Pointing the joints
Neaten the mortar joints by running a piece of hosepipe along them, forming a rounded profile. For a more decorative finish, rake out the joints with a chisel once the mortar has stiffened, and repoint the gaps using a coloured mortar mix.

Hollow blocks
For a more substantial screen with a simple pattern, use hollow concrete blocks, laid sideways and mortared in stretcher bond. These come in a range of finishes and are relatively inexpensive compared with purpose-made screen blocks. Their deep cavities, making "shelves" about 12in (300mm) wide, provide surfaces for potted trailing plants.

Completing the screen wall

4 Butter the outer edge of the first block with mortar and butt the second block up to it. Tap level and square with the stringline.

5 Build the second or intermediate pier at the other end of the screen wall, incorporating any reinforcement necessary.

STRENGTHENING SCREEN WALLS

You should add reinforcement to the piers and the blocks, especially if the walls are to be semi-loadbearing—for example, if they support a plastic carport roof.

Reinforcing the blockwork

Tall screen block walls over 6ft (1.8m) high should incorporate additional reinforcement to prevent the stack-bonded joints from simply "zipping open". As you build each horizontal course, embed a strip of $2\frac{1}{2}$in (60mm) wide galvanized steel mesh in the joint mortar to help tie the vertical joints together. Press the mesh in place, then add more mortar before laying the next course of pierced blocks.

Tying in the piers

Where the wall adjoins an existing masonry wall, it is sensible to link the supporting piers to the structure for added stability.

Tie the pier to the wall with angled metal strips hooked into the hollow of every third pilaster and slotted into a raked-out mortar joint in the brickwork. Alternatively you can use preformed galvanized metal frame ties, the flanges of which are screwed to the wall, with the right-angled splayed arms set in mortar joints between pilasters.

Tie the pier to an adjoining wall with angled metal ties mortared into the hollow pilasters; embed metal mesh in the horizontal joints, as described above.

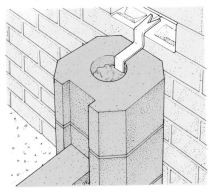

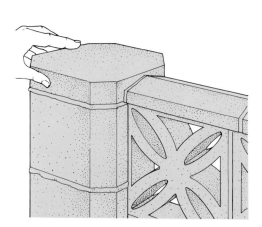

6 Complete the wall by bedding square capping pieces on top of the piers and bevelled coping stones along the top of the screen blocks.

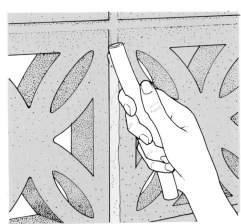

7 Point the joints neatly by running an offcut of hosepipe along the stiffening mortar to produce a softly rounded profile.

Dry-stone walls

A natural stone wall has a distinctly rugged appearance which ideally suits a country-style garden. The wall can be constructed without mortar as a freestanding structure, or as an earth-retaining support. Soil can be packed into the dry joints for plants.

Stone for dry-stone walling can be obtained from larger garden centres or local stone merchants. Choose the hardest, most impervious stone that is available, such as granite or basalt. As for quantities, you will need to allow about 1 tonne per cubic metre (just under 1 ton per $1\frac{1}{3}$ cubic feet) of wall.

Aim to have the load of stone dumped close to the site. If you need to move the stone some distance, hire a sturdy builder's wheelbarrow.

How dry-stone walls are made
A dry-stone wall, although apparently random in construction, must be made to a strict formula for rigidity and strength. It comprises:
Foundations Well-compacted and stable subsoil with large flat foundation stones on top.
Edging blocks Fairly regularly shaped edge blocks laid on the foundation stones to form the front, rear and end faces of the wall, with a cavity in the centre.
Infill stones Small irregularly shaped "heart-ing" stones used as infill for the cavity between the edging blocks.
Through stones Long, flat stones called "random throughs" placed at random intervals across the wall, from front to back, in order to tie the outer faces together.
Coverband A row of large, flat stones laid at the top of the wall, on which the copings are laid.
Coping stones Flattish stones laid on edge along the top of the wall; they may be laid in a "buck-and-doe" format, consisting of stones laid alternately flat and on edge to create a turreted profile.

Setting the batter
A dry-stone wall must be built with a broad base becoming narrower at the top for rigidity and to transmit the loading to the foundation stones. A typical "batter", as the angled shape is called, is about 3ft (915mm) wide at the base and 1ft (300m) at the top.

Batter frames are used to set the angle during construction of the wall (see box, this page). Make up a batter frame from lengths of 2 × 1in (50 × 25mm) softwood, nailed together in the wall's proportions.

For an earth-retaining dry-stone wall the back edge of the wall should be kept vertical to counteract the lateral pressure of the damp earth: fix the back upright straight and the front one angled back towards the bank.

You will need a batter frame for each end of the wall.

Making the foundation
Mark out the shape of the base using string-lines stretched between pegs driven into the ground at the perimeter. Dig the trench to depth (see Strip foundations, pages 8–9) removing the soft topsoil as far as firm subsoil. Compact the subsoil with a sledgehammer or garden roller.

Choose some large, flat foundation stones with at least one straight edge and lay in the base of the trench, interlocking the irregular edges for strength. Tap the stones down firmly with the shaft of a club hammer.

Building up the ends
Stand the batter frames in position at each end of the foundation trench and link them

---

BATTER FRAMES

The angled shape of a dry-stone wall is formed by wooden frames assembled to give the correct "batter". On free-standing structures the wall is narrower at the top.

with stringlines as a guide to building.

Stack edging blocks on the foundation stones to form staggered vertical joins between courses. Lay through stones alternately to bond the smaller stones.

Erecting the wall
Build out from the ends of the wall using edging blocks, linking them with the end blocks with staggered joints. Follow the shape of the batter when placing the stones, so the sides start to slope inwards.

When you have laid three or four courses add smaller infill stones to the cavity between the edging stones. Tie in the two leaves or "skins" of the wall with through stones.

Fitting the coverband and coping
When you reach the top of the wall, lay the large, flat coverband stones across the top, forming a sort of lid to the shell. Finish off the dry-stone wall by setting a row of coping stones on edge, tilting them slightly one way to throw off rainwater.

Building a dry-stone wall

1 Lay one layer of large, flat foundation stones on the compacted earth sub-base, interlocking the irregular edges for strength.

2 Build up the ends of the wall by several courses of regularly shaped edging blocks alternated with large, flat through stones.

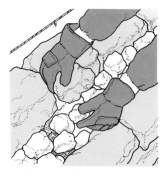

3 Place small infill stones into the cavity formed between the front and back facing blocks. Ram the stones down firmly.

4 Link the outer leaves of the wall by laying large, flat stones across the wall at random intervals. Continue building the wall with the squarer edging blocks.

5 Fit a row of coverband stones across the top of the wall to close off the structure from rain. Ideally the row of stones should slope slightly for drain-off.

6 Place a row of coping stones along the top of the coverband, setting them on edge with a slight lean to one side, or in decorative buck-and-doe format.

Fences: types 1

There is a vast range of fencing styles, either custom-made or prefabricated, which serve numerous functions in the garden. You may want something practical yet attractive to stake out the boundaries of your property, form a demarcation for the individual planting areas—for example, vegetable patch, lawn and flower beds—or simply make a utilitarian barrier that will confine the family pets and keep out neighbourhood strays. From a safety point of view, fencing may be used to prevent young children from wandering onto the highway.

Certain types of solid fencing are admirably suited to providing a windbreak for the patio, while some semi-solid types will allow a gentle breeze to filter through at the same time as giving privacy from passers-by.

Attractive fencing can also be used to conceal an unsightly vista—say, the compost heap at the end of the garden, the dustbins, or even a neighbouring house or industrial unit that overlooks your home or spoils the view from your house or patio.

Post-and-rail fences

There are various versions of the post-and-rail fence, which is generally used at property boundaries. It basically comprises a number of horizontal rails nailed to or notched into the posts. The posts themselves may be round and the rails half-round in section, and they frequently still have their bark attached for a more rustic appearance. Alternatively, the posts and rails may be sawn square to give cleaner lines. Within this category, these are the most commonly found fences:

Ranch-style Ranch-type fences have thin, planed planks of $\frac{3}{4}$in (20mm) thick softwood nailed horizontally to short posts of 5 × 3in (125 × 75mm) or 5 × 4in (125 × 100mm) softwood, or housed in slots cut in the posts. The main posts are usually fixed at about 6ft 6in (2m) intervals, often with intermediate posts of 3in (75mm) square timber midway between them.

Usually no more than 4ft (1.2m) high, ranch-style fences up to about 3ft (915mm) high have planks about 3in (75mm) wide and above this height the planks may be 5 or 6in (125 or 150mm) wide; the planks themselves are spaced so that the gaps between them are about 3 to 4in (75 to 100mm). Ranch-style fencing may be painted, usually in white gloss, or left bare and treated with preservative.

Easy-to-assemble ranch-style fence kits in white plastic are available from specialist suppliers. Although they look very similar to wooden types they will not rot, and require nothing more than an occasional hose down to maintain their neat, clean appearance.

Double ranch-style A semi-solid variation of the basic ranch-style fence, the double version has additional planks fixed to the opposite side of the posts in such a way that they coincide with the gaps between the planks on the other side.

Picket Often known as "paling" or "palisade" fencing (although in fact different from a true palisade type: see page 75), picket fencing forms an elegant boundary popularly used in front

Popular fencing types

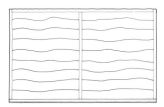

Wavy-edged fencing with horizontal overlapping planks is available in various panel sizes.

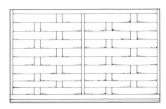

Interwoven panels make a lightweight, economical boundary fence.

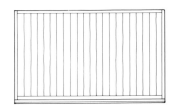

Closeboarded fences, normally built on site, are the strongest solid boundaries.

gardens, particularly in rural areas, and is traditionally painted in white gloss or treated with preservative.

The fence—which is not normally higher than about 4ft (1.2m)—comprises vertical "pales" nailed to horizontal "arris" rails fixed between posts, which are spaced between 6ft 6in and 10ft (2 and 3m) apart. The pales are usually arranged to have spaces of about 2in (50mm) between them.

Pales are commonly pointed or rounded at the top, or else ornately shaped. Custom-made types sometimes feature pales of varying heights to produce a zig-zag or undulating shape to the top edge of the boundary.

Picket fences are available in kit form, with prefabricated sections intended for securing between posts with metal brackets.

Palisade True palisade fences are similar to picket types, but differ in that the vertical pales are butted close together side by side, forming a solid fence.

Prefabricated panel fences

Prefabricated panel fences provide the quickest and most economical means of creating a solid barrier at a property boundary, within a plot, as an efficient windbreak for the patio, or for demarcation of different areas within the garden. However, bear in mind that panel fences are not the most rigid of structures, being generally constructed of inexpensive, fairly thin timber. Their strength lies in the way they are attached between the posts. Protection against the elements is provided by the bevelled coping strips which are nailed

SUPPORTING POSTS

Whatever the type, all fences have one thing in common: the supporting posts. These may be made of preservative-treated timber, concrete, metal angle iron, or even rot-free, low-maintenance plastic.

Posts are traditionally erected in a hole and encased in concrete, although metal fixing spikes are increasingly used to support timber posts because they can be installed so easily. Spikes are driven into the ground using a sledgehammer and the post fitted in the square collar at the top. Because the timber is not set in the earth, rot attack due to dampness is far less likely.

Another means of supporting a timber post is to fit a precast concrete spur set in concrete at the base. This is commonly used as a means of repairing existing posts which have rotted at the base.

The tops of timber posts are normally rounded, angled or pointed in order to throw off rainwater before it can soak into the vulnerable end grain. If post tops are left square it is usual for them to have bevelled capping nailed on top.

along the top to shed rainwater.

Basketweave The most popular type of prefabricated panel fence, basketweave panels are made from thin slats of larch or pine about 3in (75mm) wide: these are woven horizontally

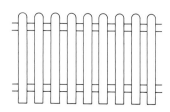

Picket post-and-rail fencing, for front garden boundaries, is usually painted white.

Wire mesh fencing may be utilitarian or, as shown, hoop-topped and decorative.

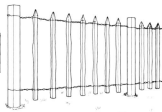

Split-chestnut paling consists of rough-hewn stakes strung between taut wires.

Fences: types 2

around vertical slats in a basketweave pattern, the resultant panel being framed in slim softwood battens. The panels measure a standard 6ft (1.8m) wide and are available in a range of heights, normally 2, 3, 4, 5 and 6ft (0.6, 0.9, 1.2, 1.5 and 1.8m).

Panels are fixed between timber or concrete posts by driving galvanized nails or bolts through the framing battens. With any panel fence, it is quite straightforward to trim the individual panels in width to fit any span; some suppliers will stock odd widths.

Wavy-edged A version of the basketweave prefabricated panel fence. The horizontal planks have irregularly shaped lower edges, often with the bark attached, and overlap to form a solid barrier. The planks are fixed within a thin softwood frame, which is again nailed between the posts.

Trellis Trellis panels are often used to give additional height to a basketweave or wavy-edged panel (or a closeboarded fence: see below). Trellis can be used as a lightweight fence in its own right, and is ideal for supporting climbing plants. Semi-solid trellis makes an excellent screen for rubbish bins or a compost heap, where only a lightweight structure is needed.

Prefabricated trellis comes in square or diamond pattern, and panels are in heights between about 1 and 6ft (300mm and 1.8m). The slats from which the lightest trellis is made commonly measure only about $\frac{5}{16} \times \frac{5}{8}$in (8 × 16mm), and are assembled using metal staples or pins; more heavy-duty trellises require thicker slats and sturdier fixings.

Some manufacturers supply trellis panels with slats arranged in an elaborate design instead of the traditional square and diamond patterns. These include a herringbone arrangement between intermediate vertical battens. Square-pattern trellis panels sometimes have a concave or convex curved top edge.

Intended only as a fence top, or for wall-fixing as a support for climbers, a diamond-pattern trellis is often sold in fairly flimsy concertina format, which can be expanded to various heights and widths.

Closeboarded fences

Where good security at a property boundary is called for, perhaps the best type of fence is the closeboarded variety, which may be anything between about 2 and 8ft (610mm and 2.4m) high. This type of fence is generally erected on site from separate components.

It comprises stout posts with two or three horizontal triangular-section arris rails fixed between, usually housed in mortices (specially cut sockets or holes) cut in the sides of the posts. Vertical boards are attached to the rails in overlapping fashion. The boards, which measure about 4 or 6in (100 or 150mm) wide, are feather-edged, so that one edge is thinner than the other.

Bevelled coping strips are attached to finish off the top of the boards, protecting the vulnerable end grain from penetration of rainwater. At the base, the boards are set on a horizontal "gravel board" which is a 4 or 5 × 1in (100 or 125 × 25mm) piece of timber nailed to short battens which are fixed at the

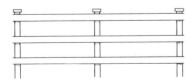

Ranch-style fencing (above) is a popular paddock boundary, often painted white.
Herringbone trellis (right) panels can be used to screen an unsightly view.

base of the posts, in order to protect them from damp rising from the ground. When the gravel boards become rotten, they can simply be levered off and replaced.

Prefabricated versions of the closeboarded fence are also available, although they are generally constructed from thinner, cheaper wood and are consequently less rigid than tailor-made types.

Wire mesh fences

For practical fencing—for example, to run around the vegetable plot or to confine animals—a wire mesh fence may be suitable. Although this fencing is often of extremely utilitarian appearance, more elegant decorative types are also available. The mesh can be fixed between timber, concrete or angled metal posts. The outer posts are usually fitted with diagonal braces to counteract the tension of the line wires that are stretched between straining bolts. The mesh is then fixed to the line wires with wire ties. Intermediate posts are fixed between the outer ones to prevent the mesh from sagging.

There is a variety of wire mesh formats for different uses in the garden:

Open-mesh Sold in 33, 83 or 164ft (10, 25 or 50m) rolls, open-mesh fencing is made in heights from 1 to 6ft (300mm to 1.8m). The size of the mesh may be $\frac{3}{8}$ to 4in (10 to 100mm) square. As protection against rusting, the wire may be coated in green plastic; alternatively the bare metal will be galvanized against corrosion.

Decorative wire Often found hooped at the top, decorative wire mesh is sold in 33 or 83ft (10 or 25m) rolls in heights from 4in to 3ft (100 to 915mm). The larger sizes must be attached to posts as for open-mesh fencing, but the pointed ends of the smaller types can be simply pushed into the ground to enhance a lawn edge, for example.

Welded mesh Chain-link, or welded mesh, fencing is the toughest of the wire structures, the steel wire being welded at each junction. Rolls are normally 20 or 100ft (6 or 30m) long and heights range from 1ft 6in to 6ft (460mm to 1.8m). The mesh itself can be anything from $\frac{1}{2}$ to 2in (12 to 50mm) square. Galvanized or plastic-coated versions are available for greater durability.

Split-chestnut paling Stockade, or split-chestnut paling, fences are assembled from cleft chestnut stakes connected at the top and bottom with galvanized wire. It is produced and sold in rolls about 30ft (9.1m) long and between 3 and 6ft (915mm and 1.8m) high. The line wires are attached between stouter posts of 4in (100mm) square softwood, usually diagonally braced, with intermediate posts to prevent sagging. Alternatively, thick chestnut poles are used at each end.

Spiked chain Used purely for decorative effect or to mark out a boundary without forming a solid barrier, spiked chain fencing consists of steel chains—often with diamond-shaped spikes interlaced—strung loosely between short posts of timber, metal or concrete. Chains are often plastic, or metal coated with plastic, or are finished with a glossy black, or "japanned", effect.

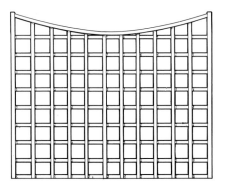

Spiked chain fencing (above) is a purely visual, often decorative way to mark off areas.
Square-pattern trellis (left) may have a curved top, and is ideal as a support for climbers.

Fixing fence posts 1

Cutting and treating the posts

Preservative-treated fence posts are sold in standard lengths, although you will probably have to cut them to size. Remember to allow for sufficient depth of post to be sunk in the ground, plus an allowance for the posts to extend a few inches above the top of the fence panels (see below for details). Cut the posts to length using a woodsaw and mark the required above-ground height clearly around their girth.

If the posts have already been treated with preservative, soak the cut ends of the posts in a bucket of preservative overnight so that the vulnerable end grain absorbs the fluid. If the posts are untreated, make a preservative bath and soak the posts thoroughly (see box page 81).

Marking out the run of fencing

The first job in erecting a fence is to mark out its position on the ground so that you can determine the number of panels, timber or wire mesh and supporting posts needed. Stretch stringlines between pegs driven into the ground to mark the run of fencing, then use a batten the length of one fencing panel plus the width of one post to determine how

---

CONCRETE POSTS AND FENCES

Most fences are supported by square-section timber posts either 3 or 4in (75 or 100mm) in size. Concrete posts, however, are available for a rot-free, durable fixing for all types of fences. They are generally 4in (100mm) square, reinforced with lengths of iron rod embedded in them. Various moulded formats are made to cope with different fencing styles: drilled concrete posts are intended for supporting wire mesh fences, while mortised posts accept the arris rails of closeboarded or post-and-rail fences. Notched posts are made also, to accept the end of a diagonal brace needed for some types of fencing. Channelled posts are made especially for concrete fences, in which solid panels are used to replace the usual timber type.

---

many panels and posts you will have to buy. Do not forget the final post.

Post fixings

While concrete posts are best set in a hole dug in the ground and encased in concrete, timber posts can be concreted in the same way, attached above ground level to concrete spurs, or fixed using a proprietary metal fence spike. Where a post is to be fixed to a solid surface, such as a concrete base slab, either embed it in the slab itself or attach it with bolt-on metal plates—these have a socket which takes the end of the post.

For posts which stand up to about 4ft (1.2m) high, dig a hole 18in (460mm) deep, but for taller posts dig down 24in (610mm) to provide more support below ground. (Remember to allow for this extra length when ordering or cutting the posts.) Excavate the hole by a further 6in (150mm) to allow for a base of hardcore, which will let surplus water drain away, and remove the danger of rot.

Using a post-hole borer

Although a spade can be used to dig the hole, a post-hole borer can readily be hired and involves much less effort. It removes a core of soil less laboriously using a corkscrew action. To use the tool, place the blades at the required post position and turn the handle to gouge out the earth. The core of earth is removed by lifting the tool.

Place hardcore or a couple of engineering bricks at the base of the hole and ram down thoroughly, using an offcut of post. Do not forget to wear thick gloves to protect your hands against splinters. Stand the post in the hole and support it temporarily by pinning a pair of timber braces to adjacent sides.

Setting the post upright

Ensure that the post stands perfectly vertical by holding a spirit level against each face in turn and adjusting it as necessary. Pack more rubble around the post to within 6in (150mm) of ground level.

Mix up a fairly dry concrete mix in the proportions 1 part Portland cement : 4 parts all-in aggregate, or use a dry ready-mixed fence-post concrete which is sold pre-packed in conveniently sized bags by builder's merch-

Concreting in a post

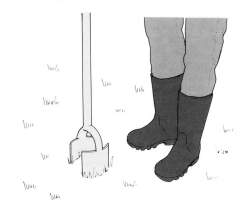

1 Dig the hole using a spade or, for ease, a hired post-hole borer, which lifts out a core of earth. Make sure you position the hole correctly according to stringlines.

2 Prop the post in the hole on a brick, with temporarily pinned-on braces, and set it perfectly vertical by checking each side in turn with a spirit level.

3 Ram hardcore into the hole around the propped-up post to support it firmly. Stop the hardcore short of ground level by about 6in (150mm).

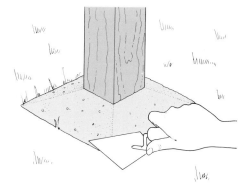

4 Trowel in the fresh concrete around the post and compact it to dispel air bubbles. Shape the mound so that rainwater will run off quickly.

ants and DIY stores. Shovel the concrete into the hole around the post so that it is just proud of the surrounding ground level. Compact the concrete with the offcut of post to dispel air bubbles, then shape into a neat mound so that rainwater will not be able to collect at the base of the post and encourage rot.

It is best to leave the concrete to harden for about two days before attaching the fencing panels. If you use fence spikes, however, the panels may be attached as soon as the posts are correctly positioned.

Using fencing spikes

Fencing spikes come in various sizes to suit different heights of fence and sizes of fence

Fixing fence posts 2

post. For fences over 4ft (1.2m) high you should use a spike 30in (760mm) long with a 3 or 4in (75 or 100mm) square post; for fences up to 4ft (1.2m) high use a spike 24in (610mm) long with a 2 or 3in (50 or 75mm) square fencing post.

A fencing spike consists of a galvanized steel spike with a square, wedge-shaped collar at the top, into which the post fits, to be gripped by internal flanges. Some makes of spike have sockets which must be closed around the post with integral bolts. These bolts can cope with irregularly-sized posts (post dimensions are given only nominally, and sometimes you may have to pack offcuts of wood between post and collar to obtain a tight fit).

Push the spike into the ground at the post position, then fit a short offcut of post into the collar. Some makes of spike come with a fixing accessory into which the offcut is fitted. Drive the offcut (and hence the spike) into the ground using a heavy sledgehammer until the base of the collar is level with the ground surface.

Be sure to check at frequent intervals that the collar is vertical by placing a spirit level against each side in turn. Once the collar is in position, remove the offcutt of post.

To fit the post, wedge it into the collar and secure by tightening any integral nuts or driving nails into the pre-drilled holes.

Plot the positions of the other post holes with your gauge batten and fix the remaining posts in the same way.

Concrete spurs

As with fencing spikes, concrete spurs avoid direct contact between ground and post, minimizing the risk of rot. Spurs are bought ready-made, with a single bevelled end and holes for attaching the post. Set the spurs in concrete, with the angled end uppermost. The lowest fixing hole should be just above the plug of concrete, so that the post is held close to, but not on, the ground. Ensure that the spurs are vertical using a spirit level. The post will be attached to the taller spur-front, so calculate the distance between the spurs accordingly. Allow the concrete to set completely before bolting the wooden posts onto the spurs.

Aligning the posts

If the fence is to be straight and rigid, without warps, the posts must be erected so that they are precisely the correct distance apart to accept the panels (or other components such as arris rails), and properly straight and upright.

As you fix the posts check that they are aligned with the stringline. Test-fit a panel or rail between posts. Check also that the posts are fixed to the same depth by placing a long straight-edged plank on top and resting a spirit level on it. Adjust the depth of the posts accordingly.

Wall-fixing a post

The first post in a run of fencing is likely to be attached to the wall of the house, garage or outbuilding. Use $\frac{1}{4}$in (6mm) diameter expanding coachbolts to secure it, three if the post is over 5ft (1.5m) high, otherwise two.

Drill holes through the post for the bolts, then select a slightly larger drill bit to make a countersunk hole for the bolt head. This is important so that the edge of the fence panel can fit flush against the side of the post.

Position the post vertically against the wall and mark the position of the bolts through the holes. Drill the wall using a masonry bit, then replace the post and slot in the bolts. If necessary, pack out between the post and the wall with offcuts of wood so that the post is set vertically. Tighten the bolts with a spanner.

Fitting a brace

For chain link fences you must brace the outer posts to counteract the pressure of the tensioning wires. Make a brace from a length of the same stock of post timber. Cut a notch in the side of the post and shape the top end of the strut to fit it. Secure the brace by nailing through it and into the post, angling the nails so that they will not pull out.

Set the post in a hole as previously described, or fit with a fence spike. Dig an 18in (460mm) deep trench from the post to take the brace. Place a brick underneath the brace, then pack around brace and post with hardcore. Fill the trench and hole to ground level with concrete. At a corner post you will need to fit two braces at right angles.

WEATHERPROOFING

Capping the post tops

Trim the tops of the fence posts to a single slope or point to ensure that rainwater runs off rapidly. Treat the cut ends by soaking the posts overnight in a bucket of preservative, so that the liquid has a chance to be absorbed into the vulnerable end grain.

Alternatively, you can fit a preformed wooden cap to the square top of the posts, by simply nailing it on: the cap, bevelled at the top, will slightly overhang the sides of the post and deflect rainwater. Another method of rain-proofing a timber post is to fit a zinc, lead or bituminous roofing felt cover, this is simply taken onto the sides of the post and secured with galvanized nails.

Making a preservative bath

Soaking the fence posts for a few days in a bath of preservative will benefit them in the long term, warding off possible attack by rot as a result of contact with damp ground. Construct a preservative bath by building low dry-laid walls of brick that are stacked in stretcher bond but without mortar. The bath should be large enough to hold all the fence posts you are going to treat.

Line the inside of the bath with a sheet of heavy-duty polythene, lapping over the sides of the brick walls. Fill the bath with preservative and lay the fence posts inside so they are completely submerged. Any other wooden fencing components such as gravel boards, coping strips, caps and even panels may also be treated, if there is space.

Leave the timber to absorb the preservative for a few days (according to the manufacturer's instructions) turning each piece at regular intervals to ensure complete coverage.

Installing a fence spike

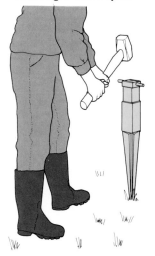

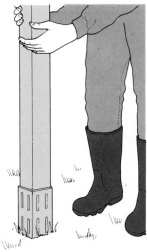

1 Drive the spike into the ground at the post position with a sledgehammer and offcut of post (and fixing accessory).

2 Check that the spike is vertical by holding a spirit level against each side in turn at frequent intervals.

3 Push the post into the collar of the fence spike. You may have to tighten integral bolts to secure.

Erecting a panel fence 1

Mark out the run of fencing on the ground using stringlines and pegs. Remember, if you are erecting a boundary fence, that all your posts and fencing must be on the property side of the stringline.

Fix the first fence post (see page 78). Although you can erect all the fence posts first, spaced the correct distance apart, you may find it easier to fix them one at a time, using the next panel in line as an accurate spacing guide. This avoids the problem of misaligned posts: it is better to adjust a post before it is fixed firmly than to find that a panel will not fit in properly afterwards.

With this progressive method of erecting a panel fence, it is better to use spike post fixings than to have to wait for each concrete support to harden before moving on.

Fixing gravel boards

You can, if you wish, install gravel boards beneath the panels to prevent the risk of damp earth touching the fence itself: the gravel boards are thus sacrificed in favour of the panels, as they are easily replaceable.

At the base, nail 6in (150mm) lengths of $1\frac{1}{2}$in (35mm) square timber vertically to the

inner faces of the posts. Measure between these supports to establish the size of the gravel boards and cut lengths of 6 × 1in (150 × 25mm) softwood to fit. Treat with preservative and allow to dry.

Position a gravel board between the posts and set it horizontal, checking with a spirit level placed on top. Nail the board to the vertical supports using galvanized nails.

Nail-fixing prefabricated panels

Prefabricated fencing panels can simply be slotted between the posts and secured by driving nails through the outer frame into the posts near the top and bottom and in the centre. First drill pilot holes through the frame pieces to prevent the thin wood from splitting when the nails are hammered in.

Place one of the panels between the first two posts on the run. Mount the panel on bricks so that it will be sufficiently high above ground level to prevent dampness, or else fit horizontal gravel boards and mount the panels on these (see above).

Align the fence panel accurately so that it is vertical in all directions, then place a spirit level on top of the panel to check that it is

Erecting a panel fence

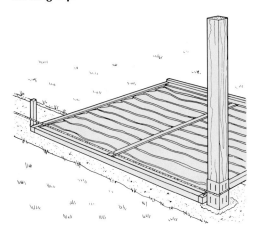

1 Mark out the fence run on the ground from the position of the first fixed fence post. Use a panel as a guide to fixing the remaining posts and a stringline and peg as a visual aid.

2 Use two-piece metal brackets to fix the fence panel to the posts. Make a T-shaped gauge to set the first half of the bracket the correct distance from the edge of the fence post.

horizontal. Hammer 3in (75mm) galvanized nails through the pre-drilled holes.

Bracket-fixing prefabricated panels

Because the outer frame of prefabricated fence panels is quite thin, it is quite likely that in severe winds splitting could occur, and the fence may even blow down.

For a stronger fixing it is best to use proprietary galvanized metal support brackets, of which there are two commonly available types: a one-piece U-shaped channel (see box, page 85); and a pair of L-shaped fittings, as shown in the fixing sequence illustrated below.

One-piece brackets Mark a centre line down the length of the inner face of each post and attach a pair of one-piece metal brackets centrally and squarely to the post, one near the top and the other near the bottom, using 2in (50mm) long galvanized nails.

You might also find a further type of one-piece bracket (see box, page 85), which has an L-shaped section, that is nailed to the inner face of the post and the outer frame piece of the fence panel. A further L-shaped bend in the bracket, which has a triangular leg, slots behind the timber frame piece to hold the panel tightly against the post.

Two-piece brackets Fix the brackets in pairs, one about 1in (25mm) above the other, with the raised flanges at opposite sides, forming what is essentially a staggered channelling. This type of bracket provides greater resistance to winds, as the staggered formation supports the fence panel at a greater width than the one-piece brackets.

To ensure that you position both halves of the bracket accurately, make up a simple gauge from offcuts of timber and use this as a spacing guide. The gauge comprises a short length of wood with a cross-piece nailed on at right angles, so that it protrudes by the distance the brackets must be set away from the edge of the fence post. Hold the gauge against the side of the post with the cross-piece resting on the inner face, to which the brackets will be attached. Butt each bracket up to the end of the cross-piece and nail on.

Fitting the panels

With either type of bracket fixing you will have to lift up the prefabricated panel and slot it into the channels. With two-piece

3 Fix the second half of the bracket to the post about 1in (25mm) above the first half, using galvanized nails. Ensure that the brackets are fixed squarely or the panel will not fit.

4 Feed the fence panel into the gap between the two parts of the bracket from below, then pivot it downwards and slot it into the channel formed by the lower pair of brackets.

Erecting a panel fence 2

brackets it is best to push the panel between the top brackets from below, then pivot it down carefully and lower the bottom edge between the lower bracket fixings.

With the one-piece brackets you must lift up the panel and lower it into the top brackets, then gently feed it downwards and into the lower brackets.

With either type of bracket, secure the panel by hammering 2in (50mm) long galvanized nails through the pre-drilled flanges and into the slim panel edge framework.

Once the panels are held securely, you can remove the bricks from beneath them.

Cutting down a panel
As your fence run is unlikely to be an exact number of whole prefabricated panels long, you will probably have to cut a panel to fit the gap at one end.

Hold a full-size panel in the gap, against the posts, one end overlapping the previously fixed panel in the run. With a pencil, mark down the panel against the post to indicate the overlap. Continue the line around to the other side of the panel.

Use a claw hammer to prise away the

upright batten on each side of the panel, at the overlap end. Reposition the battens on the inside edge of the pencil guidelines. One of the battens will be longer than the other, and this should project at the bottom of the panel.

With the panel lying flat on a hard surface, hammer galvanized nails through the upper batten, through the panel's slats and into the lower batten. Nail at each slat for a secure fixing. To prevent the nails from pulling out again, place a brick or concrete slab underneath, and use long nails which will protrude and be turned at the ends.

Support the panel firmly and saw off the protruding end of the longer framing batten. Next, saw off the surplus ends of the panel slats and the coping and bottom rails, using a panel saw. Cut as closely as possible to the outer edge of the newly repositioned side frame pieces.

Fit the cut-down panel between the posts using nails or brackets as normal.

Dealing with sloping ground
Some types of fencing, such as chain link and ranch styles, can be erected to follow the

5 Stand the fence panel on a brick (or fit a gravel board first) so that it does not come in contact with the damp earth. Secure the panel by nailing through the bracket flange.

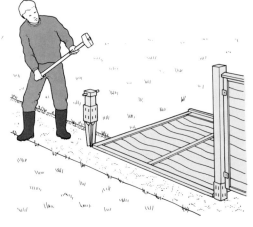

6 Fix the subsequent posts on the fence run by lying a panel on the ground, one end butted up to the previously fixed post; then drive a metal post spike into the ground at the other end of the panel.

slope of the land. A panel fence, however, because of its rigid format, cannot follow such contours and instead must be erected in a stepped format between vertical posts.

The triangular gaps left beneath each panel can be filled with shaped gravel boards if the gap is not more than about 6in (150mm) at its deepest. For greater gaps than this you will have to build plinth walls of bricks, reconstructed concrete walling blocks or natural stone. Build the walls once the fence posts have been erected, setting horizontal foundations into the slope so that the masonry can be laid straight.

Should the ground slope across the proposed line of fencing, the best solution is to build masonry retaining walls that will hold back the earth to form a terraced effect. Incorporate the fence posts into the wall, then erect the fence panels on top of this in the normal manner.

Fitting a trellis top

If you want to increase the height of a fence it is quite simple to add a trellis top. Allow for the depth of the trellis when calculating the length of the posts you will need, and fix the panels so that the appropriate space remains above the top of the fence panel.

With heavy-duty square-pattern trellis you can simply nail the outer uprights to the posts. With the lighter-weight type—especially the flimsy expanding diamond pattern—you should nail short vertical battens of $1\frac{1}{2}$in (75mm) square timber to the inner faces of the posts and attach the trellis to these. Alternatively, simply nail the trellis directly to the front faces of the posts.

Using concrete fence posts

Panel fences are easy to install using precast concrete posts. Other such posts have channels moulded in their sides, into which you can slot the panels without the need to make additional fixings. It is vitally important—as with any fencing job—to set the posts perfectly upright so that the panels will fit snugly in the channels.

Another type of concrete post has a recess in each side in which the fence panel is retained by metal brackets screwed to the outer frame pieces.

ONE-PIECE FENCE PANEL BRACKETS

One-piece fence panel fixing brackets are nailed to the inner faces of the posts and the prefabricated panels slotted into the channels they form, to be secured with galvanized nails. There are basically two types of bracket.

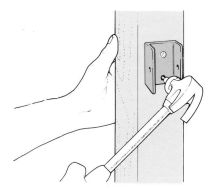

U-shaped brackets have holes predrilled in their backs for fixing direct to the fence post. Holes in the protruding flanges are for nailing the brackets to the panels.

Fence clips are nailed to the post and the side upright frame pieces of the panel, and the bracket clips around the frame to hold the panel securely against the post.

A closeboarded fence 1

Methods

Although closeboarded fences are available in prefabricated versions, this type of durable boundary is normally erected on site from separate components.

The posts may be ready-mortised to take the horizontal arris rails, or you can use solid posts and cut the mortises yourself. A far easier option, however, is to fit the arris rails with special galvanized metal arris rail brackets. With the latter method you can fix up all the posts in the fence run first, then attach the arris rails afterwards; with the former methods you would have to install posts and arris rails alternately.

With the closeboarded arrangement it is possible to disguise slight inconsistencies in the level of the posts with the vertical cladding, but you should nevertheless strive to set them as accurately as possible.

Cutting mortises

Mark the positions of the mortises for the arris rails on the posts. The arris rails should be set about 12in (300mm) from the top and bottom of the fence.

Use a 1in (25mm) flat bit fitted in a power drill to drill out the bulk of the waste wood within the 3 × 1in (75 × 25mm) mortises, then neatly square off the corners with a wood chisel.

Preparing the arris rails

Arris rails are usually triangular in section for greater resistance to pressure from wind. They commonly measure 4 × 3 × 3in (100 × 75 × 75mm), are made of preservative-treated softwood, and have ends that must be hewn to fit into the post mortises—although for bracket fixings the ends of the arris rails can be square. If the arris rails are not already shaped to fit the mortises, or if you need to cut one rail down to fit a narrow stretch of closeboarding, use a small axe to trim to the necessary wedge shapes.

Stand the rail on a piece of board and chop the sides and pointed top edge to a neat wedge. Do not chop away too much at once or you may make the wedge shape too small for the mortise: a loose arris rail would make the entire fence unstable. You could use a planer file or even a saw to shape

the arris rails if you do not feel sufficiently confident using an axe.

Treat the newly cut ends of the arris rails with preservative, preferably by standing the rails overnight in a bucket containing the fluid. Apply preservative also to the mortises on the posts, using a brush.

Erecting mortised posts and rails

For the traditional method of erecting a closeboarded fence, set the first post in concrete with its mortises facing the direction of the run. Prop up the second post in its hole and insert the first pair of arris rails in the mortises. Make sure the flat backs of the rails face the back of the fence. Drive 3in (75mm) galvanized nails through the post into the ends of the rails to secure them. Where possible it is a good idea to hold a club hammer behind the post as you hammer from the opposite side: this lessens the jarring that would otherwise make the nails difficult to hammer home.

Check that the arris rails are horizontal by placing a spirit level on top: adjust the level of the second post accordingly by raising or lowering it.

Erecting a closeboarded fence

1 Set the first post in concrete and prop the second post in its hole. Fit the arris rails in their mortises, then level the entire assembly using a spirit level for accuracy.

ARRIS RAIL FIXINGS

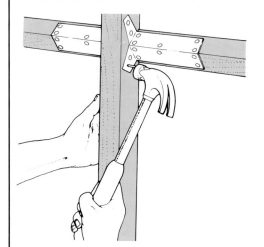

Galvanized metal arris rail brackets are nailed over the triangular-section arris rail and the pre-drilled flanges are nailed to the inner faces of the fence posts.

Mortised fence posts take the wedge-shaped ends of arris rail; nails are hammered into the rail through the posts, using a club hammer to prevent jarring as they are driven in.

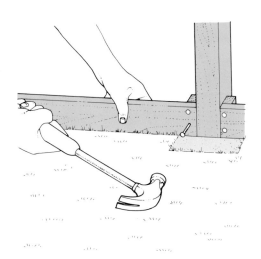

2 Nail gravel boards of 6 × 1in (150 × 25mm) timber to short support battens nailed to the inner face of the posts. Recess the battens so that the gravel boards are flush with the posts.

3 Place the first feather-edged board on the gravel board, with its thicker edge butted up against the post and its top edge aligned with a string guideline stretched between posts.

A closeboarded fence 2

Assemble the next post-and-rail section in the same way; repeat to complete the run.

Using arris rail brackets
To erect a closeboarded fence using arris rail brackets, first install all the posts the correct distance apart and upright. Cut lengths of arris rail to fit snugly between the pairs of posts, then nail on the metal brackets: these are shaped to fit over the triangular section of the rails, and have right-angled pre-drilled flanges which fit against the face of the post.

Hold the rail in position at the correct distance from the top or bottom of the posts and set horizontal with the aid of a spirit level. Drive nails through the flanges to secure the rails to the posts.

Fitting the gravel boards
Nail 6in (150mm) lengths of 1$\frac{1}{2}$in (35mm) square timber vertically to the inner faces of the posts as supports for the horizontal gravel boards on which the feather-edged cladding will stand. Each gravel board, cut from 6 × 1in (150 × 25mm) softwood, should be flush with the outer face of the fence post, on the front elevation. Hold the board in place, set horizontal with the aid of a spirit level, and fix it to the support battens with two 1$\frac{1}{2}$in (35mm) galvanized nails per upright.

Attaching the feather-edged boards
Mark out and cut the feather-edged boards to the height required for the fence, between the top of the gravel board at the base and the underside of the coping strip at the top. The feather-edged boards are positioned so that the thick edge of one overlaps the thin edge of the other by about $\frac{1}{2}$in (12mm).

The boards are attached to the arris rails with 2in (50mm) galvanized nails driven through the thick edge and either into the thin edge of the board below, or just missing it. The final board in each section between pairs of posts can overlap by about $\frac{1}{2}$in (12mm), or else you can trim it to width. For a better fixing, this final board is often turned so that its thick edge lies against the post, and it is also nailed to the post.

Stretch a stringline between posts to indicate the top edge of the feather-edged boards, then stand the first board on the

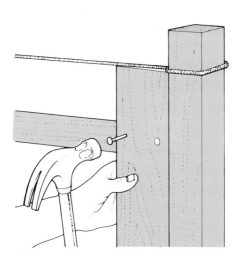

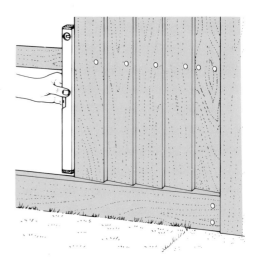

4 Drive two nails through the board into the top arris rail. Check the level of the board, then hammer in another two nails at the lower arris rail.

5 Add subsequent feather-edged boards using one nail per rail. Check frequently with a spirit level that the boards are perfectly vertical. Tapping gently with a hammer may be enough to adjust.

WEATHERPROOFING THE FENCE

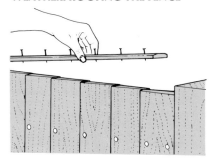

Fitting coping strips

Coping strips throw rainwater from the face of the fence and prevent moisture from seeping into the vulnerable end grain of the feather-edged boards.

Cut lengths of bevelled coping strip to fit between the posts and place them on the top of the feather-edged boards. Drive nails carefully through the top of the copings and into the ends of the boards at regular intervals.

Fitting post caps

Weatherproof the top end of each fence post by nailing on a preformed chamfered post cap. The cap is slightly broader than the girth of the post so that rainwater will be thrown clear without trickling underneath and causing rot.

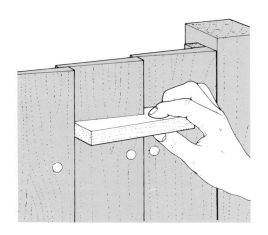

6 Make a spacing gauge from an offcut of timber and use to set each feather-edged board so that it consistently overlaps its neighbour. Fix the board at the top, then slide the gauge down.

gravel board with its thick edge against the first post. Drive two nails through the board into the arris rail at the top and bottom.

Position the second feather-edged board on the gravel board, overlapping the thin edge of the first by $\frac{1}{2}$in (12mm). Drive a single nail through the boards at each arris rail. Continue to work across the fence run fixing the boards vertically. Hold a spirit level vertically against the outer edge of the boards at intervals to check that they are upright, and adjust by levering out the nail and repositioning if necessary.

You can make a useful gauge as a ready reference for the spacing of each board: cut a notch in an offcut of timber that is equal to the width of a single board minus its overlap of $\frac{1}{2}$in (12mm). As each board is positioned on the gravel board, place the notch of the gauge on the previously fixed board and butt up the loose board to the end of the gauge. Make the fixing at the top arris rail, then slide the gauge down the fixed board to set the bottom of the board you are fixing the correct distance away.

Ranch-style fencing

Post-and-rail fences, comprising vertical posts with horizontal rails nailed across them, take a variety of forms; all are quite straightforward to erect.

Ranch-style fences can be erected on site using separate components, while picket (or palisade) types come in optional kit form for easy assembly. With this type of fence, in which there are many vertical pales to attach to the rails, kit assembly saves time; however, check before you buy that the quality of the panels is acceptable, and the fixings strong, particularly where the pales are already attached to the rails.

PLASTIC RANCH-STYLE FENCING

There are numerous makes of plastic ranch-style fencing, and assembly details vary. Most, however, consist of hollow PVC posts which are concreted into the ground, with cellular plastic planks which push-fit into slots in the post, or which are connected by plastic sleeves themselves attached to the posts with plastic screw fittings.

Plastic caps have flanges which slot into the post tops, and they are normally glued into place. Likewise the hollow ends of the planks at the end of a run are fitted with end caps, which simply slot into place.

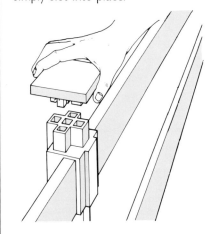

Dimensions
Ranch-style fencing is an open-plan format for boundaries, usually painted white (or sometimes a colour) but often available simply treated with preservative stain for a more natural appearance. It consists of posts fixed at regular intervals, with horizontal cross-pieces of $4\frac{3}{4} \times \frac{3}{4}$in (120 × 20mm) planed soft-wood meeting at the centre of alternate posts.

Extremely adaptable, ranch-style fencing can be any height from a few feet up to about 6ft (1.8m). The planks should be spaced so that they present an aesthetically pleasing effect. There may be a gap of about 4in (100mm) between each pair of planks, for example, and between the top of the post and the top of the first plank, with a larger gap at the bottom between the ground and the base of the lowest plank.

Erecting single ranch-style fencing
Set main posts of 5 × 4in (125 × 100mm) timber in concrete in the ground at 6ft 6in (2m) intervals, with smaller intermediate posts—say, $3\frac{1}{2}$in (90mm) square—midway between. The combination of larger and smaller posts will create an attractive rhythm.

As the planks are fitted to the outer faces of the posts, it is essential that the posts are precisely in line: check this during erection by placing a long straight-edged plank of wood across the outer faces of the posts.

Lengths of plank should meet in the centre of a post. However, to avoid a clean break down the fence where the planks meet, it is best to stagger the joints on alternate rails. Fix the first plank so that one end is flush with the outer edge of the first post on the run. Secure it in the middle to the intermediate post, then fix the other end halfway on the next main post. Run another length of plank from this post, across the next intermediate post and on to finish halfway at the new main post.

The next plank down should start at the end post and finish halfway at the intermediate post; a further plank should run from the intermediate post, fixed at the middle to the next main post, and finish halfway at the next intermediate post. This method will produce a more solid fence.

Attaching the planks

Nail fixings Ranch-style planks can be simply nailed to the posts using 1½in (35mm) long galvanized wire nails. At a butt-join use two nails, one above the other about 1in (25mm) in from the end of the plank. At an intermediate join, again use two nails but stagger them diagonally for a firmer fixing. To prevent the risk of the nails being pulled out, drive them in at a slight inward angle to each other.

Screw fixings Using screws to attach the planks to the posts gives a much more secure fixing than using nails, although it takes longer to insert them. You will need a helper to hold the planks in place against the posts while you mark them in pencil to show the positions of the posts. Remove the planks and drill clearance holes through them using a $\frac{3}{16}$in (4.5mm) twist bit to take 1½in (37mm) No. 8 galvanized countersunk woodscrews. Recess the screw holes with a countersinking bit so that the screw heads will be sunken.

Hold the planks in place again and mark through their screw holes. Remove the planks and make starter holes for the screws in the posts using a ½in (2mm) diameter twist bit. Replace the planks, insert the screws and tighten with a screwdriver.

Installing double ranch-style fencing

Double ranch-style fencing is erected in the same way as the single variety, except that identical planks are fixed to the opposite side of the posts to coincide with the gaps between the planks on the first side. Stagger the butt-joins the opposite way.

Notching the posts

A more durable and rigid form of ranch-style fencing can be constructed by notching the posts to take the horizontal planks. Before fixing the posts, lay them on the ground and mark the positions of the planks on one face, using a plank as a template. Remove the plank and mark the sides of the post with the thickness of the plank minus about ¼in (6mm) so that the planks will protrude this distance from the posts. Chisel out the waste wood within the pencil lines to form the notches, then test the fit of the planks.

Double ranch-style fencing

1 Screw or nail planks to the main and intermediate posts, with butt-joins between lengths occurring at the centre of a post. Ensure the planks are fixed horizontally.

2 Stagger the joins between planks on alternate rows to avoid a continuous break line down the fence at one post, which would tend to weaken the assembly.

Picket fencing

Assembling a picket fence

Although ready-assembled picket panels are available, you may prefer to make up this attractive boundary fencing from scratch so that you can vary the design to suit your preferences and your garden. Pales are normally spaced about $1\frac{1}{2}$ to 2in (35 to 50mm) apart, but you may prefer a wider or narrower spacing, or you may want to fit an arrangement of long and short pales to give a curving or zig-zagging top to the fence.

It is, nevertheless, sensible to assemble sections of picket fence flat on the ground and to secure the resultant panels to the posts in the same way as ready-made panels. If you were to assemble the posts and arris rails first, the non-rigid rails would make it difficult to hammer in the pale-fixing nails properly.

Cutting the rails to size

Set the 3 × 2in (75 × 50mm) posts in the ground between about 6ft 6in (1.9m) and 9ft (2.7m) apart, using concrete or using metal spikes. Cut arris rails of 2 × 1in (50 × 25mm)

softwood to span between posts. If the post is an intermediate one, the rail should finish halfway across and another length of rail should be butt-joined to it; on end posts the end of the rail should be flush with the outer edge of the post.

Mark on the posts the proposed positions for the arris rails. For a fence about 4ft (1.2m) high, the lower arris rail should be about 12in (300mm) up from ground level and the upper rail about 6in (150mm) down from the top of the pales. Measure the distance between the rails. Lay the rails on a hard flat surface, spaced the correct distance apart, with their ends aligned.

Fitting the pales to the rails

Cut the pales to length as required and lay out on the pair of arris rails, spacing them about $1\frac{1}{2}$in (35mm) apart (or as you require). Place a long spare length of arris rail against the shaped tops of the pales to align them correctly, then secure each pale to the rails with two $1\frac{1}{4}$in (30mm) long galvanized nails per fixing. Place the nails diagonally apart

Picket fencing

1 Assemble the picket fence on a flat surface by laying out the arris rails and securing the pales over them. Use a spacer to determine the positions of the pales.

2 Nail the picket panels to the fence posts, driving in two nails per arris rail. Ensure that the rails are horizontal and the pales are vertical by checking with a spirit level.

for a firmer fixing, and angle them inwards slightly: this arrangement helps to prevent the rails from being pulled out, which is a common problem.

Use a piece of timber the same length as a pale, and the width required for the gaps between pales, as a gauge to spacing. Place the gauge in each gap and push the pales up to it as you work across the section.

Fix all the pales to the rails, leaving about 4in (100mm) of rail protruding at each end for attaching the assembly to the posts.

Fixing the pale-and-rail assemblies

The procedure for fitting the pale-and-rail assemblies to the posts is identical to that for fixing prefabricated picket panels. Hold a panel against the posts, propped up underneath on bricks so that the pales clear ground level by about $2\frac{1}{2}$in (60mm). Place a spirit level on the top arris rail and set the panel horizontal.

Nail through the end of the top arris rail into the posts at each side, then recheck for the correct level before securing the bottom rail to the posts.

Make up and fix subsequent panels in the same way to complete the fence.

Bracket fixing The arris rails of a picket fence can be attached to the posts with metal angle brackets, which enable you to set the fencing behind the front edge of the posts. This type of arrangement can, however, appear utilitarian from the back – which is usually the side visible to you from the house.

TURNING CORNERS

There are no particular problems involved in turning a right-angled corner with either ranch-style or picket fences, because the same post can be used for attaching both sections.

Fix the planks of a ranch-style fence or the arris rails of a picket type so that those on one side of the corner overlap the ends of those on the other side of the corner. The overlapping plank or rail should be on the front elevation of the fence for the neatest appearance.

Drive a nail through the overlapping plank or rail into the end of the overlapped plank or rail so that the join will not part.

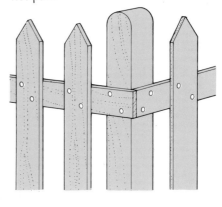

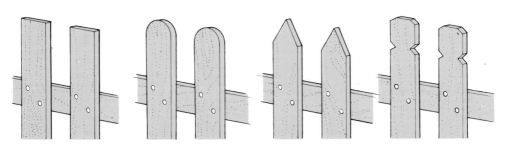

Four common styles of pale are the plain square-ended type, a softer rounded top, an angular pointed top, and a more ornately shaped Queen Anne format. One of these pale patterns can be used throughout a run of fence, or two or more alternated to create a more individual design.

Post-and-wire fencing 1

Wire mesh fencing

Wire mesh fencing, used as a practical boundary marker or a means to keep animals in or out, is stretched between posts of timber, concrete or steel. It is available in long rolls, in a choice of chain mesh (which may be welded for extra toughness), lightweight chicken wire, or a more decorative mesh with a hooped top. Most suppliers will sell a kit containing all the hardware needed for the type of mesh fence and post you want.

Wire fencing is less expensive than timber. It also provides a boundary that makes minimal disruption of the view. Although its appearance is not in itself attractive, wire mesh makes a good support for climbing plants; however, you need to choose suitable, lightweight varieties as most wire meshes are weak in comparison with alternative fencing materials.

Choosing posts

Concrete posts are available with holes to take the straining wires on which the mesh is stretched, while timber posts will probably require holes to be drilled for this purpose. Steel posts, which come in square, triangular or L-shaped section, are usually pre-drilled to take the wire. One advantage steel posts have over concrete and timber is that the intermediate posts can simply be hammered into the ground rather than being set in concrete.

Preparing the posts

Concrete and metal posts need little preparation other than fixing in the ground with their pre-drilled holes facing along the run of the fence. However, timber posts (which should preferably be pre-treated with preservative) must be prepared prior to sinking them in the ground. Mark the height of the fence on each post, including an allowance for the post to protrude about 4in (100mm) at the top of the mesh. Mark the positions of the straining wire fixing holes and drill through the posts at this point using a $\frac{3}{8}$in (10mm) wood bit. Treat the holes with preservative.

Set the main strainer posts in concrete, having made the post holes broader at the bottom than at the top to counteract the tensioning of the line wires. Fit the diagonal braces to the outer posts (see box, page 95), and then erect the intermediate posts. The purpose of the diagonal braces is to counteract the pressure imposed by the tightening of the straining wires.

Turning corners

If your mesh fence is to turn a corner you will need to install a special corner straining post. This type of post features a pair of diagonal braces set at right angles, and pre-drilled holes for the tensioning bolts and for other fittings.

Erecting on sloping ground

Although mesh fencing is flexible enough to cope with minor irregularities in the level of the ground—you simply set the base of the mesh a little way above the ground—it cannot accommodate a steeply sloping site. In this case you will need to create a series of steps in line with the gradient. At each change in level you must erect a two-way straining post and fit shorter lengths of mesh between, so that they can be tensioned individually.

On a slope, braces will be needed at each side of the straining posts to provide equal support in both directions. With timber posts you can drill the holes for the fittings as

Erecting a wire mesh fence

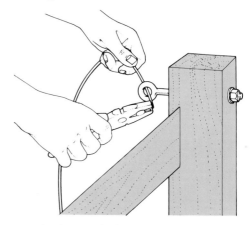

1 Fit the first eyebolt to the post without tightening fully, then attach the line wire and twist it around itself using pliers.

BRACING THE OUTER POSTS

Install the upright strainer posts first and let the concrete harden fully. Dig a hole for each of the diagonal braces needed. Cut the braces to length from timber the same size as the posts.

To mark a brace for cutting, hold it in place against the side of the upright post, its bottom end resting on a brick in the hole. Mark the brace against the side of the post in pencil to give the correct angle for cutting. Saw along the line, then return the brace to the post, holding it against the side. Mark a notch about $\frac{3}{4}$in (20mm) deep on one side of the post, then continue the cutting lines around to the opposite side.

Saw down the notch depth lines, then pare away the waste wood using a wood chisel. Slot the angled end of the brace into the notch and secure it by driving two nails, dovetail fashion, through it into the post.

Add concrete to the post hole to secure the diagonal brace and leave to cure in the normal way (see page 78 for instructions on the use of concrete with posts).

Set the main upright post first, then notch a diagonal brace of the same size timber into the inner face, about 6in (150mm) from the top of the post. Secure the brace to the post with two nails driven in at opposing angles to prevent it from pulling out. Set the base of the brace on hardcore, then pack around with coarse concrete. Allow to harden before fitting the straining wire to the post.

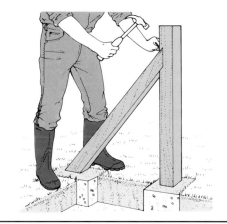

2 Thread a stretcher bar onto the end of the mesh roll, then attach the bar to the brackets attached to the eyebolts.

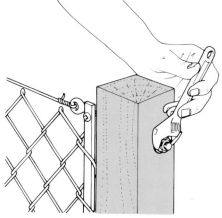

3 Tension the line wires using an adjustable spanner to tighten the nuts on the eyebolts, or tighten the turnbuckle.

Post-and-wire fencing 2

necessary, but with steel and concrete posts you will probably have to order special posts made by your supplier following a plan of the sloping or terraced area. Note that the posts must also be longer than usual to cope with the difference between levels.

Attaching the straining wire

Eyebolts are used to attach the straining wire to the posts, and to the bolts you must fit stretcher bar brackets, which keep the mesh taut along its height.

Slot the eyebolt into the hole in the post and attach the stretcher bar brackets, plus their washers, to the other end. Do not tighten the fittings at this stage.

Thread the end of the straining wire through the eyebolt, turn it back on itself and twist the end around the taut wire several times using a pair of pliers.

Fitting a turnbuckle

A fitting called a turnbuckle can be fitted between the eyebolt and the straining wire to make it easier to adjust the tension of the wire. To fit this, attach the wire to the eye at the end of the turnbuckle and hook the other end onto the eyebolt attached to the post. Do not tighten the turnbuckle until the fence is ready for tensioning.

Tensioning the wire

Run the wire to the other end of the fence and cut it off the roll leaving about 6in (150mm) extra for attaching to the post. Fit a second eyebolt and connect the wire by threading it through the eyebolt and twisting it around itself.

Start to tension the wire from the turnbuckle or one of the eyebolts, tightening with an adjustable spanner. Tighten the fittings equally at each end of the wire. Over-tightening the wire could result in it snapping, so stop adjusting the eyebolts or turnbuckle when the kinks have straightened out and the eyebolt or turnbuckle becomes difficult to turn.

With metal or concrete posts you can fit additional straining wires in holes which are provided along the posts' length. With timber posts a straining wire at top and bottom is sufficient.

Intermediate fixings

The straining wires must be held against the intermediate posts to prevent the mesh from sagging, although the fixings must not hinder the tensioning of the wires via the eyebolts. With timber fences you can simply hammer staples over the wires to hold them in place, but with concrete and steel types you will

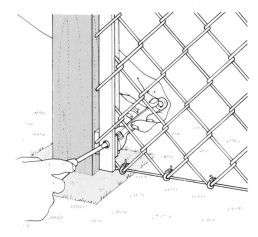

4 Secure the mesh to the line wires by winding on twists of galvanized wire at intervals along the run to prevent sagging.

5 At the other end of the fence, slot on another stretcher bar and attach to the eyebolt brackets.

need to fit wire "stirrups".

Cut lengths of $\frac{1}{8}$in (3mm) galvanized binding wire and slot two through the pre-drilled hole in the post, then take them around the sides of the post and twist the ends around the line wire, which is stretched across the face of the post.

Fitting the mesh

A stretcher bar is fed through the end of the mesh to keep it taut along its height. Slot the bar through the free end of the roll of mesh, then bolt the bar onto the brackets attached to the eyebolts. Tighten the bolts with an adjustable spanner.

Unroll the mesh along the length of the fence and loosely tie it to the straining wires with twists of wire wound on using pliers. Shake the mesh as you go to even it out. At the opposite end of the fence, feed on a second stretcher bar at the line of links which just reach the straining posts.

Unravel a strand of the mesh beyond this stretcher bar by untwisting the top link with a pair of pliers. Bolt the second stretcher bar to the brackets attached to the eyebolts.

Tensioning the mesh

Pull the mesh taut on the straining wires by tightening the nuts on the eyebolts; these

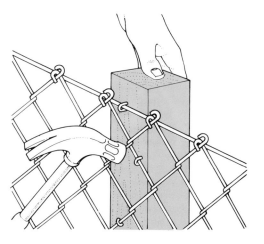

6 When the mesh is taut, secure it to the intermediate posts; hammer in wire staples (or fit stirrups on metal or concrete posts).

pull the stretcher bar brackets against the post. Once the mesh is evenly taut, secure it to the straining wires at 6in (150mm) intervals using twists of wire. Should the mesh appear to sag, remove the stretcher bar and move it along the mesh one or more links to tighten it; then repeat the straining procedure.

Line wire plant supports

Wire frameworks enable you to support a growing climber while it is becoming established and to train it into the most suitable shape. Wires can be stretched horizontally between freestanding posts, forming a type of fence within the garden.

Post fixing It is not necessary to concrete the posts into the ground. Use 3in (75mm) square timber which has been treated with a horticultural grade of preservative, which is harmless to plants.

Trim the bottom ends of the post to points with an axe and, using a sledgehammer, drive them into the ground vertically about 3ft (900mm) deep at each end of the run.

Braces To counteract the tension of the line wires and the weight of the growing climber, brace the uprights with diagonal lengths of 3in (75mm) square timber nailed to the inside face about 6in (150mm) from the top. The brace should be sunk into the ground at the base. Dig a hole for the brace and place a brick or large stone in the base to wedge the brace against, then fill in with the earth.

Intermediate posts Drive in intermediate posts of 3in (75mm) square timber, without diagonal braces, at 4ft (1.2m) intervals.

Line wires Drill $\frac{3}{8}$in (10mm) diameter holes through one of the outer posts, 5in (130mm) apart. Slot in galvanized straining bolts and retain with washers and nuts. Attach $\frac{1}{10}$in (2.5mm) gauge galvanized wire, or plastic-coated wire, twisting it back around itself.

Attach screw-in cup hooks to the opposite end post and attach the free end of the wires. Fasten the wires to the intermediate posts with wire staples hammered in: the wires should be held against the posts by the staples but not so tightly that they cannot be tensioned by the straining bolts.

Tighten the nuts on the straining bolts to stretch the wires taut, using an adjustable spanner.

Trellis

Trellis is a versatile extension to a solid fence; it can serve, for example, as a means of increasing the height of a standard panel size. However, it is also useful as a lightweight fence in its own right. Trellis can also be fixed to a wall or against a fence as a means of supporting climbers and shrubs.

Prefabricated trellis comes in numerous patterns and sizes, although making your own is quite straightforward and requires few carpentry tools other than a tenon saw, chisel and hammer.

Trellis supports
Prefabricated wooden trellis panels in square or diamond pattern make an attractive, less utilitarian type of support for climbers than line wires and mesh fences. Numerous types are widely stocked by garden centres, in planed hardwood or sawn softwood. The former, more costly, is used where appearance is important; the latter, cheaper option, is for inconspicuous general use.

Standard panels Pre-treated with horticultural preservative, standard trellis panels are commonly 6ft 6in (1.9m) high in a choice of widths, typically 12, 24 and 36in (300, 610 and 915mm).

Expanding trellis Sold in folded form, expanding trellis opens out concertina-fashion to make diamond-pattern panels 6ft 6in (1.9m) high in 12, 20, 24, 36 or 47in (300, 510, 610, 915mm or 1.2m) widths.

Fan-shaped trellis Consisting of three or four uprights arranged side by side at the base, but fanning out to a broad top with cross-pieces pinned on to maintain the fan shape, this type of trellis arrangement is intended to be fixed against a wall, where it is an ideal support for single climbing plants or shrubs.

Fixing the trellis
You will find that some trellis panels are pre-drilled for wall-fixing. To fix a panel to a wall, first hold the trellis in position and mark through the screw holes. Set the trellis down and drill holes in the wall to take wallplugs. Push in the wallplugs, then mount the trellis.

It is a good idea to set the trellis against old cotton reels or wooden blocks as spacers. This serves to hold the trellis away from the wall sufficiently to allow the climbing plant to wind around the support.

Drive fixing screws through the trellis, through the cotton reel spacers and into the wallplugs.

Hinging trellis panels
Trellis fixed to a wall or fence can be a problem when you need to repaint the wall behind or treat the fence with preservative. While you could probably untwist the climber itself, or prune it back, the trellis would have to be removed completely.

One way around this problem is to hinge the trellis panel to the wall at the bottom, and attach it to the wall at the top using a simple hook. When required, you simply release the hook and pivot the trellis down from the wall (see diagram, page 99).

Home-made lightweight trellis
To make a lightweight trellis in diamond pattern for fixing to the top of a solid fence or wall, first draw out the area you want to fill as a square or rectangle on the ground. Cut pieces of 1 × ¼in (25 × 6mm) softwood to length and lay them diagonally across the marked-out area, parallel to each other and spaced about 2 to 3in (50 to 75mm) apart.

Cut more strips of timber to length and lay these diagonally opposite to and across the first rows of strips, forming the diamond pattern. Hammer ½in (12mm) tacks through the slats at the intersections, then turn over the lattice arrangement and tap the ends of the tacks to bend them over slightly, so preventing the strips from pulling apart.

Nail the trellis to a thin frame of softwood to give it additional support, then attach the frame itself to the fence posts.

Making a jointed trellis
If you want to make a sturdier trellis up to about 6ft (1.8m) square and freestanding, you must use 1in (25mm) square timber, assembled with simple "cross-halving" joints for added strength—these joints, which are half the thickness of the timber, restore its original thickness when brought together.

Cut the pieces to length and place them on a flat surface side by side with their ends aligned. Wrap adhesive tape around the strips to hold them together while you mark out and cut the joints.

Determine what size squares you want for the trellis and mark off the lengths of timber accordingly. Allow for the thickness of the timber at each point. Do not forget to include the ends for an outer frame member. Continue the marks across all the lengths of timber, using a try square for accuracy.

Remove the adhesive tape and continue the cutting lines down the sides of each strip of timber. Now set a marking gauge to $\frac{1}{2}$in (12mm)—half the thickness of the timber—and scribe down each side of the strips of timber, between the pencil guidelines. This gives you the depth of the cross-halving joints.

Tape up all the strips of timber again marked joints uppermost, and saw down the width lines as far as the thickness lines using a fine-toothed tenon saw. Release the strips and place them one at a time on a board of scrap timber. Use a 1in (25mm) bevel-edged wood chisel to chop out the waste timber to the gauged line. Do not chop out too much timber at once or you may split the joint: pare off a little at a time until the notches are complete.

When all of the notches have been cut you can assemble the trellis on a flat surface by piecing together the joints. Apply PVA woodworking adhesive to the meeting faces and reinforce each joint by hammering in a 1in (25mm) long galvanized nail.

Finally, nail the trellis between stout ground-fixed posts or attach it to the wall as necessary.

Fixing trellis above a wall

Should you want to erect a trellis along the top of a masonry wall, you will have to attach it first to long upright battens, which you can screw to the wall.

Lay the trellis on the ground and position lengths of $2 \times \frac{3}{4}$in (50 × 20mm) sawn softwood, preservative-treated against rot, along its outer uprights. The battens should be just over twice the depth of the trellis members for a firm fixing to the wall. Nail the trellis to the battens, then lift the assembly and ask a helper to hold it in place against the wall you are fixing it to.

Drill holes through the battens protruding from the base of the trellis at top, bottom and centre, and into the masonry. Push hammer-in frame fixings (which consist of a plastic wallplug with screw attached) into the holes and tap with a hammer to seat fully. Use a screwdriver to tighten the fixings; this causes the plugs to expand within the wall and secure the battens.

Attach the trellis to a wall with old cotton reels as spacers so that the plants can twine around the support.

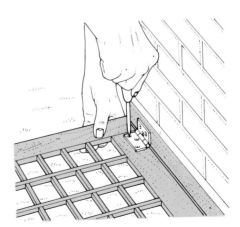

Hinge a trellis panel to the base of a wall and hook it at the top so that you can pivot it down when you need to redecorate the wall.

Fences on sloping ground

When constructing most types of fences and walls, it is not difficult to cope with slight unevenness in the ground level by digging out the earth so that the structure can be erected on the horizontal. Where the ground level is very uneven it is usually necessary to build a fence or wall in a stepped format.

Stepping the structure

With rigid types of panel fencing such as closeboarded, woven or overlapping versions it is best, on sloping ground, to create a stepped foundation.

Position the fence posts vertically, with their top edges set to a consistent slope. Check that the slope is consistent by placing a long plank across the tops of the posts, with a spirit level incorporating a diagonal vial or a special angle-finding device placed on top.

Fix the panels as normal, leaving triangular gaps between their bottom edge and the slope.

Fill in the gaps under the fence panels by cutting spare panels to fit the shape, or else remodel the earth underneath the square-based panels. Where the gap is not too deep it may be possible to cut tapered gravel boards of softwood to fit under the panels.

Alternatively you could construct solid masonry plinth walls underneath the fence.

Stepping the foundation

In order to make solid plinth walls beneath a panel fence built on a slope, or to support a masonry wall built on a slope, you will have to construct a stepped concrete foundation.

Lay the concrete strip foundation between each post position using as formwork lengths of board spanning the trench and supported by timber stakes at each side. Work from the top of the slope, casting each horizontal section of strip foundation on the roughly shaped earth base. If you use the trench-fill method of casting the concrete, no side formwork is necessary, as the sides of the trench will support and mould the mix.

When the first step is formed, move the board formwork down to the vertical edge of the next step and cast another section. Repeat this process to the bottom of the slope.

Cast the fence posts in the concrete slab at the given points, then leave the concrete to set before building the plinth walls. Where a solid wall is to be built on the plinths, construct piers at the step positions as you build the wall.

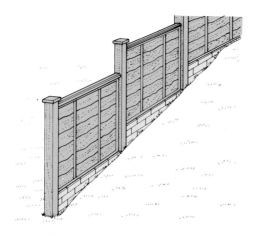

Rigid fence panels must be stepped down a slope and the triangular gaps beneath filled with broad gravel boards, cut-down panels or brickwork plinths.

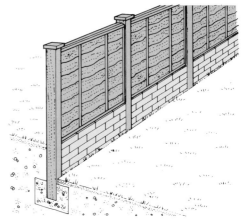

Build a retaining wall where a slope runs across the garden and erect the fence or wall on top of this.

Construct plinth walls in bricks or blocks on the stepped concrete strip, so that the steps are linked by one or two courses of masonry shared by adjacent sections. The top edge of the plinths will, of course, follow the stepped form of the foundation. The fence panels or masonry walls are erected between the posts (or piers) on these walls.

Setting fences on a slope

It is possible to erect post-and-rail fences such as picket, palisade and ranch types on ground that slopes quite considerably. Set the posts vertically as before, then fix arris rails at an angle that follows the general lie of the land. Cut mortises in the posts to take the arris rails so that they slope at the correct angle: drill out the mortises first, then finish off with a chisel for accuracy.

Fix the vertical pales of picket or palisade fencing vertically, with the bottom ends cut to a slope as necessary. Set the top edges to the same angle as the arris rails. The pales will be uneven in length, but each must be vertical for the fence to appear correct.

With ranch-style fencing, simply set the normally horizontal planks to an angle that follows the general slope of the ground. Cut the ends of the boards diagonally and butt-join between lengths. You can use a sliding bevel or combination try square (a wooden tool with a metal blade, rather like a try square, with a sliding blade which can be set at any angle) as a guide to setting the angles.

PLANNING A SLOPING BOUNDARY

Checking gradients

Before you can plan out the route a fence or wall will take on a sloping site, you will have to measure its approximate gradient. This will enable you to draw a side elevation diagram of the proposed structure— a vital aid for calculating material requirements and sizes of components, and to visualize the finished effect.

Water levels One method of measuring the gradient of a shallow slope is to use a device called a "water level", which can be improvised using an ordinary garden hosepipe.

Plug a hosepipe at either end with transparent plastic tubing. Attach one end of the hosepipe to a peg driven into the ground at the top of the slope so that the open end faces upward. Lead the hosepipe along the ground to the bottom of the slope. Ask a helper to hold the hosepipe so that it rises vertically from the low-point of the slope.

Using a funnel and watering can, fill the pipe with water from the top of the slope until the water overflows. The water will settle at the same level at both ends of the hosepipe. Measure the level the water reaches in the pipe at the lower end of the slope. The height of the drop is the height of the water level above the ground at the lower end of the slope minus the height of the water from the ground at the top of the slope.

Adjusting a slope over a large area

Where the site is very uneven, and perhaps sloping too, work out the overall level and carry out any remodelling of the earth that may be necessary. For this exercise, use "boning rods", which, together with a straight-edged plank and a spirit level, enable the level to be established by sight.

Boning rods are stakes with short pieces of wood nailed across near the top and bottom at right angles. Fix a short boning rod in the ground at the top of the slope and a longer one further down. Lay the plank between the two rods at the top and adjust the depth of one of the rods until the spirit level shows you that the plank is level. Then place a third rod lower down the slope, lining its top cross-piece by eye with the bottom cross-piece of the second rod. Proceed in this way down the slope. Then measure the various vertical dimensions and add them all up. Don't forget to subtract the height of the cross-piece from the ground at the top of the slope.

Contours/planters 1

Shaping the contours of the land to suit your requirements is one of the basic principles of planning a garden, but one that is often neglected. Many people put up with gardens that are nothing more than flat, featureless expanses of earth, with no visual relief or outstanding features to attract the attention. This is particularly so with newly constructed houses, where the garden is likely to be a muddy wasteland of débris left behind by the builder. In fact, you can flatten a sloping site, if that is what your garden design requires; but often it is better to turn the slope to advantage. If you start with a flat site, you can create terraced planters or undulating shapes without too much difficulty.

A log roll planter
A planter need not be a high structure between two ground levels. Even adding a contrasting edging to a flower border or a slightly raised lawn can provide a subtle but significant change of level that adds to the interest of the design.

Several manufacturers stock preformed half-round log sections, with flat backs, connected in a log roll. These are intended as an edging for borders, but equally well serve to make a raised planter or a division between terraces.

The heights of the individual logs in the rolls are typically 6, 12 and 18in (150, 300 and 450mm), and they come in 3 ft 3in (1 m) lengths. Durable half-round cedar edging also comes in roll form, in 6 and 12in (150 and 300mm) heights and 6ft (1.8m) lengths, and this, too, can be used to create curving raised planters.

The benefit of log roll edging is that it is very flexible and can cope with quite complex curves. To install the edging, simply dig a shallow trench around the path, lawn or border, then unroll and insert the edging, and backfill with earth to hold it in place. Although the timber is durable, it is sensible to fix heavy-duty polythene behind the rolls in order to prevent the damp earth from touching them.

Reasons for changing the contours
Faced with a plain plot the most radical option of all is altering the shape of the ground. This is not just a means of creating more visual interest—it also provides the opportunity to erect original structures which will serve as additional planting areas.

Introducing earth-retaining walls into a basically flat site will immediately create a series of terraces, which you can plant out. Terracing a steeply sloping site has the benefit

Making a log roll planter

1 Mark out the area of the planting bed and dig a shallow trench at the perimeter to take the rolls of log edging.

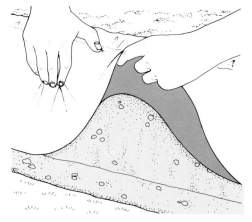

2 Drape heavy-gauge polythene over the back wall of the trench as a damp-proofing precaution to protect the timber edging.

of making the plot more usable, workable and attractive to the eye.

Changes of level in a garden can provide shelter from prevailing winds or frost, and hence may be useful in the provision of, say, a kitchen garden or a swimming pool. (A flat area, on the other hand, may be ideal for games such as croquet.) Slopes can also have the function of concealing an unsatisfactory boundary.

Introducing slopes

Remodelling the earth can produce interesting undulating profiles, often with the benefit of improving drainage to promote healthy plant growth. Beware of too drastic alterations, however, as the point of the exercise should be to make adjustments, not to introduce dramatic change.

Slopes should lie at an angle of not more than 30 degrees, because a bank steeper than this is liable to erosion by surface and underground water movement. The gentler a slope is, the wider the area it will require; but remember that steep slopes will be difficult to traverse, especially with garden equipment.

A gradient of 30 degrees is manageable comfortably with a cylinder lawn mower. A hover mower can cope with a steeper slope—up to 45 degrees. When planting a steep

3 Unroll the log edging and set it in the trench, with its back edge against the polythene. Backfill the trench with soil.

bank, it is advisable to plant through a sheet of coarse netting pegged into the soil; this will retain the earth until the roots get established.

When introducing slopes into the garden, it is important to relate them to the main views. A view at right angles to the contour lines tends to be more appealing than a view that falls away to one side or the other.

Cutting-and-filling

Using the "cut-and-fill" technique you can alter the existing levels.

For the sake of economy, the cut should be equivalent by volume to the fill. Carting away excess earth, or bringing new earth to the site, can be an expensive operation. The procedure involves removing the fertile topsoil from the whole area of ground to be reshaped, removing the subsoil from one area of the site and moving it to another, then returning the topsoil to both levels. Take care not to leave subsoil exposed as a surface covering. Unlike topsoil it is not rich enough in nutrients to support growing plants.

Drainage of the site

Free drainage from the higher terraced area is necessary to prevent the roots of plants from becoming waterlogged. Building rubble can be used to form the core of a raised planting bed. A problem with these structures is that the soil is likely to drain too rapidly denying the plants much of the nourishment they need and making it necessary to water the plants more frequently. This can be prevented by laying turves, grass side down, on top of the drainage material.

The retaining walls of planters—whether constructed from brick, stone or timber—should incorporate some form of drainage to avoid trapping water. A simple plastic or clay drain pipe inserted across the thickness of the wall, protruding from the face near the base, will act as a channel for excess moisture. On masonry walls it is sufficient to omit the mortar from a few vertical joints between bricks or blocks. This in no way affects the stability of the wall, but it does keep the back face of the structure well drained.

Materials for planters

Raised planting areas are an ideal means of

Planters 2

compartmentalizing your garden, and are especially convenient for the elderly or infirm to work in because the height of the planting areas can be designed to be reached without stooping—or even from a wheelchair. They can be constructed from a wide range of materials, the choice of which is often determined by the style of garden you want to create. For a formal patio-style town garden, for example, neat, angular brickwork planters are an ideal choice, perhaps linked to brick walls and terraces, flanking sets of steps, or built within an area of paving slabs. Choosing second-hand bricks and incorporating curves in the planter walls will lessen the angular appearance while still creating an effect that is well organized and neat.

If you would prefer to create a more natural-looking effect—for example, in a rural garden—timber enclosures or dry-stone retaining walls are perhaps more appropriate. Timber types can be constructed from planed, preservative-treated timber, jointed for strength as a sturdy framework to contain the earth; or they may be nothing more than a series of rough-hewn logs sunk end-on in the ground as a basic retaining wall.

Natural stone walls will always appear rugged and random, although their assembly follows a rigid formula (see pages 72-3). Reconstructed walling blocks with riven or exposed aggregate faces offer the outward appearance of a natural material combined with the "manufactured" regularity of brickwork.

Whatever material you choose, you should strive to soften the structures with masses of plants, either spilling over the edge of the planter, or actually growing from between the stones or timbers.

Around the planters

The treatment of the planters' immediate surroundings is as important as the choice of materials. If you have planned the garden so that it will provide easy access for equipment, a paved or gravelled area surrounding the raised planting beds is ideal. This also reduces the amount of weeding that will need to be done.

Alternatively, turfing the area around the planters will help them to blend in with the garden. The planters may also be made to rise from conventional flower borders, so that they are surrounded by plants. Paths wending their way through the plot will, of course, be needed with such a design, for access with equipment and for tackling periodic maintenance tasks.

Building retaining walls

Constructing an earth-retaining wall to introduce terraces to the plot is not a straightforward matter (see pages 66-7). The sheer weight of earth that must be held back calls for a structure that is built to rigorous standards. If it is to be over about 4ft (1.2m) in height, you should obtain advice on the structure from your local authority's Building Control Department.

Railway sleeper walls

Ex-railway sleepers, sold by some garden centres or specialist suppliers, are a tough, durable material to use in planter construction. When laid as a single layer they require no support or fixings other than their own considerable weight. The sleepers, which generally measure 52 × 10 × 5in (1.3m × 225 × 125mm), can be laid directly on the ground as the edging to a border, path or other feature. A single height of sleeper will create a substantial low bed, but you can also stack the sleepers to make a high retaining wall (see box, opposite).

Log walls

Logs can be used to make sturdy planters with a natural, rustic quality. Stakes of the same wood can be used to secure the walls; they need to be sturdy and rammed well into the ground to brace the weight of soil in the planter.

Lay the bottom logs on the ground to plot out the position of the planter. Decide on the height of the planter in advance and cut the stakes accordingly. Drive the stakes in close to the end of each log.

At a corner where two logs meet, two stakes will be required; the ends of the logs should be bevelled. Build up the layers of logs behind the stakes, staggering the ends of each course of logs in relation to the course below. Attach the logs to the stakes using galvanized nails.

Interlocking logs

Another way to make a raised planter (or a fishpond or tree seat) is to buy flat-backed, round-faced logs with notches cut in their edges. Adjoining logs interlock to create a rigid yet lightweight structure, and it is possible to construct rectangular, hexagonal or other shaped units. Preformed panels made of a row of connected logs can be attached with dowel fixings so that a planter can also double as a practical bench unit in the garden. Because of the interlocking construction, no further fixings are necessary.

Damp-proofing provisions

Any timber structure will succumb to rot unless it is specially treated, so it is essential that some kind of damp-proofing provision is made in the planter construction.

While a thorough treatment with preservative is vital, additional protection can be provided by a waterproof barrier between the retaining walls and the earth in the planter. Heavy-gauge polythene placed behind a log roll border or railway sleeper wall will act as a moisture bar, so that the surplus water drains away safely.

Sandwich the polythene sheet between the timber and the earth, allowing it to protrude slightly at the top and bottom: future planting will conceal the polythene from view.

A further provision against dampness rising into the timber is to bed the retaining walls on a fine layer of gravel, which has the advantage of being free-draining.

MAKING A RAILWAY SLEEPER PLANTER

When stacking sleepers to form a planter, stagger the vertical joins between them in alternate rows, just as you would when laying bricks. It is important to anchor two or more sleepers, using metal hoops driven into the ground, if you stack them with their short side uppermost. Backfill with subsoil, then topsoil.

Some manufacturers produce miniature versions of the original railway sleepers. These often have one or more rounded faces for a softer, more natural appearance.

1 Construct a raised planter from railway sleepers laid horizontally. Butt-join the sleepers at the corners.

2 Build up courses of sleepers to the height required for the planter. Stagger the vertical joints to give a strong, rigid bond.

Planters 3

CONSTRUCTING A TIMBER PLANTER

This timber planter provides a neat growing area you can work on without having to stoop. The structure can be formed from an existing sloping site, or else created on flat ground and filled with imported subsoil and topsoil. No complicated carpentry joints are required to construct the planter, as the assembly makes use of the weight of the earth the box contains to force the side planks against the supporting timber posts.

Preparing the timber

Construct the planter from 3 × 2in (75 × 50mm) sawn softwood for the supporting posts and 6 × 2in (150 × 50mm) sawn softwood for the plank sides. Try to purchase pressure-treated timber or, failing that, treat all of the timber with preservative before assembly, preferably by submerging the lengths in a home-made bath of the protective fluid so that it soaks in over a few days.

Planning the structure

Draw a simple sketch of your garden and draw in the position and size of the planter to see how it relates to other features. Work the sketch into a scale plan drawn on graph paper so that you can calculate the quantity of timber you will need to buy. Draw a side elevation so that you can work out the height of the various bays that divide the planter.

Sinking the posts

Mark out the overall shape of the planter on the ground using stringlines stretched between wooden pegs driven into the ground at the post locations. Dig the post holes using a spade or hired post-hole borer, then add hardcore to the holes to provide a firm foundation and free-draining base. Set the uprights in the holes, propped vertically, and pour in fresh concrete. Leave the posts for a few days until the concrete is fully set: they will have to support a considerable weight of soil in addition to holding the plank sides of the planter.

Alternatively you can use metal fencing spikes to set the posts: these are simply hammered into the ground without the need

Constructing a timber planter

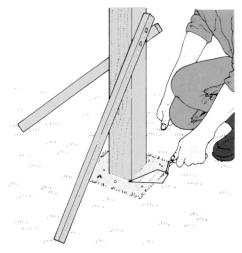

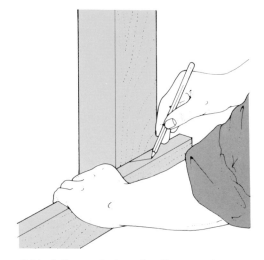

1 Set the perimeter posts in concrete, or use fence spikes to support them around the marked out area of the planter. The posts must be positioned at each corner of the design.

2 Mark the angled cutting lines on the top edge of the planks so that the mitres thus formed will be forced against the back of the posts by the pressure of the contained soil.

to dig holes, and have a collar at the top into which the bottom end of the post slots.

Check that the posts are set level across their tops by spanning across them with a long straight-edged plank with a spirit level on top. If they need adjusting, raise or sink one of the posts as appropriate.

Fitting the plank sides
The plank sides are cut to fit behind the pairs of posts—finishing at the posts' centre point—and their ends cut to mitres so that they will be forced flush against the inside face of the posts by the pressure of soil within.

Hold each plank, which should be longer than required, behind pairs of posts and mark off the cutting lines in pencil. It is a good idea to cut the planks to size using a power circular saw or jigsaw, both of which have an adjustable sole plate. By setting the angle of the sole plate to the precise angle required for the mitres you will be able to ensure an accurate fit for each plank.

Cut the planks as marked, then position them behind the posts on a layer of fine

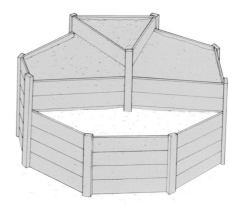

A plank-and-post timber planter can be built on flat ground, or into a slope. It consists of a number of posts supporting stout planks stacked one on top of the other to create a basic box to contain the soil. The box can be any angular shape, and divided into a number of bays.

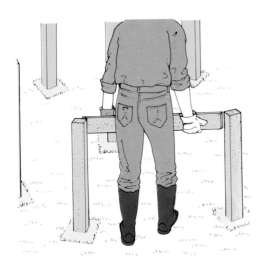

3 Place the bottom planks behind the pairs of posts. They should be long enough to allow the bevelled edges to finish at the middle of the posts.

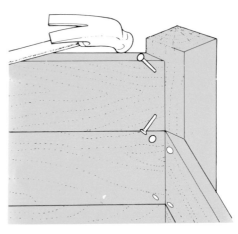

4 Stack the planks behind the posts, level them carefully using a spirit level, then secure them to the back of each post using 3in (75mm) long galvanized nails, driven in dovetail fashion.

Planters 4

gravel to ensure rapid drainage of rainwater. You should aim to sink the bottom row of planks about 4in (100mm) below the surrounding ground level so that soil will not leak out onto the paving or other surface. Place a spirit level on the top edge of each plank and tap the plank horizontal with the shaft of a club hammer.

Stack the planks one on top of the other until you reach the finished height—about 1in (25mm) below the top of the posts.

Secure the planks to the posts by driving in two 3in (75mm) long galvanized nails at each end. Drive in the nails at an angle to each other so that they resist pulling out.

Dividing up the bays

When you have constructed the outer framework of the timber planter you can start to divide it off into a number of separate bays, set at different levels. Intermediate posts can be fixed within the main box to support single planks, creating a gentle change of level, or else stacked planks can be used for a more dramatic terraced effect. Remember that the bottom planks should be bedded on hardcore and gravel both to prevent them from sinking and to improve drainage.

Adding a damp-proof membrane

Although soaking the timber in preservative will help to ward off an attack by rot, the planter will eventually succumb to the effects of the damp earth unless you provide a second line of defence.

Pin sheets of heavy-gauge polythene to the inside walls of the planter and its bays before you fill it with earth: this will form a physical barrier through which the dampness cannot penetrate. The damp-proof membrane will also help to direct surplus water downwards to the free-draining base.

Redistributing the earth

Once the skeleton of the planter has been constructed, you can fill the box with upturned turves to within about 10in (250mm) of the top row of planks. Add subsoil and compact lightly. Add topsoil to within a few inches of the top row of planks and leave to settle for about two weeks. Fill in any hollows that form with more soil.

CONSTRUCTING A BRICK PLANTER

A masonry planter is not difficult to construct, provided that you are familiar with the basic techniques of bricklaying (see pages 62-5). The structure need be no more than about six or eight courses high, so the provision of foundations is not a problem, unless the ground is especially soft. A planter can be built on an existing concrete slab patio, a crazy paving surface, or a surface made of bricks or precast concrete slabs: what is important is that the surface is sound and level.

Choosing and using bricks

To make a planter about eight bricks long, two bricks wide and six courses high, you will need about 100 bricks. This will produce a planter that measures $61\frac{3}{4}$in (1565mm) long by $17\frac{1}{2}$in (440mm) deep (front to back).

Choose facing bricks, which have an attractive colour and facing texture, if the planter is to be a freestanding unit, or try to obtain bricks similar to those used in other features in the garden or the walls of the house.

An ordinary stretcher bonding pattern (with bricks laid end to end, overlapping by half their length in alternate courses) is used in assembly; at the corners, a brick is turned at right-angles to the others and the bond continued.

Mortar mixes

About 176lb (80kg) of mortar is needed to lay the bricks, and this should be purchased as a dry ready-mix (which already contains plasticizer) in two 89 or 110lb (40 or 50kg) bags. Alternatively, mix the separate ingredients yourself, using 220lb (100kg) of builder's sand and 44lb (20kg) of ordinary Portland cement, with plasticizer added (this comes in small containers); or use 44lb (20kg) of hydrated lime instead of plasticizer. Mix the concrete in the proportions of 6 parts sand to 1 part cement, with plasticizer added according to the manufacturer's instructions.

Add water. Mortar of the correct consistency should hold the ridged shape when a shovel is dragged across the surface.

Building the planter

Dry-lay the first two courses of bricks on the foundations, without mortar but with finger-thick gaps between each brick, to check that the stretcher bond and the mortar joint thicknesses are correct and consistent.

Set up stringlines and pegs, or profile boards, as a guide to laying the bricks accurately. Check that the corner of the planter is at right-angles using a try square. Remove the bricks about three at a time, and re-lay them on a mortar screed trowelled on the base. Tap the first brick into place with the handle of the trowel, aligning it with the stringline, so that the mortar joint is only $\frac{3}{8}$in (10mm) thick. With the trowel scoop up the surplus mortar that is squeezed out from under the brick and use to spread onto one end of the second brick, forming a vertical joint. Lay the third brick in the same way, then remove the next three loose-laid bricks and lay them properly on mortar.

Place a spirit level on top of the row of bricks you have just laid to check that they are set horizontally. Complete the first course of bricks, then lay the second on top, staggering the vertical joins by half the length of a brick. As the courses rise, use a gauge rod (see page 64) to check that the mortar joints are consistent. Place the spirit level diagonally across the face of the walls to check for bowing.

Completing the planter walls

If you are using bricks with frogs (indents) on one side, these should be laid frog upward, so that the vertical mortar joint is made as strong as possible. The fresh mortar, trowelled onto each course, fills the frog and forms a key that prevents sideways movement of the courses once the mortar has hardened.

At the final, sixth course, however, lay the bricks frog downwards, so that the flat top faces of the bricks will give a smooth top to the planter walls. Alternatively, lay a row of specially shaped coping bricks along the top of the planter. These are available with a bevelled, chamfered or rounded finish, and are laid in exactly the same way as ordinary bricks. Shaped corner pieces are also made for some special bricks.

Pointing the mortar joints

Neaten the appearance of the planter by pointing the mortar joints. To do this, use a length of hosepipe to rub the mortar, when it is just starting to stiffen, to form a neat, rounded profile.

Leave the planter for about four days so that the mortar will harden fully before you add the soil filling.

Damp-proofing the planter

As the planter will contain a considerable amount of earth, which will be damp for much of the time, it is a good idea to paint the inside of the unit with bituminous emulsion to prevent the moisture from soaking into the bricks. Leave the emulsion to dry thoroughly before adding the soil filling.

Allow surplus moisture to seep away by omitting the mortar from about three vertical joints between bricks in the first course, on each long side.

Dig over the base of the planter to ensure drainage is not impaired and shovel a layer of pea gravel 1-2in (25-50mm) deep into the base to provide free drainage. Cover the ground with upturned turves (grass-side down) to prevent clogging, then top up with fertile topsoil. Allow this to settle for about one week before filling in any hollows and planting out.

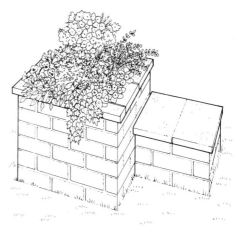

A brick planter can incorporate a low ledge, which can be used as a seat or as a plinth for a potted plant.

Pergolas 1

A timber pergola erected against the house wall or freestanding elsewhere in the garden provides an ideal way to support grapevines, climbing plants or bush or tree fruit. Once the plants are properly established, the foliage covering the pergola will also provide a cool and shady place to sit on hot summer days, made all the more pleasant by the sunlight filtering gently through. Barbecues and meals outdoors can be taken under the leafy cover.

Alternatively, a pergola can be used as an arbour, or partially covered walkway, leading to another part of the garden. Entwined with roses, honeysuckle or clematis, such a structure may simply terminate at a garden bench seat, or open into a gazebo. Built against a house wall, the pergola will even afford some measure of protection against rain, particularly if the foliage is lush.

The basic structure

A pergola is basically a stout timber framework consisting of tall upright posts with an arrangement of cross-pieces at the top, which form a semi-solid roof. The sides of the pergola may be left open, or else clad with trelliswork, planks or fence panels, or garden furniture may be positioned between posts.

Plant supports

Unless the pergola is intended exclusively to support clinging climbers such as ivy or twining ones such as honeysuckle, additional supports to train plants over the pergola will be required. Numerous options are available:

Trellis Prefabricated trellis panels, or the expanding type of lightweight diamond-pattern trellis, can simply be pinned on to the supporting posts.

Line wires Galvanized wire, ideally coated with plastic, can be stretched between the posts and the existing top and additional bottom rails to form a vertical, horizontal or criss-crossing form of support for twining plants. Secure the line wires with hammer-in staples or nails, twisting the wire around itself

A freestanding pergola

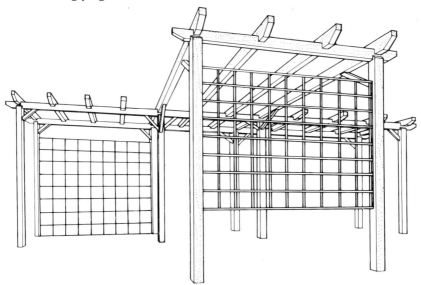

Construct a freestanding pergola over the patio to provide an area for sitting out under the shade of climbing plants entwined around the structure's main beams and trellis panels. The pergola may be a single unit, or two or three connected areas, furnished individually with patio seats, loungers, or a barbecue. Alternatively construct the pergola as a leafy walkway across the garden.

using pliers. Alternatively, purchase some screw-in vine eyes to attach the wires.

Mesh Plastic-coated chain link garden fencing can be stretched to fit across the pergola framework and secured with staples. Alternatively, choose the lightweight green plastic mesh, which is fixed in the same way.

Once the climbers become established, support their woody, quite heavy stems by tying them to lead- or plastic-headed wall nails, driven into the main supporting timbers of the pergola.

The roof structure

The roof of the pergola is usually fitted with additional supports for climbers, in the form of cane poles, trellis, mesh or line wires stretched between eyebolts. It is important that the main roof beams are made of strong enough timber—6 × 2in (150 × 50mm) sawn softwood is ideal—so that a person's weight could be supported. Snow, especially when combined with a bulky climber, can be very heavy, and the pergola must be able to withstand this loading.

The materials used to connect the roof timbers to the upright posts should be strong and rigid, and it is usual to use cross-halving joints for the longitudinal and cross-members. This joint, in which half the timber's thickness is cut away to be restored when the pieces are connected, resists sideways movement and is unlikely to separate. Posts are normally notched to accept the roof timbers, or may have metal brackets attached.

Where the pergola is attached to the house wall, a stout wall plate is normally employed, bolted to the masonry and notched to take the ends of the roof timbers. A slope can be incorporated in the pergola roof, away from the house wall, in case subsequent glazing is required to convert the structure into a carport or perhaps a covered way to the house entrance.

There is no reason why sections of the pergola cannot be partially glazed, particularly

An attached pergola

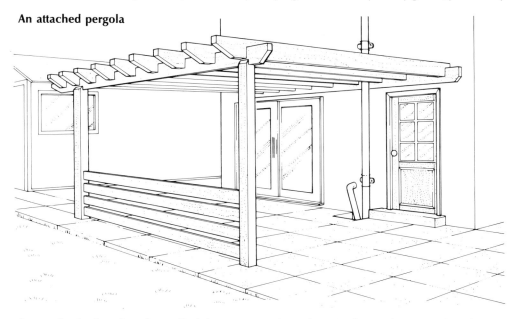

A pergola sited against the wall of the house becomes a partially covered extension to the living room, dining room or kitchen with direct access, ideally through patio doors. This type of garden structure can also double as a carport during the winter months, when built over a suitable base such as slabs or pavers.

Pergolas 2

if it covers the door to the house, offering shelter to callers when it rains. Use wired glass or corrugated plastic sheeting as the glazing so that, in case of breakage, falling fragments are held together and are not a danger.

Types of pergola post
The supporting posts need not be timber. More substantial supports can be formed by constructing piers of brickwork, natural stone blocks, tubular or angled metal, or even cast concrete. For a classical appearance, supporting columns cast in concrete could be used, possibly fluted and topped with capitals or incorporating decorative corbels or other scrollwork embellishments.

Design
The design of the structure and its size are important if the pergola is not to look incongruous in the garden. Many contemporary pergolas are made distinctive by their extending roof timbers, which are cut with bevels reminiscent of Oriental architecture: this design also protects the vulnerable end grain of the timber from the rain.

The shape of the structure may be rectangular or square, positioned over a patio or terrace. It can be made to follow the line of a path, or turn a right-angled corner in order to fit into a corner of the garden against a boundary wall or fence. More elaborate

formats are possible, too, such as changes in the overall height of the pergola, in order to traverse a slope or to climb and cover a flight of garden steps.

There is plenty of scope for attractive designs. A classic format is a timber roof structure supported on brick piers that are shaped like church buttresses, diminishing in area from bottom to top. The slopes of the buttress are capped with coping which serves to shed rain.

Another approach is to build the piers using tiles, with a coping stone at the top on which the timbers rest.

Variations in the height of the beams will give the pergola a sense of movement. This is very easily achieved by setting the poles or beams at different levels within brick or stone piers.

A rustic appearance is often more desirable than a formal effect. Complete tree trunks or straight branches will give an appropriately natural look, blending effectively with climbers trained over the structure. Bamboo poles can also be effective.

When the uprights of a pergola are of masonry, it is important to provide a substantial roof structure. Too flimsy a superstructure will look disconcertingly out of scale.

The entrance to a pergola can be emphasized in various ways. One approach is to place a pair of matching ornamental features at either side of the entrance—for example,

Additional support for plants

Galvanized chain link or plastic mesh can be stapled to the pergola posts and cross-rails as a plant support.

Line wires can be stretched vertically, horizontally or in criss-cross fashion from eyes fixed to the pergola.

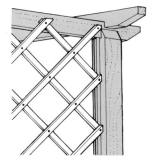

Prefabricated trellis in diamond or square pattern can be cut to fit across the posts and pinned on.

substantial containers, each planted with a tree or shrub, or a pair of urns or vases, or even statuary. Another way to provide emphasis is to add decorative braces between the supports and cross-pieces of the first arch.

To enhance a pergola and set it off from other parts of the garden, it may be worth building it on a stepped base.

It is also possible to construct a roughly circular pergola, using short roof timbers to connect the posts, arranged around a central feature, say a bird bath, statue or fountain.

BUILDING A GAZEBO

A gazebo is, strictly speaking, a summer-house, belvedere or pavilion sited in the garden in such a position that it will command an attractive view. In many gardens, the best position will be the corner of the plot, in the angle formed by the walls or boundaries with a view into the garden itself. The often elegant structure can also be a feature in its own right, containing built-in or freestanding seating, and possibly a table. Climbers can be trained up the sides of the gazebo and hanging baskets attached to the rafters.

Some gazebos have solid panelled walls, glazed windows and a door, while simpler versions may be just a lattice-roofed screen with trellis panels as walls.

Gazebos are available in kit form from major fencing manufacturers. It is easy, however, to construct a gazebo using standard fencing materials and trellis.

Mark out the plan of the gazebo on the ground using stringlines and pegs—it may be square, rectangular or a more complex hexagonal shape—and erect posts of 3 × 3in (75 × 75mm) sawn softwood about 7ft (2.1m) high at the corners.

Although the posts may be set in concrete, it is simpler to use fence post spikes. Where the gazebo is being assembled on a solid paved surface, use a post-fixing plate: the spike is replaced with a broad, flat plate which you bolt to the ground. Another version has an extension which is set in fresh concrete, for use where a spike is impractical.

Connect the tops of the posts with horizontal rails of 3 × 2in (75 × 50mm) timber, nailed into place, and fit diagonal braces at the upper corners. Construct a roof, pitched on four sides by linking rafters of 3 × 2in (75 × 50mm) timber to a central finial, shaped to a point and positioned at the apex of the structure. Notch the lower edge of the rafters to fit over the horizontal rails at the top of the posts and secure by skew-nailing (driving nails in through the sides of the rafters into the rails).

Clad the roof with preformed trellis cut to the triangular shape of each elevation and pinned on, or pin on a latticework arrangement of $1 \times \frac{1}{4}$in (25 × 6mm) slats cut to fit. Fix trellis to one, two or three sides of the gazebo, leaving at least one side open as a viewpoint.

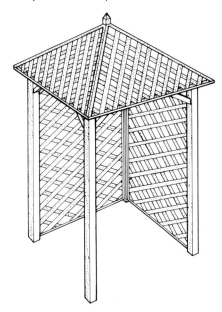

A gazebo made from four upright posts with a pitched roof is clad with trellis panels as a shady sitting area looking over the garden or to an attractive view beyond.

Constructing a pergola 1

The position of a pergola will influence its finished effect on the garden, and the kind of use you are able to put it to, so careful planning is required.

Planning the site
Because the structure is inherently angular, it is essential to align it with straight-sided features such as a garden wall or outbuilding to avoid a disjointed appearance, with spaces alongside that are awkwardly shaped and unlikely to be accessible.

Because of its height—probably in excess of 8ft (2.4m)—a freestanding pergola can appear to loom over surrounding features, or even to cast them in shadow. Conversely, if the pergola is placed in the centre of a lawn, for example, it might look marooned, or may block a pleasant view from the house.

It is best to opt for a site where the pergola can be made to blend in with its surroundings: for example, place it in a corner formed by boundary walls or the wall of a house and its extension, or run it along the side of a wall or fence, even attached to it. Where there is a narrow pathway running alongside the house, leading to a side entry or back door, consider erecting the pergola along the path as a leafy walkway.

A sunny aspect is important if vines or fruit trees are to be trained against the pergola, and one of its long sides should face a southerly or easterly direction (in the northern hemisphere) where it will receive sun for most of the day. Avoid placing the pergola in a location that is predominantly shaded by tall trees or buildings, or on a wall where it will receive little or no sunlight.

If the pergola is to be erected on a sloping or terraced site, remember that the top of the structure must be stepped to follow the gradient; otherwise it will appear too lofty.

Estimating materials
If one of the numerous kit pergolas available is to be used, everything needed to erect the structure to a given size will be provided. However, if the pergola is to be constructed to your own specifications, you will have to draw a detailed plan and side elevation, both to enable you to decide on the design of the structure and to calculate the lengths of

timber and other materials you will require.

The greatest expense will be the timber, although if you choose a size that corresponds to standard floor joists—6 × 2in (150 × 50mm) and 4 × 2in (100 × 50mm)—you might be able to obtain secondhand timber from a demolition site at much reduced rates. You will probably have to spend some time removing old nails from the timber. Treat all the timber with preservative by soaking in a makeshift bath of fluid. If you buy new timber, make sure it has been pressure-impregnated with preservative.

Fitting a wallplate
For a single-sided pergola that is to be built against the house (or other) wall, a stout wallplate of 6 × 2in (150 × 50mm) timber will need to be fitted as a support for the roof timbers. Cut the wallplate to length and drill 1in (25mm) diameter holes through the face using a flat bit at the centre, 16in (400mm) in from each end, then at 20in (50mm) intervals.

Cutting notches for the rafters
The roof timbers can be located in notches cut in the top edge of the wallplate. Mark

Constructing an attached pergola

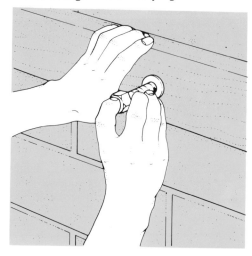

1 Secure the wallplate using steel anchor bolts. Remove the outer shell of the bolt and push into the wall before inserting the bolt through the hole in the wallplate.

out the position of each notch on the top edge with a pencil and a try square. Mark notches 2in (50mm) in from each end of the wallplate, then spaced at about 28in (700mm) intervals between. Continue the lines down the front and back of the wallplate for about 2in (50mm).

In order to incorporate a slight slope in the roof timbers, away from the house wall, make the depth lines of the notch about 2in (50mm) at the front and $1\frac{1}{4}$in (30mm) at the back. Draw a horizontal line at each side to indicate the depth of the notches.

Cut down the sides of the notches with a tenon saw, angling the cut toward the front if you are making sloping notches, then use a chisel and mallet to chop out the waste timber. Chisel out small pieces rather than attempting to remove large chunks, to avoid splitting the notch. Test-fit a length of roof timber in each of the notches.

Using metal brackets

Attaching the roof timbers to the wallplate with galvanized metal U-shaped brackets avoids having to cut separate notches, and the fixings are quite inconspicuous. Mark the positions of the roof timbers on the top edge of the wallplate only and fit the brackets after the wallplate has been secured to the wall.

Position the brackets and secure by hammering galvanized nails through the pre-drilled holes in the base of the channel. With the bracket-fixing method you cannot allow for sloping roof timbers unless you bevel the top edge of the wallplate accordingly.

Attaching the wallplate

Measure up the wall the height for the roof—up to about 10ft (3m)—and draw a horizontal line in chalk at this point using a spirit level and a plank as a rule. Lift the wallplate into place on the wall (with the help of an assistant) and align its bottom edge with the chalk line. Mark through the drilled holes in chalk, then remove the wallplate and drill holes in the wall using a $1\frac{3}{8}$in (35mm) diameter masonry bit to a depth of $4\frac{1}{2}$in (115mm).

Raise the wallplate again and align correctly, then insert $6\frac{1}{2} \times \frac{2}{3}$in (165 × 16mm) steel anchor bolts in the holes. With an adjustable spanner tighten the bolts in succession until you can feel the wallplate being pulled tightly against the masonry.

2 Set the supporting posts in concrete or with fixing spikes or bolt-down plates, with the top notches aligned with the wallplate. Check that all the posts are vertical.

3 Metal U-shaped brackets offer the easiest fixing for connecting the roof timbers to the wallplate. Position the bracket and secure with galvanized nails.

Constructing a pergola 2

Preparing the posts

Cut the posts to length according to the calculations on your plan. The top of the main support posts should be notched to take the edge of the roof timbers, although intermediate posts can be fitted with brackets as for the wallplate.

In the top end of each main post, mark out and cut notches that are about 3in (75mm) deep and the width of the roof timbers. Bevel the square top of the posts on two sides so that rainwater will run off easily: neat bevels are also more aesthetically pleasing than square tops.

Erecting the posts

Erect the pergola posts after marking out their positions in relation to the wallplate and the drawn design. Use stringlines and pegs to mark out the shape of the structure on the ground.

Fit fence post spikes (or socketed plates for fixing to a concrete surface) and slot in the posts, making sure the notches point toward the wallplate. Check that the posts are vertical by holding a spirit level against all four sides. Make any adjustments necessary. If the posts

are to be set in concrete, leave them for about two days before continuing with the construction, so that the concrete will set properly.

Fitting the roof timbers

Measure the length of the roof timbers, allowing for an extension beyond the outer posts of about 6 to 12in (150 to 300mm). Bevel the ends of the timbers or mark out a more ornately shaped end and cut using a scrolling jigsaw whose blade is able to turn on its axis to the left and right.

Fit the roof timbers by lowering their back ends into the wallplate notches or brackets, then slot the front lower edges into the slots cut in the top of the main posts. Secure the timbers by driving nails through the pre-drilled upstands of the brackets, or hammer nails through the top edge of the wallplate into the sides of the notches.

Adding cross-piece rafters

The design of the pergola may include rafters fixed over the roof timbers at right-angles to them. These rafters, which can be made of thinner section 4 × 1in (100 × 25mm) soft-

4 Lower the end of the roof timber into the channel formed by the fixing bracket and secure by hammering galvanized nails through the holes in the upstands.

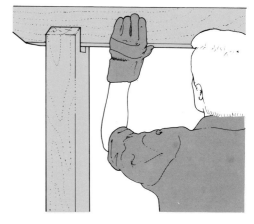

5 Locate the outer shaped end of each of the main roof timbers in slots cut in the top end of the supporting posts. The top of the post is bevelled for rainwater run-off.

wood, should be bevelled or decoratively shaped at each end, and should extend beyond the sides of the pergola by about 12 to 16in (300 to 400mm).

The rafters can be notched into the top edge of the main roof timbers, or fixed with U-shaped brackets in the same way as the main timbers are attached to the wallplate.

Bracing the structure

For rigidity, fit cross-braces between the roof timbers and the posts, and spanning across the roof timbers at a corner. This will help to prevent the pergola from flexing sideways or twisting during high winds. The best fixing is to set the bracing timber—use 2 × 2in (50 × 50mm) softwood—in notches cut in the roof timbers and posts. Cut the braces to length and hold in place so that the posts and roof timbers can be marked accordingly; then cut the notches.

Fit the braces and secure with nails driven through the top.

Shaping the rafters

Cutting bevels on the underside of the rafters and roof timbers has both decorative and practical functions. You can create a highly ornate effect by cutting complex curves in the protruding ends of the timbers—you could even create a fretwork effect by drilling holes in decorative patterns through the timbers.

Remember to treat all cut ends of the timber with preservative, even if you are using the pressure-treated type.

Maintenance

When climbing plants are pruned in the autumn, the pergola that supports them should be inspected for signs of rot. If possible, climbers should be released and the framework fully checked. Any infected wood must be replaced. New woodwork, and the cut ends of old woodwork, should be treated with preservative or paint. Make sure that the preservative has dried before you restore the climber to its position.

Check any other materials used in the pergola. Replace any weakened wires and strengthen the fixtures if necessary.

6 Rafters made of thinner timber can be fixed at right-angles across the main roof timbers. Notch the rafters into the roof timbers or fix with metal brackets.

NOTCHING THE TIMBERS

Bracket fixings are quick and easy to make but you might consider that they look too utilitarian—you will be able to see the metal upstands of the brackets, where the roof timbers and rafters are slotted into the channels.

Notching the tops of the support posts makes for a stronger joint, and one that looks more craftsmanlike. Mark out the notches using a pencil and try square, allowing a few millimetres extra for fitting tolerance. Measure the actual thickness of the timber you are using for the rafters, as sizes are nominal only, and there may be some slight difference. A loose-fitting joint is both untidy and unsound.

Secure the roof beams in the notches with galvanized nails driven through the sides of the post; secure the rafters to the roof beams by nailing at an angle through the top edge of the roof beam and into the sides of the rafters.

Making a rustic arch 1

A rustic timber arch will add a touch of rural charm to your garden, and serves a practical purpose as an informal division between areas such as the lawn, vegetable plot or patio.

Natural poles, with or without bark, are used to construct the arch. These are readily available from garden centres. Sizes are usu-ally standardized. For example, peeled, pressure-treated poles commonly come in 8ft (2.4m) lengths and 2 to 3in (50 to 75mm) diameters.

The natural timber poles can be assembled into a freestanding structure without having to resort to complicated carpentry. The arch

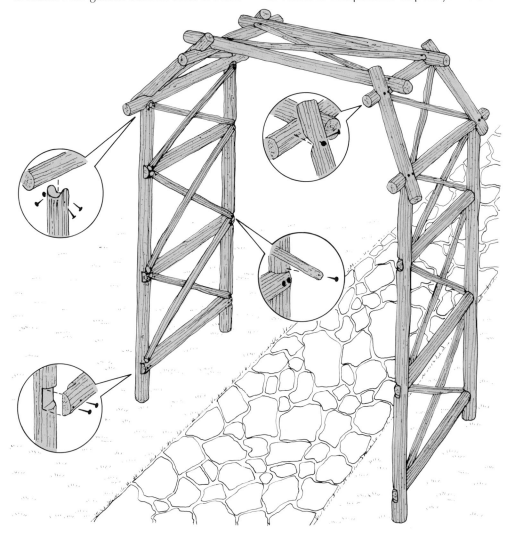

The framework of the rustic arch consists of stripped or bark-covered irregular poles about 3in (75mm) in diameter with smaller diameter poles used as intermediate bracing and decorative design. V-shaped or, as here, cross-halving joints are used in construction, strengthened by nails and screws.

is mainly decorative and is not normally structurally strong—nor does it need to be—although climbing plants such as honeysuckle, clematis and roses can be successfully trained to climb up and over it.

Consider adding more rails or braces to the arch, or even connecting it to flanking screens of rustic poles, which will help it to blend in more with its surroundings.

Built against a hedge, an arch of this construction can be used as an arbour.

Designing a basic arch

A basic rustic arch should comprise two pairs of uprights concreted into the ground at each side of a path with a pair of horizontal rails fixed at the top and bottom, an intermediate pair of rails, and thinner 1 or 2in (25 or 50mm) diameter diagonal braces between. The top of the arch is made from two pairs of 3in (75mm) diameter poles fixed to a top piece, and to the side uprights. Further rails and braces can be added to create an attractive design. Although the supporting frame poles, rails and arch formers have basic joints cut for rigidity, the thinner bracing pieces can be simply fixed with nails.

Cutting the joints

All the joints used to assemble the arch can be made with a panel saw and either a coping saw or a padsaw. You will also need a chisel to chop out the waste from some joints.

There are two ways to make the joints. In the first method, the top rails are located in 1in (25mm) deep V-shaped notches cut in the top end of each upright pole. Form the notches using a coping saw or a padsaw. Cut V-shaped notches about halfway down the poles, at right-angles to the direction of the top notches: these take the intermediate rails which link the pairs of poles. Cut the rails to about 24 to 36in (600 to 900mm) lengths and form inverted V-shaped ends to fit into the notches in the poles.

For the second method (or where a pair of poles cross), cut cross-halving joints: mark the diameter of each pole using tape and cut down the inside edges of the tape, on both sides, to half the depth of the poles. Then remove the waste wood between the cuts using a chisel.

Treating the timber against rot

Lay out the poles and rails for each side of the arch on the ground and test-fit the joints. If you are satisfied with the fit, disassemble the components and treat each joint thoroughly with preservative.

Poles with the bark left on will probably not have been pressure-treated with preservative, and it will be difficult to get preservative to soak in through the bark. Instead, apply several coats of polyurethane varnish to seal the wood.

The poles will need extra protection against rot at the bottom where they will be inserted in the damp ground. Stand them in a bucket of preservative overnight so that they soak up the liquid. As a second line of defence, coat the bottom 18in (450mm) with creosote. Alternatively, seal the pores of the timber by scorching the ends with the flame of a blowtorch, but take great care not to burn the wood.

Assembling the frames

Assemble the sides of the arch with the upright poles laid out on the ground, then position the cross-pieces. Secure all the joints by driving 4in (100mm) long galvanized wire nails, which will not rust, through the joints themselves. Drive in the nails dovetail fashion so that they will resist being pulled apart. Nail the thinner cross-pieces to the side pieces to give the frames extra rigidity.

Erecting the side frames

Dig four holes in the ground to take the ends of the side frame poles and add a layer of hardcore to give a firm foundation and help drainage of rainwater from the holes. Ram the hardcore down with a stout length of timber or a sledgehammer.

Stand both assembled side frames in their holes and temporarily nail timber battens between the uprights to support the structure while the concrete hardens. Buy a bag of dry-mixed fence post concrete and mix with water, then tip into the holes. Pack the concrete around the poles to dispel air bubbles. Use a trowel to form a slightly domed top to the concrete infill; this will aid rainwater run-off. Leave the concrete to set hard overnight before fixing the arch top.

Making a rustic arch 2

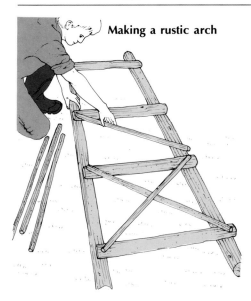

Making a rustic arch

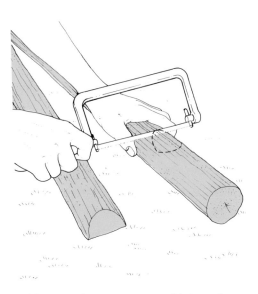

1 Assemble the arch sides on the ground before cutting the joints, with the braces of thinner section laid over the side uprights and cross-rails.

2 Use a coping saw to cut a V-shaped notch about 1in (25mm) deep in the side of the uprights, then trim the ends of the cross-rails to inverted V-shapes to connect.

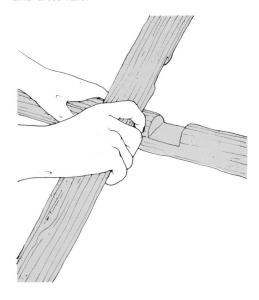

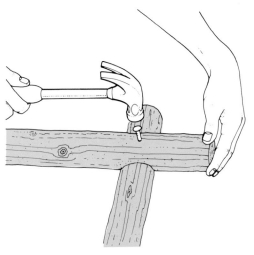

2b Alternatively, cut cross-halving joints where rails intersect. Mark the diameter of each pole using tape and cut and chisel down the inside edges half the pole depth.

Secure all the joints with galvanized nails driven in at an angle so they will resist the natural flexing of the structure. Nail the diagonal braces in place.

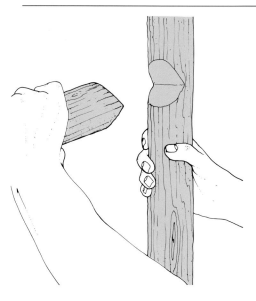

Fitting the arch top

Lift the arch top into position on the top of the side frames. There will be sufficient play in the upright poles to enable the joints to be pulled together, should they not align properly.

Attachment of the top depends on the method of construction used. If the arch sides have a flat cross-rail at the top, laid in notches without protruding vertical members (as in diagram 3 below), the arch top should be notched on the inside edge of the angled poles, about 1in (25mm) in, to fit the cross-rail. If cross-halved joints have been used, notch the angled poles on their sides and attach to the extended ends of the side uprights (see diagram 4 below).

It would be difficult to nail the arch top into position because the natural springiness in the frames would prevent the nails from being driven in properly. Instead, drill holes through the arch pieces into the top rails of the frame sides and insert 4in (100mm) long rustproofed screws to secure the structure.

Bring together the rail and upright to test the joint. Trim with a chisel. Nail the joints together and nail on the diagonal braces.

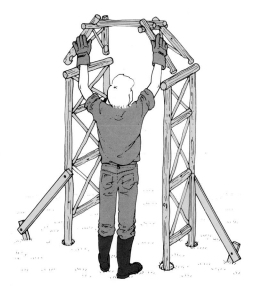

3 Erect the side panels of the arch with uprights sunk in concrete-filled holes; prop them up while the concrete sets. Assemble the arch top and lift onto the side panels.

4 Secure the arch top to the side uprights as here, or to the top cross-rails using rustproofed screws. Nailing is not possible due to springiness of the structure.

121

Gates and accessories 1

Choosing a garden gate

Whether you want a gate to confine children and pets to the garden, to keep out neighbourhood strays, to improve your frontage with an attractive entrance, or to provide a measure of security against intruders, ready-assembled gates are available in a choice of materials and a whole host of styles to complement the types of fencing available. Choose a design of gate with care, as what looks totally at home in a rural setting could appear incongruous fronting an urban plot.

Some gates are nothing more than a length of fencing—such as picket or closeboard—with additional braces for strength, while others are strongly-jointed, purpose-built units made to fill a specific role. In general the choice is between a timber gate and one made of metal (although plastic types are available to match plastic fencing systems).

Timber gates

Timber gates will generally suit most locations, although styles differ considerably.

Front entrance gates To mark a boundary in front of a garden path, and at the same time restrict the movements of young children and animals, look for a gate that is about 3 or 4ft (900mm or 1.2m) high, which corresponds with the popular height of fencing and garden walling. Standard widths for these gates are 3ft, 3ft 6in, 4ft and 5ft (900mm, 1050mm, 1.2m and 1.5m).

A gate of this type is normally constructed from a timber such as redwood and comprises a pair of side uprights, with horizontal rails and, usually, exterior-grade plywood lower infill panels. Variations on this design include shaped vertical infill panels—often with diamond-shaped cut-outs—fixed to horizontal rails, or a simple design with horizontal rails braced with a diagonal rail.

Gates to match woven, closeboarded or overlapping fence panels are also made, in heights of 3 or 4ft (900mm or 1.2m).

Side entrance gates Usually more utilitarian in appearance than front entrance gates, and normally about two or three times the height to discourage intruders, side entrance gates are traditionally the ledged-and-braced type. Three horizontal rails are braced with diagonal rails, and the cladding may comprise feather-edged vertical boards to blend with a close-boarded fence, tongued-and-grooved vertical boards, or else pointed-top vertical pales spaced a few inches apart in the style of a picket or palisade fence. Woven or horizontally overlapping panel gates are also available to fit into a run of prefabricated panel fencing of similar format.

The popular width for side entrance gates is 3ft (900mm), and they are generally available in heights of 3, 4, 5 and 6ft (900mm, 1.2, 1.5 and 1.8m).

Drive entrance gates To fill a drive width of up to about 10ft (3m), you can install a pair of standard front entrance gates, but for wider than normal drive entrances you can choose from various models of farm-style gates.

A traditional five-bar gate consists of a pair of upright posts with five equally spaced horizontal bars between, and a diagonal brace fixed to the back to prevent the gate from sagging. The brace normally spans from the low part of the hinge side to the top part of the opening side.

A variation on the basic five-bar gate, which is more suitable for residential areas, includes a cladding of closely spaced vertical pales. Another option, the yeoman gate, features a large curved hanging stile (the upright part of the gate's frame) with a slanting brace attached.

Smaller versions of these gates doubled up with their larger counterparts are often sold as a means of providing pedestrian access at the side of a drive entrance. This avoids unnecessary use of the large gate, which is typically fixed by means of a drop bolt at ground level. A band of metal usually links the two inner posts of the gates as a catch.

Farm gates come in widths from about 4 to 12ft (1.2 to 3.6m).

Hardware for gates

Most gates come without latches, hinges or other hardware, and you will have to buy these separately. Choose fittings that have a "japanned" finish (black glossy lacquer) or a matt black coating to prevent rust attacking the metal. Alternatively choose galvanized metal fittings which, although their grey finish is less decorative than blacked types, have greater resistance to rusting and can be overpainted to blend with the gate if required.

There are numerous options for hinges and latches, the choice of which largely depends on what you are fixing the gate to.

Choosing hinges

Strap hinges Double strap hinges consist of a single strip of metal bent to fit along both sides of the horizontal rails of a timber gate. A preformed loop at the end slots onto a matching hinge pin, or "hook", which is either bolted through the side post, hammered in, or set in the mortar joints of a brick pier. These hinges allow the gate to be lifted off the hooks.

T-hinges The simplest type of gate hinge, the T-hinge consists of a screw-on hinge flap for attachment to a wooden gate post with an elongated flap which is screwed to the rails of the gate.

Hook-and-band hinges With this heavy-weight hinge, a separate screw-on hinge pin connects with a bolted-and-screwed-on metal strap fixed to the gate; again the gate can be lifted off its hinges.

Reversible hinges A hinge which can be used either way up (and therefore at either side of the gate, as required), the reversible hinge has a pin which is housed in a pair of screw-on cups; this prevents the gate from being lifted off the hinges.

Choosing latches

All latches are fitted on the inside of the gate and its post, and are typically based on a lever, which is operated by pushing down one end to disengage it from the staple, or by turning a ring handle and spindle to lift the lever. Another type is a simple lifter bar, which you pull up to disengage via its integral knob. There are variations of these latches, operated from both sides.

Suffolk latch Used mainly for tall, side-entrance, closeboarded or tongue-and-groove clad gates, the Suffolk latch has a thumb-operated pivoting "sneck" (catch), which passes through a slot in the gate. A lifter bar and keeper are fitted to the other side of the gate and its support.

Automatic latch This consists of a hook screwed to the inside face of the gate's top rail, which links with a thumb-operated latch attached to the post: the latch fastens when the gate is pulled closed, and can be released by pulling the thumb latch toward you.

Gate accessories

There are numerous other devices that can be fitted to gates to hold them in the open or closed position, or to ensure the gate closes of its own accord:

Spring closer A metal spring attached to the back of the gate at a diagonal angle between

Gate types

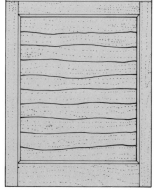

Overlapping board gate: intended to match a run of wavy-edged, lap fencing.

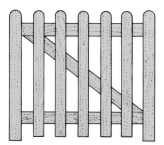

Paling gate with diagonal brace: the ideal complement for a picket fence.

Diamond-slatted front entrance gate: a more rustic design.

Gates and accessories 2

FITTING GATE POSTS

Although gate posts may be set in concrete in the same way as fence posts, you should link the post holes with a bridge of concrete to form a single unit. This will make the sagging of individual posts less likely, and so reduce the possibility of the gates sticking or jamming.

Spacing out the posts

To set the correct width between posts, lie the gate on the ground and place the posts at each side, leaving a gap of $\frac{1}{2}$in (6mm) from the gate stiles. Place hardboard packing between the gate and posts, then temporarily pin battens of wood connecting the posts at top and bottom with an intermediate batten fixed diagonally.

Lift up the connected post assembly and position in the previously dug post holes. Prop the posts vertically with struts of timber while pouring in the concrete.

Dig a trench about 1ft (300mm) deep between the post holes, add hardcore to the base and top with fresh concrete. Compact the concrete level with the surrounding path surface.

Leave for a few days until the concrete has hardened before hanging the gate.

Fitting timber packing at the piers

Where new piers are being built for a gate, the hinge pins and latch keep should be built in during construction. But when you are fitting a gate between existing masonry piers, it is easier to attach vertical lengths of timber packing to each pier and secure the gate hinges and catches to these. This procedure saves your having to cut into the masonry in order to fit the mortar-in type of fitting.

Stand the gate between the piers and measure the gap for the thickness of packing timber needed. Cut the packing posts, drill holes for the fixing bolts, then mark the positions of the holes on the piers. Drill holes for the bolts, then attach the posts using expansion bolts.

Drive gate posts

A heavy drive gate requires stout fixings at the posts to prevent the gate from sagging. At the opening side a standard fence post fixing can be used, but at the hinge side it is best to dig an extra-wide hole and secure a length of timber horizontally near the base of the post to act as an anchor.

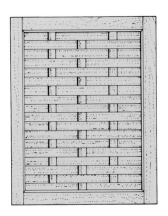

Woven panel side entrance gate: made to fit in a run of basketweave fencing.

Ornately scrolled metal gate: most suitable for an elegant front entrance.

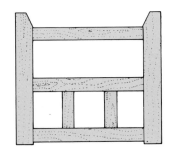

Standard timber front entrance gate: with plywood infill panels below.

the hinge post and the hinged stile of the gate, properly tensioned, will push the gate into the closed position when released, engaging the latch.

Drop bolt Fixed near the bottom of the gate's opening stile on the inside face, a drop bolt can be released and engaged in a plate fixed to the ground to prevent a drive gate from swinging too far when it is closed.

Gate stop Fulfilling the same role as a drop bolt, the gate stop consists of a cast-iron seating fixed in a hole in the ground, with a lift-up flap to prevent the gate from swinging too far.

Gate holder To hold a gate open, a holding device consisting of a pivoting latch is fixed at ground level at the point at which the gate swings open, engaging with a loop.

Cabin hook To secure a single gate in the open position, a cabin hook consists of a slim length of hooked metal fastened to a screw-on plate, which is attached to the gate. A second plate with a loop is screwed to a post or wall at the end of the gate's swing, to take the hook.

Metal gates

Metal garden gates are made either of mild steel, a less expensive option for lightweight gates, or wrought iron, a heavier and more durable material. Styles of gate for path and drive entrances are similar, and consist of traditional ornamental scroll designs or plainer modern infills within an outer framework. Side entrance gates are usually taller than front gates, but based on similar designs.

Latches are usually attached to the gate during assembly, and are normally of the lever variety used on timber gates. Hinges, likewise, are normally fitted to the gate during assembly, and there is usually no way of altering the inbuilt "hand" (gates hang from one side or the other; they are either "left-handed" or "right-handed").

Metal gates are largely used for their highly decorative appearance, and the larger types are frequently installed within a delicate brick-work arch, which complements the ornate scrollwork or curved top. Such gates are popular for side entrances.

There is a wide range of standard-width metal gates available, usually supplied with matching metal posts with hinge pins and latch fastenings attached. However, you can also have gates made to fit between a given post spacing, by a local metalworker or blacksmith. Most gate suppliers will offer a custom manufacturing service, too, allowing you to specify the type of decorative scroll-work you would like incorporated into the design.

This could include the addition of a house name or number, created with scrollwork metal lettering welded into the frame of the gate, or else a flat plate pierced with the required letters or numbers.

Gate posts

Gates may be hung between timber, metal or concrete posts, or else fixed between brick, stone or concrete block piers attached to a masonry wall. Select a material that will complement or blend with the gate and adjacent boundary.

Timber Gate posts made of timber should be no less than 4in (100mm) square, increasing to 5in (125mm) square for a gate that is more than 6ft (1.8m) high or more than 3ft (1 m) wide. The posts must be long enough to enable 18in (450mm) to be set underground for a gate up to 3ft (1 m) high, and 2ft (600mm) underground for a gate that is higher or wider than 3ft (1m).

Large farm-type gates will require stout posts 6 or 7in (150 or 175mm) square, and these must be long enough for 3 or 4ft (1 or 1.2m) to be sunk in the ground.

Metal Available in circular, square or rectangular section, metal posts are supplied to suit the type of gate they are to support. Ask the supplier which shape he recommends to suit your choice of gate.

Concrete Use standard-sized concrete fencing posts to which $4 \times 1\frac{1}{2}$in (100 × 38mm) preservative-treated timber has been bolted. The timber additions enable the gate hinges to be attached.

Piers Piers of brick, stone or concrete walling blocks must be built on substantial foundations and sunk below ground level by about 20in (500mm) to support the gate properly. The pier must be a minimum of a brick-and-a-half square, which is roughly $13\frac{1}{2}$in (340mm) square, to avoid the possibility of collapse.

Constructing a gate 1

Constructing a gate to your own specifications is quite straightforward, and uses only basic carpentry techniques and tools. With the rigid outer framework assembled, fit the type of infill cladding which best suits your surroundings.

The frame components

The frame consists of a pair of stiles of 4 × 2in (100 × 50mm) hardwood (or planed softwood as a less expensive option) with top and bottom horizontal rails of 3 × 1½in (75 × 40mm) timber tenoned into mortises cut in the stiles. A diagonal brace of 4 × ¾in (100 × 19mm) timber is fixed between the stiles.

The infill cladding may be a row of vertical tongued-and-grooved boards, pointed-top pales, a latticework arrangement of thin slats, or plain plywood, perhaps with diamond or other shaped cut-outs. The cladding is fixed to battens of ½in (12mm) square timber screwed to the inner perimeter of the outer frame members.

Marking out the joints

Mark out and cut the stiles to length and bevel the top ends inward for rainwater run-off. Mark out and cut the top and bottom rails to length, including an allowance at each end for forming the stub tenons: these should penetrate mortises cut in the stiles by about 3in (75mm).

To prepare the tenons for cutting, first mark their length on each end of the top and bottom rails and square the lines around the timber using a try square and marking knife.

For accuracy, use a tool called a mortise gauge to scribe the tenons on the rails. Set the gauge's twin pins to the width of the tenon—½in (12mm). Then with a rail set upright in a vice, score parallel lines down the sides as far as the scribed length marks and across the top of the timber. Mark out the other end of the rail, and the second rail, in this way.

Cutting the tenons

With a rail clamped in a vice at an angle of 45 degrees away from you, use a tenon saw held horizontally to cut down the waste side of the gauged lines as far as the length marks.

Now reverse the rail in the vice and cut down from the other corner. Set the rail upright and saw down the triangle of waste that is left. Repeat for the other side of the tenon, then hold the rail flat and saw along the length mark to remove the waste. Complete all four tenons in this way.

Make shouldered tenons by making ¾in (19mm) in from each side of the tenon and cutting down these lines. Turn the rail on its side and cut down the side of the tenon at the length mark to remove the piece of waste wood.

Cutting the mortises

Place the stiles side by side, inner faces pointing uppermost, and mark lines across both 6in (10mm) from the top and 1in (25mm) in from the bottom, using a try square. Place a tenon on the stiles, aligned with the pencil lines and mark the width of the tenon. Square the line across, then use the mortise gauge set to ½in (12mm), as before, to scribe twin lines between the joint width lines. This gives the width of the mortise. Repeat for the other three mortises.

Traditionally, mortises are cut solely with a mortise chisel, which takes some time and patience to learn and which is quite time-consuming to carry out. Instead, it is acceptable to drill out the mortises using a ½in (12mm) diameter auger bit fitted in a power drill: first measure the length of the tenon (in this case, 3in/75mm) and wrap adhesive tape around the bit as a guide to drilling to the correct depth.

Clamp a stile horizontally in a vice or the jaws of a workbench, mortises uppermost, and drill out the bulk of the waste in a series of closely spaced holes within the mortise lines. Remove the bit when the tape guide reaches the top of the timber.

The mortise must, of course, be square-sided, so use a mortise chisel to pare away the remaining waste carefully. Repeat this procedure for all the mortises, then test-fit the tenons in the slots.

Assembling the frame

Sand all the joints thoroughly and wipe off dust, then apply PVA woodworking adhesive to the tenons. Slot the tenons into the mortises and clamp the entire frame with a pair of sash cramps which fit across the gate pulling the stiles inwards. Check with a try square that the internal angle between rails and stiles is 90 degrees: if there is some misalignment you may be able to correct this by repositioning the sash cramps to pull the frame square.

Using a damp rag, wipe off any smears of adhesive that have squeezed out from around the joints, then set aside the assembly for the adhesive to dry.

Cutting the diagonal brace
The diagonal brace fits into the top opening-side corner and the bottom hinge-side corner.

Cut the brace slightly overlong and hold in place. Mark the brace for cutting against the stiles and rails, then saw off the corners as marked. Fit the brace to the inner frame to which the cladding is attached.

Fitting the inner frame
Cut two lengths of $\frac{1}{2}$in (12mm) square timber to fit horizontally between the stiles, and two more to fit between the first two, once they have been secured to the top and bottom rails.

Attach this inner frame, butt-jointed at the corners, with 1in (25mm) long rustproofed countersunk woodscrews. Recess the heads beneath the surface by countersinking the

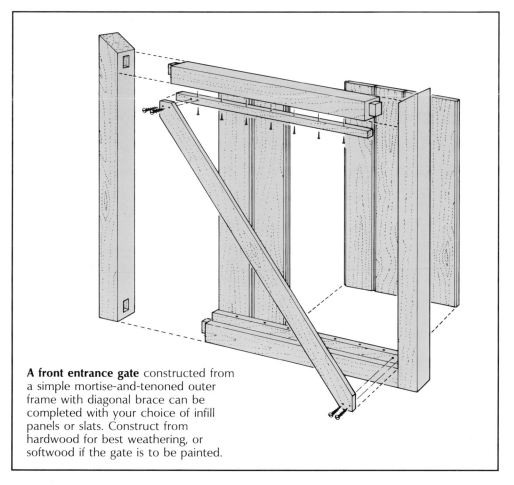

A front entrance gate constructed from a simple mortise-and-tenoned outer frame with diagonal brace can be completed with your choice of infill panels or slats. Construct from hardwood for best weathering, or softwood if the gate is to be painted.

Constructing a gate 2

mouths of pre-drilled clearance holes with a countersinking bit.

If the cladding material is to fit within the top and bottom rails, position the inner frame back from the front face of the gate the thickness of the material you are using. Where you want the cladding—say, decoratively shaped pales—to protrude above the top rail of the gate, set the inner frame flush with the front face of the gate.

Screw the diagonal brace to the back edge of the inner frame, then invert the gate and nail on the cladding.

Attaching the cladding

The cladding can be attached with $1\frac{1}{4}$in (35mm) long galvanized lost-head nails. For pales, use 2, 3 or 4in (50, 75 or 100mm) wide softwood, $\frac{3}{4}$in (19mm) thick, with two nails per fixing to the inner frame. With panelling, drive in nails around the perimeter at 3in (75mm) intervals.

Hanging the gate

Before fixing the gate between the posts, check that there is sufficient clearance underneath for the gate to swing open fully by positioning it against the hinge-side post and

chocking it up in the fully open position, prior to fixing it between the posts or piers.

If there is sufficient clearance, chock up the gate between the posts or piers, with a clearance gap of $\frac{1}{4}$in (6mm) at each side, using wedges of wood. Raise the gate by 2in (50mm). How the hinges are fitted depends on the type you are using. The following types are the most commonly encountered:

T-hinges With the gate in position, hold the hinges in place along the top and bottom rails and mark through the screw-fixing holes. Remove the gate and drill starter holes for the screws. Fit the long hinge flaps to the gate, then offer the gate up to the post and screw on the narrow hinge flaps.

Strap hinges Attach the strap part of the hinge to the gate, after drilling any bolt holes necessary, then prop up against the post, but in the open position. Mark the screw holes for the hook on the post, then screw the hook on.

Reversible hinges With the gate propped between the posts, straps attached, screw the bottom cups onto the post, then fit the top cups, retaining the hinge pin.

Attach a spring-closer across the gate and post by screwing the top bracket to the post

Hanging the gate

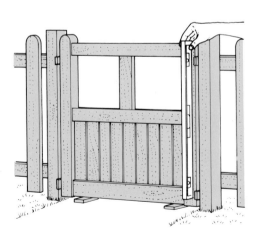

1 Prop the gate vertically between the posts or piers on wooden blocks, with a gap of $\frac{1}{4}$in (6mm) at each side and 2in (50mm) below.

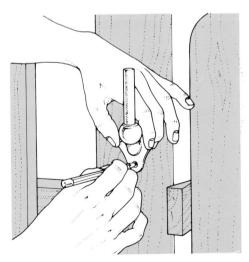

2 Fit the strap hinges to the gate first, prop in position and screw the lower cups onto the end of the hinge pins.

and the lower one to the hinge stile of the gate. Fit the latch to complete the installation: with the gate closed, screw the latch mechanism or keep against the post, then fit the locking bar and screw on.

Dealing with sloping ground

No part of the gate should come into contact with the ground when the gate is opened or closed, but this can be awkward if your garden path slopes down towards the gate. If this is the case, work out the height the gate must be hinged at by getting a helper to hold it between the posts while you work. There must be a minimum clearance from the highest point on the ground of at least $1\frac{1}{4}$in (30mm).

With the gate held in position, mark the top and bottom positions of the gate on the posts, then cut wedges of the correct size to prop the gate in place while you secure the hinges.

Where the ground slopes across the line of the gate, you will, of course, still have to fix the gate vertically, and tolerate a gap at one side: hinge the gate at the higher side of the slope, so that it will swing freely without the risk of scraping the ground.

FITTING A SPRING-CLOSING DEVICE

A **spring-closer** is useful, especially where child safety is a consideration. This device, screwed across the post and gate on the hinge side, will pull the gate shut even when it is left open. An automatic latch will hold it shut.

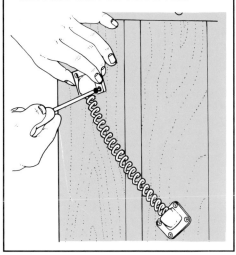

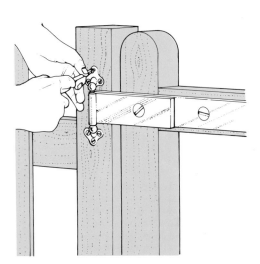

3 Fit the top hinge cups to retain the hinge pins. Note that the bottom corner of the diagonal brace is on the side of the hinge.

4 An automatic latch is screwed to the gate post and its locking bar to the gate; a thumb-operated lever releases the bar.

Building a dustbin screen

It is not very appealing when sitting in the garden to have to look at the rubbish bins, but often they need to be near the house for filling and collection. Similarly, a compost heap is best hidden from view, yet the compost must be contained and easily accessible. Although it is not usually convenient to have rubbish bins completely enclosed, they can be concealed from view by constructing a simple screen from pierced concrete walling blocks (see page 68). The pierced blocks still allow air to filter through—to avoid smells that would linger in a solidly enclosed structure—while providing a visual barrier that will suit most styles of garden. Compost, too, needs to be aerated, and screen blocks provide the ventilation necessary.

The screen wall is constructed from blocks laid in stack bond one on top of the other: there is no need to create the overlapping or stretcher bond arrangement that is used for a brick wall as the structure needs neither the strength nor the height of a brick building.

Designing the screen

A basic dustbin or compost heap screen can be an open-ended, three-sided structure consisting of two end piers formed by pilaster blocks and two corner piers, with pierced screen blocks laid between them, housed in the pilasters' channels.

If the screen is to be used to conceal dustbins, it should be built on concrete raft foundations (see page 14), with the solid base doubling as a dry base for the bins themselves. For a compost heap screen, lay concrete strip foundations (see page 11) at the perimeter of the wall, with the compost laid straight onto the earth.

Building a pier

Start the construction by dry-laying (laying without mortar) the first row of blocks and pilasters on the base, then mark out on the concrete base the shape of the screen wall by drawing around the blocks in chalk. Remove the blocks.

Mix some bricklaying mortar on a large board on a nearby hard surface (such as the garage floor) or in a wheelbarrow. It is easiest for a project of this size to use a pre-bagged dry-mixed mortar to which just water is

added, rather than buying the separate ingredients and making up the mortar.

Trowel a bed of mortar onto the base in the position of the first pier, furrow the surface to aid adhesion and suction, and lower an end pilaster onto it. Tap down the pilaster with the shaft of your trowel and check that it is level by placing a spirit level across the top. The mortar joint should be about $\frac{3}{8}$in (10mm) thick. Mix up a little sloppy mortar and pour it into the hollow centre of the block as reinforcement.

Trowel more of the stiff mortar onto the pilaster and place a second pilaster on top. Continue in this way until you have laid a pier that is five blocks high. Hold your spirit level against each side of the pier in turn to check that it is vertical.

As you build, pour more sloppy mortar mix into the hollow pilasters.

Laying the pierced blocks

Trowel a screed of bricklaying mortar onto the base along the line of the proposed wall, using the chalklines as a guide. Furrow the mortar with the point of your trowel. "Butter" one edge of a pierced block with mortar by scraping it off the trowel blade, then furrow

Building a dustbin screen

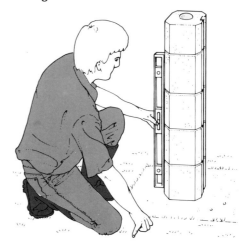

1 Build the first pier five pilaster blocks high, checking that it stands vertically. Add sloppy mortar to the hollow centre.

the surface. Place the pierced block on the mortar screed, slotting the mortared edge into the channel in the side of the pilaster block. Tap it down and check with a spirit level that it is horizontal along the top, and vertical at the side.

Butter one edge of subsequent blocks with mortar and lay them side by side on the screed. Check that the blocks are level with each other across their tops. To contain a pair of dustbins you will need to lay a wall at least four blocks long.

Completing the first side

To lay the second and subsequent rows of blocks, trowel a screed of mortar along the top of the first row, furrow the surface, then lay the blocks one on top of the other. Repeat for the third and final course.

The mortar joints between blocks must be consistently $\frac{3}{8}$in (10mm) thick, and this should be checked frequently as the wall is built. It is also important to ensure that the wall does not bow outward. Check this by holding a spirit level or straight-edged length of timber across the face of the wall: any unevenness will be obvious. Correct any misalignment before the mortar hardens.

Building the other side walls

Once the first side has been built, you can construct a pier at its other end, using pilaster blocks with slots on two adjacent sides, so forming a corner. Pour sloppy mortar mix into the hollow centre as reinforcement. Erect a second screen wall of pierced blocks as previously described, then build another corner pier at the other end.

Finally, build a third screen wall and a second end pier to complete the basic structure of the screen.

Fitting capping and coping

Neaten the appearance of the wall and help deflect rain from its joints by bedding bevel-topped coping stones along the three side walls. These 24in (600mm) long stones overhang slightly at each side. To protect the tops of the piers, fit square cappings on the pilasters, bedding them on mortar.

Smooth all the mortar joints by running an offcut of garden hose along the setting mortar to give a half-rounded profile.

Leave the screen blocks bare, or alternatively paint the structure with exterior emulsion paint to camouflage it or to blend with other paintwork.

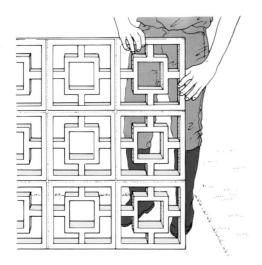

2 Erect the first wall of pierced screen blocks out from the first end pier, to three courses, using a simple stack bond.

3 Tap down each block as you go. Check the levels are accurate using a spirit level.

Compost containers

Types of compost heap
The ideal size for a compost heap, which will produce the most rapid results, is about 6ft (2m) square, and 5ft (1.5m) high. Where space is cramped, plan a heap of about 5ft (1.5m) square. A selection of proprietary ready-made compost bins are available, or you can make the enclosure yourself.

Ready-made containers Metal-framed compost containers are commonly wire-mesh boxes fitted with a hinged access panel, or else little more than a strong, black polythene sack held in a metal cradle: holes in the side of the sack provide the necessary aeration.

Plastic containers include an open-topped round format with preformed holes in the sides for aeration. There are even tough plastic compost containers available which are mounted on a cradle. If these are turned every day, they can produce compost in as little as 21 days.

Timber compost containers are available constructed from a number of interlocking planks, which enable you to disassemble the surround for access to the compost it contains.

Home-made containers Do-it-yourself assembly compost containers take many forms. Erect side walls from breezeblocks stacked up without mortar, alternate courses staggered by half their length. For airflow to the base of the compost heap, raise the container walls on bricks laid on edge. Another method is to create a wooden container from preservative-treated planks nailed to vertical posts set in concrete or to fencing spikes. For access to the heap, the front planks of the container should be removable, preferably slotted into a channel formed by slim battens fixed to the supporting posts: simply slide the planks up and over when needed. Again, provide aeration by spacing the planks apart by about 2in (50mm), using timber spacers. Fit a lid of corrugated plastic.

Corrugated iron or plastic panels, held between an arrangement of timber posts driven into the ground, can be used as the basis for the walls of a compost container. Rest the panels on bricks on edge, or on drainpipes laid on the ground, to introduce an air supply to the centre of the heap.

Dividing the heap
So that there is always enough compost for use in the garden, it is sensible to divide the heap into two, by introducing a simple divider in the container. A panel of corrugated plastic, or of timber slats held between intermediate posts, can be slid out if necessary, but in the meantime it will serve to separate the compost under production from that which is already usable.

MAKING A COMPOST HEAP

Fork the ground lightly to allow earthworms into the heap. Spread a layer of woody prunings over the soil as a means of aerating the base, then add a layer of garden and kitchen waste which has been mixed with a little water.

Fork the mixture into the container and compact it lightly. Pour on a thin layer of nitrogen-rich activator such as poultry manure, blood or fishmeal, if the compost heap is being made up during the autumn or winter.

Add another layer of waste matter, then if your soil is acidic, add a sprinkling of ground limestone which will maintain the correct pH within the heap. A layer of soil or wood ashes is added to slow down the escape of ammonia gas from which microorganisms extract essential nitrogen.

Fill the container with these layers, then cover with a sheet of punctured black polythene followed by a piece of old carpet or sackcloth. Fit the lid, and leave the heap for about one week to heat up. When the material has shrunk down to about one-third of its volume, top it up with the same layers.

After several weeks, fork the cooler outsides of the compost into the warmer centre to assist the breakdown of material. After about four months the dark brown, crumbly compost will be ready for use.

Types of compost container

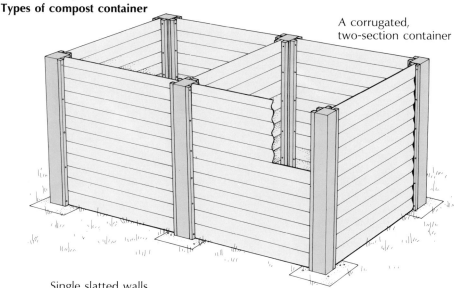

A corrugated,
two-section container

Single slatted walls

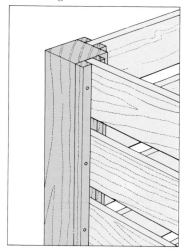

Double slatted walls

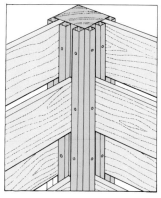

Make a compost container from 4in (100mm) square, preservative-treated, sawn softwood posts, fixed vertically at each corner of the proposed unit, bedded in concrete or fixed with fence spikes. Where you are making a two-section container, include intermediate posts (top). Fit pairs of 1in (25mm) square vertical battens to the sides of the posts to form a central channel to take the wall panels (above left). The walls themselves may be nothing more

than sheets of corrugated PVC roofing material (as in the top diagram: the side of the container is cut away to indicate the corrugations of the material). Alternatively, use prefabricated sections comprising horizontal planks nailed to uprights: the planks should be spaced about 2in (50mm) apart for aeration of the heap (above left), or else staggered at each side of the uprights (above right).

Barbecues 1

Barbecues, now very popular adjuncts to the garden, can offer a versatile summer extension to the kitchen. They may be purchased in a wide range of designs, or constructed for use in a permanent position in the garden.

Siting the barbecue
Although correct design of a barbecue is crucial to its working efficiently and safely, picking the best site for it is of equal importance.

Bear in mind that the spot needs to be accessible from the kitchen for bringing utensils, crockery and food, so avoid a position that is too remote.

Do not position the barbecue below overhanging trees, which could be seriously damaged by the intense heat. Similarly, do not place the unit too close to a timber fence.

Avoid siting the grill close to open windows, where curtains could billow out and catch light or where smoke is likely to waft through neighbours' windows or into their washing.

Bear in mind that if the unit is built on an existing lawn the grass will almost certainly become worn by the heavy foot traffic it will receive. It is best, therefore, to surround the barbecue with paving slabs or brick pavers. Ensure that the surface is broad enough to accommodate several people, either standing or sitting, or if it covers a smaller area that it is set flush with the surrounding turf so that your guests can move freely in the area.

Designing the barbecue
The barbecue unit is usually box-shaped and built of non-combustible materials such as bricks, concrete blocks or stone. It has an open back (where the cook stands) and an

---

MAKING A LOOSE-BRICK BARBECUE

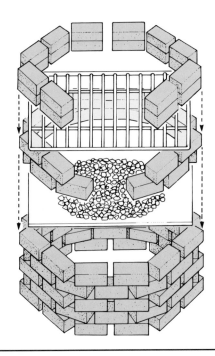

A temporary barbecue, which can be dismantled for storage during the winter, can be made by stacking bricks dry, without mortar. Not only is the unit inexpensive and easy to construct in a matter of a few hours, but it is also a very efficient structure: the honeycomb bonding arrangement used to raise the walls ensures a plentiful supply of air to the charcoal for good combustion.

The barbecue can be built in a circular, triangular, square or hexagonal shape, as preferred. A basic circular unit will use about 100 bricks; other shapes need more.

Lay the bricks in the chosen format on the prepared base with 2in (50mm) wide gaps between each brick. Lay the second course on top, staggering the joints by half the length of a brick so that the bond will be strong. Continue to stack bricks, alternating the staggered bond with each course, until you reach the seventh course. Place a sheet-steel panel across the top of the brick walls as a charcoal tray, then add two more courses of dry-laid bricks before fitting a slatted grill on top. Add another two or three courses of bricks around the back of the unit to act as a windshield for the cooking area.

open top. There are various factors listed below that need to be taken into account in the basic design:

Cooking height The barbecue should be constructed so that it is perfectly stable, with its grill set at the most convenient height for cooking—normally about nine or ten courses of bricks from ground level.

If the grill is too low you will have to stoop to attend to it; if it is built too high you will find it awkward to tend to the food without dropping it off the edge, or scorching your face by being too close to the hot charcoal.

The grill and the tray which contains the charcoal can be supported by metal rods fitted in the mortar joints between rows of bricks (or whichever material is being used), or on brick ledges protruding in from the outer walls of the unit. They should be removable for cleaning and storage out of the barbecue season to protect them from rusting.

Cooking control The barbecue needs a supply of fresh air to burn correctly, and this can be provided by building in an updraught flue to the grill area.

Storage facilities Sketch out the basic shape of the barbecue and work out how cupboards shelves and worksurfaces can best be incorporated into the unit for convenience while you cook. Include space for stacks of plates and a dry area for spare charcoal, which may be needed during the course of cooking.

Utensils such as a spatula, tongs and a wire brush for cleaning down the grill can be hung on hooks attached to the sides of the barbecue unit.

If a gas barbecue is being installed, an area beneath the charcoal tray will be needed for the gas canister.

Grill and charcoal tray Proprietary kits are available containing the grill, charcoal tray, brackets and accessories needed for mounting them, all in a home-made barbecue unit. This is by far the easiest way to assemble the cooking area of the unit.

Alternatively, an ordinary sliding slatted grill from a conventional indoor cooker may be used as the cooking surface. Ideally, the grill area should be wider than the fire area itself, so that cooked food can be moved from the central position to the sides, where

it will keep hot without burning.

A tray beneath the grill is needed to contain the hot charcoal, and this can be made from a sheet of mild steel (bought from a builder's merchants, cut to the size required). A second narrowly slatted grid mounted just above the tray makes an alternative holder for the charcoal, allowing the ashes to fall into the tray for easy removal.

Some form of windshield should be provided around the cooking area, so that the grill will be protected. This can be allowed for by extending the brickwork of the barbecue above the grill at the back and sides.

Building a brick barbecue
Construct a permanent barbecue on concrete strip foundations, from half-brick thick walls arranged in a U-shape. The grill and charcoal tray are placed either on adjustable-height brackets set in the mortar joints, or on fixed supports formed by turning bricks at right-angles in relevant courses to protrude from the walls.

A worksurface adjoining the cooking area is supported between the outer wall of the barbecue and a low brick plinth wall. The top may be a panel of exterior grade chipboard or plywood, or slats of preservative-treated softwood, or a precast concrete paving slab.

The basic design can easily be extended by building extra plinth walls to support further worksurfaces. Raising these plinth walls a few courses will convert them into seating. Raising the walls still further—virtually to the same height as the top of the barbecue—will allow a tabletop made of timber or slabs to be added, around which people can sit close to the cooking food.

Laying the bricks
Prepare strip foundations using profile boards and stringlines as a guide to setting out.

Realign the stringlines to indicate the position of the walls of the barbecue unit, then trowel a $\frac{3}{8}$in (10mm) thick screed of bricklaying mortar onto the prepared foundations at one side of the barbecue. Furrow the surface and lay the first course of bricks end to end. At the corners, turn a brick at right-angles so that its end abuts the side of the last brick on the side wall, forming a mortar joint

Barbecues 2

between the two. Check with a spirit level that the brick course is horizontal and ensure that it is aligned with the stringlines.

Lay the second course of bricks, starting with a brick cut in half across its width to maintain the stretcher bond. Continue to lay courses of bricks, staggering the vertical joints alternately, until you reach the fifth course, on which the support ledge is built.

Building the support ledge
At the fifth course, lay a row of bricks at right-angles to the walls, abutting them side by side and placing them on edge rather than flat down. The bricks should overlap the walls at each side evenly. Continue this row of bricks along the back wall of the unit.

Add a further three courses of bricks in stretcher bond on top of the overlapping bricks: this forms a narrow ledge on which to rest the cooking grill and the charcoal tray. A sheet-metal shelf could be fitted to support the charcoal tray, if a tray large enough to span the ledges at each side is not available.

Build another ledge at the tenth course of bricks, then add another three courses in

stretcher bond to complete the main part of the barbecue unit.

Using rod supports
As an alternative to forming a brick-supporting ledge, continue to lay bricks in stretcher bond, setting lengths of steel rod in the mortar joint between the sixth and seventh courses. Allow the rods to protrude from the walls within the U-shaped structure by about 3in (75mm), and use these to support the grill and tray.

Build up more courses of bricks, bedding further rods in each mortar joint, to give a variety of cooking heights at which the grill can be placed. Complete the unit with a tenth course of bricks.

Building a worksurface
The easiest way to add a worksurface to the barbecue unit is to construct a low plinth wall in bricks about six courses high, set on a separate strip foundation parallel with one of the side walls of the barbecue. Lay the sixth course of the plinth wall on edge.

Cut a panel of $\frac{1}{4}$in (9mm) thick exterior-

Building a brick barbecue

1 Lay five courses of bricks, then add a sixth on edge, overlapping the side walls to form a ledge for the charcoal tray.

2 Build up the side and back walls in stretcher bond by another three courses; add the tenth on edge, then add the windshield.

grade chipboard or plywood to fit between the plinth wall and the ledge protruding from the side of the barbecue, the other side of which supports the charcoal tray. The board could be covered with ceramic or quarry tiles, stuck down with tiling adhesive, and edged in softwood lipping. Remember, however, that the worktop will have to be removed and stored indoors after the barbecue season to avoid becoming damaged by damp conditions.

A large paving slab or square of York stone makes a good alternative surface for the worktop, and can be left in position permanently.

If the plinth wall is to be connected to the main unit from the outset construct an E-shaped arrangement of brickwork up to the sixth course (the height of the worksurface and charcoal tray), then continue the side and back walls of the barbecue unit itself to the tenth course. This option gives you space underneath the worksurface for storage of charcoal, or it could be fitted with shelves and a door to store cutlery, utensils and crockery.

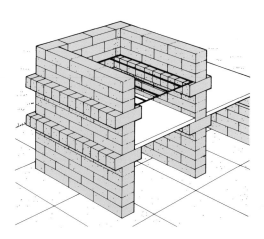

3 Place the shelf and worksurface on the ledges and slot in the charcoal tray and grill above. Point the mortar joints; leave to set.

Finishing the unit
Complete the barbecue unit and its attendant worksurface, table or seating by neatening the mortar joints. Form a soft rounded profile by running along each joint with an offcut of garden hosepipe when the mortar has just started to stiffen.

Leave the unit for a few days for the mortar to set before lighting your first barbecue, or the heat could cause the structure to crack.

Clean the barbecue after each use, to avoid an unpleasant job at the end of the summer.

PROPRIETARY BARBECUES

Purpose-made barbecues include the so-called hibachi type; made of cast iron or cheaper, thinner steel, this is the simplest model. The tabletop type is basically a simple tray which contains the charcoal, with one-, two- or three-handled grill trays; these slot in at one of several height settings for adjusting the ferocity of the cooking.

Hibachis are ideal for use on a home-made brick-built barbecue surround, because all that is required is a flat surface at the cooking height on which the feet of the tray can rest.

Freestanding barbecues made of lightweight steel (often wheeled) offer portability and a more controlled cooking environment than a simple hibachi or brick-built unit. They usually feature adjustable cooking heights via ratchet lever or multi-position grill housings, a built-in windshield, and battery-powered rotary spit attachment.

Other, even more complex, barbecues such as the kettle type are intended for freestanding use, and may incorporate wheels for mobility, but they should not be moved when alight. The kettle cover serves as a windshield when raised, and pivots or hinges over the cooking to convert the barbecue into an oven, infusing the food with the cooking aromas and smoke. Versions are available with rotating spit attachments.

Choosing garden furniture 1

The choice of outdoor furniture is largely determined by the garden's basic design and the way in which the furniture is to be used. Durability, portability, collapsibility and ease of maintenance are important factors to take into account.

Choosing styles

The design of the furniture should be chosen to complement the style of the garden. Rustic timber items, for example, are best suited to an informal, leafy or "wild" garden, whereas the frequently colourful, coordinated look of modern patio sets—table and matching chairs—in steel or plastic may be more suitable for patios. Elegant, ornate cast-iron tables and chairs may be preferred in a formal courtyard scheme.

Benches Simple benches can be used in most parts of a garden. Park benches with backrests and armrests designed in a more formal style are often effective when placed against a wall, hedge or fence. These benches sometimes feature elegantly curved or slatted backrests and shaped armrests; some types even hinge and fold so that they can be stored during bad weather.

Chairs Individual chairs are made in timber, metal or plastic in numerous designs. The basic metal types have a foldable tubular aluminium frame with a plastic fabric seat and back, while a more comfortable option is the canvas-seated, wooden-framed director's chair, which usually has an adjustable back so that you can sit upright or recline.

Cast-iron Victorian-style chairs are a durable, if rather uncomfortable, form of seating with highly ornate pierced patterns on seat, legs and back. The typical balloon-backed chairs are made to complement matching cast-iron tables. Lighter-weight, non-rusting cast-aluminium versions are also available, as are less expensive types that are moulded in tough plastic.

Dining sets Purpose-made garden dining sets comprising table and matching chairs are available in traditional hardwood to classic designs, or in lightweight metal or plastic with a modern, streamlined look; usually there is an optional central parasol. Modern garden dining chairs are typically foldable and fitted with removable upholstered cushions; the more elaborate types will adjust into the lounging position.

Rattan-framed furniture is another option, best suited to the more traditional garden.

For family picnics outdoors, a timber trestle table with integral bench seats at each side is ideal, and can be fitted with a central parasol shade if required. This type of unit is straightforward to construct—see page 142.

Loungers Deckchairs are still hard to beat for lounging in the sun, and fold flat for storage. Replacement canvas is easy to obtain and simple to fit. More elaborate types have leg and arm rests.

For sunbathing, a basic metal-framed sunlounger with fabric stretch cover is suitable. More expensive types have padded, upholstered covers and adjustable headrests. Poolside loungers, fitted with wheels, are made in timber, metal, or the cheaper plastic.

A luxurious touch in the garden can be provided by installing a swing hammock, fitted with a fabric awning. The swing seat, basically an upholstered bench seat with room for four or more sitting side by side, is commonly made with a steel tubular frame, often plastic-coated, and must be dismantled and put in storage during the winter.

Materials

Furniture falls into two main categories: that which you can leave outside permanently and that which you must store indoors when you are not using it.

Plastic is undoubtedly the most durable material, and can be left out in all weathers without showing signs of deterioration. It never needs painting—simply a wash down will keep it looking pristine. However, it can appear utilitarian, and the colours are usually unsuitable.

Metal is commonly used for garden furniture frames, although it is susceptible to attack by rust. However, galvanizing, painting and plastic coatings will usually protect the vulnerable metal—provided the surface is not chipped or scratched. Aluminium will not rust, is much lighter than iron and steel, and can be cast to make traditional-style furniture.

Timber is by far the best-quality material to use for garden furniture, but it is also one of the most expensive and one that requires

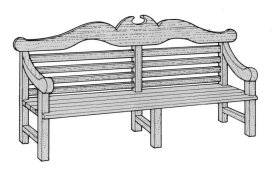

Hardwood bench Modern reproductions of classic styles are available.

Upholstered adjustable chairs Suitable for a patio or conservatory.

Swing hammock Needs to stand on foot-plates if used on a lawn.

Deckchair Comfortable, foldable for storage and inexpensive.

Plastic-framed wheelbed Suitable for a poolside situation. Also available in wood and metal versions.

Choosing garden furniture 2

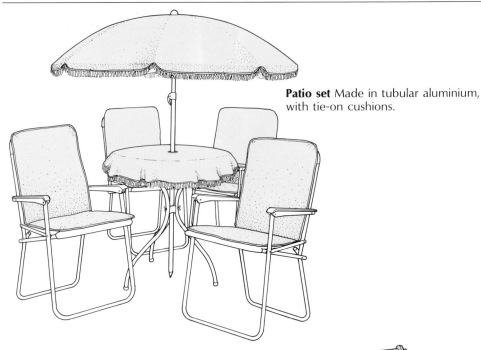

Patio set Made in tubular aluminium, with tie-on cushions.

Hardwood bench seating and low table Offers more flexibility than a table with integral bench seats.

Victorian-style cast-iron chairs and table Can be left outdoors throughout the summer. Replicas in cast aluminium have inferior detailing.

regular maintenance to resist rot. Hardwoods can be left bare to weather to an attractive tone, while softwoods (with the exception of cedar, which weathers naturally) must be treated with preservative, or else painted to withstand the elements.

Regular maintenance
Whatever type of furniture you choose, ensure that all joints are firm and sturdy, and that metal fixings are galvanized to prevent rusting. On a regular basis you should lubricate all pivots, hinges and screw heads to prevent them from binding. Protect metal-framed chairs from corrosion during the winter by applying oil or a spray-on wax moisture-dispersing product which simply wipes off the next season.

Treat softwood furniture with colourless preservative, or repaint immediately prior to the summer season. Apply stain, varnish or oil to hardwood furniture before putting away in store, or before bad weather threatens if the furniture is to be left outside permanently.

Secondhand furniture
New garden furniture can be expensive, especially if you opt for items made from hardwood, which is especially costly. As a money-saving option, chairs, tables and other items of furniture originally intended for indoor use may be obtained secondhand.

Junk shops, car boot sales and stripped pine outlets often yield bargains in the form of old church pews, dining chairs and tables which will make admirable additions to the garden. Stripped of any previous varnish, the pieces can be treated with preservative and resealed with varnish, or paint if preferred. As such pieces are not intended for use out of doors, however, it is best to keep this type of furniture under the partial cover of a pergola or awning.

Built-in garden furniture
Built-in seating and tables may be readily incorporated into a patio garden.

When building a timber deck, for example, it is not complicated to install integral bench seating or a built-in dining table, cladding the top surface with the same slats used for the decking surface (see pages 38-45).

Encircle a favourite tree in the garden with a bench seat fitted around its trunk: proprietary kits can be obtained, or a slatted top on a sturdy frame mounted on posts can be constructed (see pages 145-6).

During the construction of a brick- or stone-built terraced patio, it is possible to include plinth walls, running along the top of a raised planting bed, to form the base for a slab-topped seating unit.

STONE SEATING

Benches in stone are more for ornament than for use, although they could be temporarily fitted with cushions. They are not usually made in reconstituted stone, and are available today only as antiques: they are therefore an expensive option for a garden designed in a style of the past. They may be bought at auctions and architectural salvage warehouses.

Softer stones such as Italian limestone acquire an attractive patination very quickly, but will soon suffer erosion in harsher climates. On the other hand, a durable material such as Portland stone (very popular in the 18th and 19th centuries) has a long life, though it takes years to patinate.

Stone benches usually come in a number of individual parts—for example, a single flat seat on individual supports. Where there are parts that are not original, this should be reflected in a lower price.

The more elaborate seats include superb carving on the legs and armrests—for example, griffins, lions. Sometimes there is also carving on the back, such as scrollwork, sometimes flanking a heraldic device.

An improvised stone seat could be made from salvaged architectural capitals (that is, the decorative features that surmount classical columns) topped by a flat piece of marble.

A garden bench

Making your own garden furniture is not only a rewarding activity but also likely to be much less expensive than buying ready-made pieces. For the more complex items some carpentry skills are necessary, but the simpler pieces of outdoor furniture can be of rougher quality than for indoor furniture.

MAKING A GARDEN BENCH

A simple garden bench can be constructed by erecting two piers of bricks, natural stone or concrete blocks on a strip foundation base. The piers should be no more than about 18in (450mm) high for comfortable use.

Cut four lengths of $6 \times 1\frac{1}{2}$in (150 × 35mm) planed softwood or hardwood to fit across the top of the piers with an overhang of about 6in (150mm) at each end, and screw these to three battens of 3×2in (75 × 50mm) timber, fixed at right-angles to them near each end and across the middle. Space the planks about $\frac{1}{2}$in (12mm) apart.

The bench top can simply rest loosely on the piers, or can be attached with screws driven into wallplugs.

Adapting designs

The basic design of the bench seat may be adapted by adding a slatted plank backrest supported on vertical timber posts screwed to the back edge of the masonry piers.

Additionally, it is possible to adapt the design of the picnic table described below to create a freestanding timber bench; or, by scaling down the components, you can construct individual chairs using the same principles. Assemble the frames as for the picnic table, except that at one side of the leg frames the legs themselves should be set vertically, cut square at the bottom, and extended by a few feet beyond the top rails to form the back legs of the seat and attached backrest. Fix planks or smaller-section slats, spaced about $\frac{1}{2}$in (12mm) apart, to the protruding backrest supports. Fix slats to the horizontal top rails, which in the case of a chair will become the seat supports.

MAKING A PICNIC TABLE

The popular type of picnic table with integral bench seating at each side is straightforward to construct using no complicated carpentry

joints whatsoever: the components are simply bolted together or screwed into place.

The table is supported on three leg frames of $2\frac{1}{2} \times 1\frac{1}{2}$in (62 × 35mm) softwood, each comprising a horizontal top batten with pairs of legs bolted to it, splayed apart at the base. Planks of $6 \times 1\frac{1}{2}$in (150 × 35mm) planed softwood are screwed to the top of the leg assemblies to form the tabletop. The seats are formed by screwing pairs of planks to horizontal battens of $2\frac{1}{2} \times 1\frac{1}{2}$in (62 × 35mm) bolted across the leg assemblies, about 18in (450mm) above ground level.

Assembling the legs

Mark off six 36in (914mm) long legs from a length of timber, then saw each to length. Cut the base and top of each leg to an angle of about 30 degrees, using a sliding bevel as a guide. Mark out and cut three top rails for the leg assemblies from the same timber. These should be about 36in (914mm) long, the ends cut to an angle so that people sitting at the table will not graze their knees on the sharp edges.

Lay the legs on the ground in pairs, with the top rails on top. Drill through both pieces to take $\frac{3}{8}$in (10mm) bolts, insert the bolts, fit washers and tighten the nuts securely but not too tightly at this stage with an adjustable spanner. Repeat the procedure for the other two leg assemblies. All nuts are securely tightened when the assembly is completed.

Fitting the seat formers

Mark out and cut three 60in (1.5m) long pieces of $2\frac{1}{2} \times 1\frac{1}{2}$in (62 × 35mm) planed timber, with angled ends, to use as the seat formers; these also help to brace the leg assemblies. Lay a leg assembly on the ground and place a brace over it so that it protrudes equally at each side and its top edge is 18in (450mm) from the base of the legs.

Drill pairs of holes through the brace into each leg and insert bolts. Fit washers, then screw on the nuts. Tighten the nuts with an adjustable spanner so the leg and seat former assembly is rigid. Fit the other braces to the remaining leg assemblies.

Assembling the table framework

Cut nine $6 \times 1\frac{1}{2}$in (150 × 35mm) planks to a

A picnic table 1

length of 60in (1.5m) to form the tabletop and the seats. Assemble the table framework by drilling pairs of screw clearance holes in each end of each plank, then centrally, to coincide with the positions of the top rails and seat formers of the leg assemblies.

Screw the planks to the seat formers of the leg assemblies so that the framework will be freestanding. Next, screw the remaining five planks to the top rail of each leg assembly. Leave a gap of about $\frac{1}{2}$in (12mm) between each of the planks on the seats and the tabletop: both the seats and the tabletop will overhang the ends of the supporting frame members slightly.

Drill a 1$\frac{1}{2}$in (35mm) diameter hole through the centre of the middle tabletop plank so that you can insert the stem of a parasol: the base of the parasol can be driven into the lawn, or fitted into a proprietary parasol support under the table.

Apply preservative to all parts of the picnic table and allow to dry before using.

The design of the picnic table can be adapted to construct a basic dining table without integral seating. Simply fit braces that stop at the outer edge of each leg rather than protruding as the seat supports. A longitudinal brace can be added along the length of the table, between braces. This timber can be attached to the central brace by a cross-halving joint and nailed to the outer braces.

A picnic table: exploded view

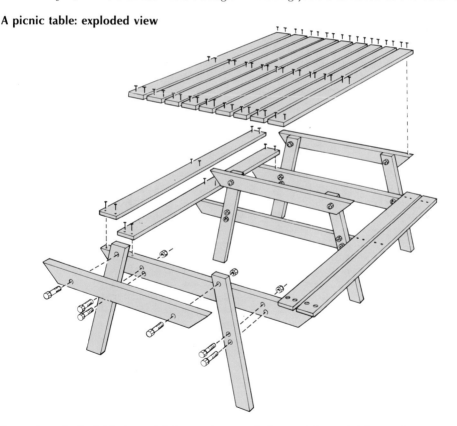

A wooden picnic table is straightforward to construct. The timber parts must be joined at the correct angles and care must be taken when spacing the slats. Drill fixing holes straight and tighten all nuts evenly to avoid weak spots. Proprietary kits are available if you are daunted by carpentry.

A picnic table 2

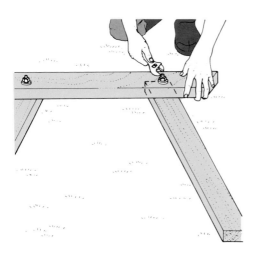

1 Bolt pairs of legs to a top rail to form the basic leg assembly of the picnic table. Make sure the ends of the legs and the rail are cut to the correct angles.

2 Cut the seat formers to length and bolt across the legs, about 18in (450mm) from the base. The formers will also act as a brace for the leg assemblies.

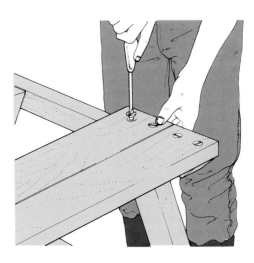

3 Assemble the table framework by screwing pairs of seat planks to the protruding seat formers. The table framework will then be freestanding.

4 Screw the planks to the top of the leg and seat assemblies, spacing them about $\frac{1}{2}$in (12mm) apart. Treat the entire picnic table with preservative.

A tree seat 1

Making a tree seat

Create a shady seating area under a favourite tree with a raised planter constructed from interlocking timber logs (illustrated page 146). These can be obtained in easy-to-assemble kit form. Attractive and practical, this wooden tree seat can be assembled in just five minutes—without the need for any tools. When filled with soil, the same design can serve as a conventional planter, which incorporates seating areas.

The logs, which are preservative-treated to ward off rot, have notched edges which interlock to form the walls of the tree seat and make the structure rigid. No other fixing is necessary.

The principles involved in constructing the tree seat are easy to modify to a home-made unit. Straight-edged timber can be used to construct a planter or tree seat, if a more formal appearance is required. If there is no suitable tree in the garden, it may be worth planting one and building the seat around it—leave room for the trunk to grow.

Alternatively, you could use the seat as a planter by filling with soil and adding small shrubs, or trailing plants which will grow through the gaps between the logs.

A proprietary kit

A basic kit comprises three thin logs which form the base of the structure, and 21 thicker logs which you build up as the hexagonal sides. There are also three thick logs which have pre-drilled holes to take seat-fixing dowels, and three slot-on seats. Two sizes of tree seat are made: 4ft 3in and 5ft 9in (1.3 and 1.7m), measured across the widest sides, but you can obtain a larger size to order from the manufacturers. Each unit is 1ft 4in (406mm) high.

Measuring the tree circumference

Measure around the trunk to work out the size of the components. Trees up to a maximum circumference of 6ft 6in (2m) will require a planter which measures about 4ft (1.2m) across the points of the hexagon; trees up to a maximum girth of 11ft (3.3m) will need a planter measuring about 6ft (1.8m) across the point. Much larger trees require a planter about 8ft (2.4m) across.

Preparing the ground

In order for the tree seat to be fixed properly, the ground at the base of the tree should be more or less flat, firm, and free from large stones and other obstructions. On an uneven or sloping surface dig out the earth to level it, but beware of cutting into the tree roots, which could damage the tree or even kill it.

Where excavation is not feasible, add more soil to the lower area and compact it to create a flat surface for the seat.

Laying out the base logs

Space three single-notched thin logs in their approximate positions on the ground around the base of the tree, with their notched edges uppermost—they will form a broad triangle that is unconnected at the ends. Move the logs around the tree until they lie as flat and as steady as possible.

MAKING LOG FURNITURE

Large-section logs trimmed to size can be used to make useful stools and occasional tables. Cut a rounded trunk to length—say, about 18in (450mm)—and fix to one end a larger, thinner round cut from a trunk to make a small table.

Make a chair by cutting an L-shaped section, 36 × 24in (900 × 600mm) notch from a trunk. The base of the notch becomes the seat itself, while the upstand serves as a backrest. Drill holes of about 1in (25mm) diameter at 12in (300mm) intervals where the backrest meets the seat, to allow rainwater to drain freely.

Smooth rough patches, but avoid overworking the surface; weathering will create a comfortable and natural appearance quite quickly.

Treat the cut surfaces of the trunk with a red oxide primer as a means of sealing it against penetration by rain: the primer also blends in with the rustic appearance of the piece.

A tree stump can also be put to use as a plinth for a bird bath (see page 185).

A tree seat 2

Making a tree seat

1 Lay out the base logs in a rough triangular shape around the tree, with the notches pointing uppermost. These thin logs will not meet at the ends.

Laying the connecting logs
Connect the thin logs by spanning between them with three of the twin-notched thicker logs, slotting together the notches. This will form the basic hexagonal shape of the tree seat. Add the remaining thick logs to build up the walls of the tree seat to their full height. The final three logs have holes to take the seat dowels. Place them on the log walls with their holes uppermost and push in the dowels so that they still protrude above the walls.

Fitting the seats
The three seats are each assembled from three thin logs fixed side by side to form a comfortable base, and are connected by battens underneath. Holes in the undersides of the seats allow them to be slotted over the protruding dowels. On a home-made unit, where such convenient anchorage is lacking, the seats can simply be nailed or screwed to the top of the log walls.

2 Fit twin-notched thick logs to connect the first three thin logs and form the hexagon shape, then lay the second course of twin-notched thin logs on top. Build up the log walls until you reach the fifth course.

3 Fit dowels into the upper logs, so that the dowels protrude into holes on the undersides of the three flat seats.

Making a shed 1

Making a shed

A shed is an essential garden feature in which to store tools and equipment as well as bulky items for which no storage space is available elsewhere. Many shed kits are available and it is not difficult to erect them, with help, in a few hours once the foundations have been prepared.

Types of shed

A shed about 6ft 6in deep × 5ft wide (2 × 1.5m) will give ample space for storage, plus room for a shelf and folding workbench. Where storage is your only requirement, a smaller shed might do, but you will probably not be able to step inside when it is full.

Pent roof Sheds with a "pent" roof, which slopes in one direction only (high on the door side; low towards the back), offer limited headroom overall. A window is normally included in the front or front side wall so that a workbench can be placed underneath for good light and sufficient headroom in which to work.

Apex roof For good headroom overall, an apex roof shed is the best choice: here, the roof slopes on two sides and has a central ridge and there is plenty of space in which to work as well as for storage. There will normally be a door on one end, or side, and windows on one or two sides.

Timber and cladding

All timber used in shed construction must be treated with preservative to combat rot. Softwoods need treatment at least every two years. Pressure-impregnated timber such as larch is the best choice, although western red cedar is one timber which is naturally durable; it will weather to a grey tone.

The wall panels of the shed will be either feather-edged horizontal boards, overlapping those below, or a tougher "shiplap" profile, in which the boards interlock with a curved rebate, so the top of one board is curved inward to produce a more desirable profile. Tongued, grooved and V-jointed boards are also used vertically on some sheds.

Building paper used to line the inside walls of the shed will minimize draughts and moisture penetration.

A shed may be built directly onto a concrete base, or may have a timber floor consisting of stout beams or framing bearers covered with plywood panelling or conventional floorboards.

Preparing the foundations

Erect the shed on a firm, flat surface such as a cast concrete base, or precast concrete paving slabs. Buy enough slabs to cover the base on which the shed is to stand with an overlap of about 4in (100mm) all round. Mark out the base with stringlines and wooden pegs, then remove any vegetation and large stones from within the area. Dig out any turf and the fertile topsoil and use them in another part of the garden if possible.

Compact the earth and flatten the surface using a garden roller, then fill in any hollows with soil and roll again. Rake a 6in (150mm) layer of sharp sand over the base, then bed the paving slabs in this (see page 30). Tap the slabs down firmly with the handle of a club hammer. Butt the slabs up against each other and check that they are level across the surface using a spirit level. Note that the entire slab base should slope gently—by about 1in (25mm)—and consistently in one direction to ensure rapid drainage of rainwater.

Assembling the shed floor

A kit shed usually has a prefabricated floor of chipboard (or ordinary floorboards), which is sometimes fitted with slim reinforcing battens resting on stout timber bearers. Place a layer of bituminous felt underneath the bearers so that damp cannot rise, and set the floor on this base. Check that the floor is firm and steady: if not, you might have to pack underneath it with offcuts of timber.

Erecting the wall panels

Shed walls are typically prefabricated, and consist of overlapping slats on a softwood framework. Most panels must be bolted together, and you will need help to hold them in place while they are being fixed. First, place the back panel and one side panel on the floor and temporarily secure this with the bolts: slip the bolts through the pre-drilled holes from the outside, fit the washers and screw on the nuts inside fairly loosely. Lift up

Making a shed 2

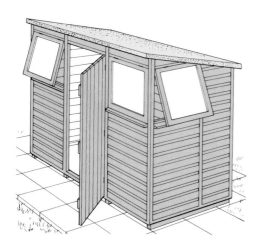

A pent roof shed has a roof that slopes in one direction, usually towards the back.

An apex roof shed has a pitched roof sloping on two sides from a central ridge.

the remaining two wall panels and fit the bolts—again, not too tightly.

Measure the diagonals inside the shed to check that the walls are square. If the framework is square, the diagonals will be equal. Tighten the nuts on the bolts with a spanner.

Position the four walls correctly on the floor—you will probably find that they are intended to overhang by about 1in (25mm)—then secure them by hammering nails through the lower reinforcing batten frame into the floor supports, at about 12in (300mm) intervals.

On some sheds there are slim trimming battens which must be pinned over the slight gap between the side walls at each corner.

Fitting the roof panel

The roofs of small sheds are normally the pent type (sloping to the back only), which is far easier to fit than the pitched type. A pent roof is usually supported at the front on a header beam, which is secured to the top of the front wall panel, and supported at the sides on tapered battens fixed to the tops of the side panels.

Position the header beam and side battens

Making a shed

1 Fix the wall panels The wall panels are lifted onto the floor and temporarily secured with bolts. Nail the wall panels to the floor (shown above), then tighten the bolts to secure them.

and secure them by driving screws up through the wall panel frames. The roof itself will simply be a panel of chipboard large enough to overhang the walls of the shed so that rainwater will run off clear of the walls. To secure the roof panel, lift it onto the roof bearers and align its edges with the walls to form a consistent overlap all round. Nail to the supports below.

To fit an apex roof on a small shed, nail the roof braces to the wall frames and reinforce underneath the ridge at each end with a nail-on plywood plate. With larger apex sheds, however, purlins may need to be fitted and rafters to support the weight of the shed roof.

Fitting the roof covering
Some roof panels are supplied already felted as protection against the weather. However, if the panels are plain, fix sheets of bituminous roofing felt to the surface to make them waterproof. Cut a strip of felt from a 33ft (10m) roll to fit across the width of the shed.

Lay the felt on the roof at the back, or lowest edge, so it overhangs by at least 4in (100mm). Fix the felt to the roof panel with $\frac{1}{2}$in (12mm) long galvanized large-headed clout nails driven in at 4in (100mm) intervals.

Fit the second strip of felt to the roof so it overlaps the previous strip by about 4in (100mm) and secure it with nails as before. With some smaller prefabricated sheds the roofing felt is simply secured by nailing slim preservative-treated battens across the overlapping layers.

Trim the excess felt so that it overhangs the roof by about 2in (50mm), then fold it over and secure with nails to the underside of the roof panel. Nail on a thin fascia board to cover the felted side and front edges, leaving the lower one, the back edge, free so that rainwater will run off.

Complete the shed by hanging the door and fitting any openable window frames that may be included with your model. Glaze the window frames without using putty by pinning the panes into the rebate.

2 Trimming battens may be required to seal the join between the panels at external corners.

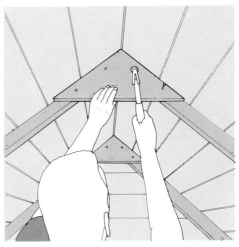

An apex roof is nailed to the wall battens, then reinforced with plywood ridge plates. The final stage is to lay felt on the roof so that it overlaps at the ridge and edges for good waterproofing.

Making a rock garden 1

A rock garden should be more than just a random pile of stones. The most successful—and authentic—type of rock garden is one that closely resembles the natural rocky outcrops that occur in mountainous regions. The rocks may be angled in the same direction to suggest geological strata.

Choosing a site

The rock garden must be constructed on thoroughly prepared foundations in a similar way to any other garden structure, so that it will not erode after heavy rain. It is very important to prepare the ground thoroughly and give special consideration to the drainage of the site. Remember that it is impossible to review the basic treatment when the stones are in place—you cannot then dig and manure the site like an ordinary border or flower bed.

Choose a site for your rock garden carefully so that it will receive plenty of warm sun and be protected from prevailing winds.

Drainage and soil types

Drainage on the site is of paramount importance, which is why a sloping design is advantageous. The gradient should not be so steep that the rocks tend to slide down or that the soil is washed away by rainwater.

It is especially important for the welfare of alpine and rock plants that the rock garden is built on soil that is well drained, particularly if the ground is fairly flat. Light, sandy soil is an ideal medium, as the excess water will drain away underground rapidly. However, if the soil is thick and impervious clay, you may have to install additional land drainage in the form of soakaways.

To construct a simple soakaway, dig a hole about 12in (300mm) deep and 12in (300mm) square. Fill the hole with hardcore and ram it down lightly: it should be firm enough not to settle unduly, but not so firm that it prevents the water from soaking away quickly.

Top the hardcore with a layer of gravel or several turves upturned (grass down) to prevent soil from silting into the hole and clogging the hardcore, through which the water must percolate freely. Compact the surface lightly before continuing with the construction of the rock garden.

Buying the materials

Natural stone can be obtained from specialist merchants or larger garden centres, some of whom may hold stocks, or can order them from a local quarry. Choose local stone for use in the rock garden if possible: this minimizes the considerable transport costs that can otherwise be incurred. Otherwise, limestone or sandstone are good choices for most rock gardens as they weather well and are usually readily obtainable.

As a rough guide to estimating the quantity of rocks needed, for a rock garden that measures about 9ft (3m) across, rising about 24in (600mm) above ground level, allow about $1\frac{1}{2}$tons (1500kg) of stone. Ask the supplier to provide large and flattish or angled rocks rather than rounded boulders, as the latter are more difficult to place naturally. Make sure that the rocks provided are not all similar in shape and size.

You will also need gravel or limestone chippings of about $\frac{1}{4}$in (6mm) for mixing with the topsoil to improve drainage. For top-dressing the rock garden, and to act as a mulch to suppress weed growth, order some larger chippings—if possible from the same supplier as the actual rocks so that they match as nearly as possible. These stones are used to cover the shapes around the outcrops and should be a mixture of smaller and larger stones to give a natural effect.

For convenience when working it is best to pile the stones and chippings near to the rock garden site so that they do not have to be moved far. When moving large, heavy rocks, use a pickaxe to lever and roll them. Do not try to lift them without assistance. Smaller rocks should not be difficult to lift but always remember to keep your back straight and bend your legs from the knees when lifting to avoid the risk of strain.

Preparing the foundations

Once the position of the proposed rock garden has been decided, mark out its shape and size on the ground using a spade, a length of hosepipe or stringlines and pegs. Map out a roughly wedge-shaped base, with the point of the wedge at the lower end if there is a gradient.

Cut away any turf from the area by slicing

Building a rock garden

1 Mark out the shape of the rock garden on the ground using strings stretched between pegs, or a garden hosepipe, then dig around the perimeter with a spade.

2 Dig out the topsoil within the area of the rock garden and retain the fertile soil for fertilizing and mixing with grit as the growing medium. Compact the base by treading lightly; trampling may impede drainage.

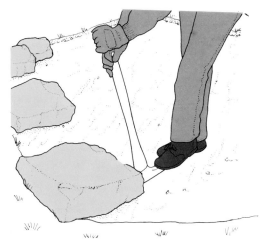

3 Roll the largest rock to the base of the proposed rock garden, as a keystone, using a pickaxe as a lever. Build out roughly V-shaped arms from the keystone with smaller rocks.

4 Fill the lower outcrop of rocks with a mix of topspoil and grit. Rake out the bedding material and compact it by light treading, but do not dislodge the stones.

Making a rock garden 2

5 Build the second outcrop of rocks on top of the first tier, but set back from its edge, leaving adequate space for planting.

6 Remove the plants from their pots and place them in holes dug in the bedding medium between rocks. Introduce plants in crevices between abutting stones, too.

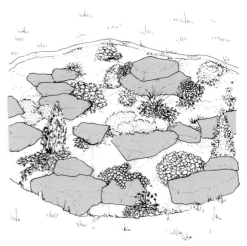

7 Continue to add rocks in smaller tiers until you reach the penultimate layer. Top with a pinnacle composed of rocks pressed together, or one large rock.

8 Complete the planting. Cover the exposed bedding mix with the chippings and the grit, which discourages weeds.

out rectangles—using a turfing iron for best results—and set the turfs aside for possible reuse elsewhere in the garden. Dig out the topsoil to a depth of about 6in (150mm) and set this aside, too, this time for use as part of the soil compost for the rock garden.

Mixing the soil compost

Ensure that the soil you are going to use is well prepared by mixing three parts of loam with one part of peat or garden compost plus, if necessary, a general fertilizer. Mix up five parts of this good, fertile topsoil with one part of $\frac{1}{4}$in (6mm) grit or rock chipping. Use a bucket to gauge the correct proportions. Shovel this mixture onto the foundations so that it is about 2in (50mm) below the surrounding ground level. Rake the surface evenly. When growing alpines, the proportions may need to be five to two.

Setting out the rock garden

As there are so many equally valid ways to approach the rock garden, the following description deals with a fairly traditional, tiered approach in which rocks are set, from the bottom working upward, to form terraces with pockets for plants. This design can be adapted according to individual needs.

Forming the first tier

In this design the rock garden is constructed in a number of V-shaped tiers, which decrease in size from a fairly broad base to a pinnacle at the back, which forms the high point of the feature. A large "keystone" is positioned at the point of each V-shape to prevent the smaller rocks from sliding down the gradient.

Select the largest rock from the pile and roll it into position at the base of the wedge-shaped foundations. Dig a shallow hole for the base of the keystone, and angle it back into the slope so that it is well bedded in the earth. Pack around its base with some of the previously prepared soil and grit mix, so that the stone appears to be partially buried.

Continue to lay smaller rocks to form the arms of the first V-shaped tier. Avoid an artificial, uniform appearance by including variations in rock size. Lay stones immediately above the keystone as well, in clusters of three, five or seven stones. Be sure that you tilt each rock back slightly so that it will not slump forward.

Start the planting (see below) before continuing with the next stage of building.

Forming the subsequent tiers

Add more of the grit-and-soil mix to the V-shaped terrace, then rake it level. Compact the surface by patting it firmly with the back of a shovel.

Lay a second outcrop of medium-sized rocks. This tier should be smaller than the first tier and set back from its rear edge by about 12in (300mm). Fill in this V-shape with more soil and grit, then rake and compact.

Setting the pinnacle

Arrange a pinnacle of small "stratum" rocks, making sure as usual that they are firmly bedded in the soil and next to each other. Pack some of the soil and grit mix between the rocks as they are being placed, to firm up the structure. Alternatively, use one large rock at the top as an "anchor" against soil wash. If the rock garden is not on a natural slope, it is useful to plant a very low, spreading conifer behind the rock or rocks.

Planting out the rock garden

It is easiest to plant alpines and shrubs as you go, after each stage of rock building. First, top up the soil and grit mix as necessary. You can plant at any time of the year, unless a sharp frost threatens. Dig a small hole with the trowel and, having removed the plant from its pot, place it carefully and scoop soil around it. Press down firmly around the edges to bed the plant properly, then sprinkle some grit around the stem and water the plant in.

Introduce plants to the crevices between rocks by first filling the crack with soil, then carefully feeding in the plant's roots. Pack more soil around and underneath the plant to support it, then water very carefully using a watering can fitted with a fine rose.

Adding the final layer

Place the smaller stones and chipping over the surface of the soil between the rocks in order to discourage weed growth and help prevent moisture from drying out too rapidly on the bank.

Garden ponds

There are many different ways of creating a pond, whether you choose to mould your own from concrete, fit a flexible waterproof liner in a hole, or install a semi-solid prefabricated version. Some approaches are more laborious and difficult to complete than others. All methods begin with digging a hole of the required shape in the ground: what is different is the type of impervious material used to line the hole prior to filling it with water.

Concrete Garden ponds are often formed by making a basin of the required shape and lining it using concrete. While perfectly acceptable as a waterproof lining—if properly laid—concrete may crack due to ground movement or frost damage. The main advantage of concrete is that it may be moulded to any shape, size and depth.

Flexible liners Waterproof liners allow the same degree of flexibility as concrete in designing a pond of virtually any shape and size. They are the most economical method. There are various types of flexible liner to choose from:

Heavy-gauge polythene is the least expensive, although most fragile and least flexible, material. Choose a sheet with a minimum thickness of 150 microns (600 gauge), and use a double thickness.

PVC produces a more flexible and durable liner with a lifespan of about 10 years. The nylon-reinforced types are the best choice because they are stronger. Commonly coloured blue on one side and stone-coloured on the other, a PVC liner is best used stone side up for greatest authenticity.

Synthetic butyl rubber is the most flexible material to use for a pond, and offers a lifespan of up to about 50 years—considerably longer than the other types. It is available in black or stone tone in a range of sizes up to 22 × 30ft (6.5 × 9m), although most suppliers will make liners to special sizes if required.

Semi-rigid liners Moulded from vacuum-pressed plastic, semi-rigid pond liners provide a ready-made pond shell which you fit into a hole that roughly conforms to its profile. They are limited in the sizes available. Shapes are either plainly rectangular or irregular for a more natural effect.

Rigid liners Liners made from rigid glass-reinforced plastic (GRP) are the toughest type, and are unaffected by frost or ice and less likely to be punctured accidentally. A range of irregular contours is made, with various depths of internal shelf. Sizes range from about 8 × 6ft (2.4 × 1.8m) to 16 × 11ft (4.8 × 3.6m). The hole must be dug to the precise contours of the shell.

Proprietary systems of nine basic glass-fibre-reinforced polyester elements are available, which can be bolted together and sealed to form virtually any size and shape of pool. The range includes square and triangular 36in (900mm) deep pools, semi-circular bows, open-ended pools, blanking pieces (end sections) and interconnecting sections.

Making a choice
Apart from the greater flexibility offered by moulding concrete into the shape required, there is no real benefit in making a concrete-lined pond. Modern lining materials are equally suitable, as they are not damaged by frost, are easy to install, and are quite inconspicuous when blended in with the surroundings. Flexible liner types can accommodate virtually any shape you choose for your pond.

Deciding on shape and size
The shape you choose, although a matter of personal taste, should reflect the overall style of the garden. In a formal garden a square, rectangular or circular pond makes a fitting centrepiece, especially when placed within a paved area or formal lawn. For a less formal garden, an irregularly-shaped pond—say with a broad kidney shape—looks more natural, and can be made to follow the natural contours of the ground more successfully.

Apart from considering the basic shape of the pond, bear in mind its proportions so that fish, plants and water can be successfully accommodated. A minimum surface area of 38sq ft (3.5sq m) is recommended for this reason, and to ensure that the water is kept well aerated and clear. Smaller ponds will require an artificial filtration system to be installed, which is expensive.

In general, the greater the area of the pond, the deeper it must be: a pond that is about 100sq ft (9sq m) in area should be about 2ft (600mm) deep, but to some extent the depth

Rigid pool liners 1

of a garden pond will depend on the kind of plants and sometimes the type of fish that are going in. Some water lilies, for example, require a depth of 3ft (915mm) or more, though others need no more than 6 to 9in (150 to 230mm). It is unlikely, however, that you will need to dig deeper than about 2ft 6in (760mm), even for a very large pond.

Water that is less than about 1ft 3in (380mm) deep is liable to overheat in the summer, which leaves the fish short of oxygen, and to freeze in winter. An important point to remember is that the sides of the excavation should slope outwards at about 20 degrees so that, in the event of a freeze, the ice will tend to move upward and reduce the pressure on the sides of the pond.

To grow marginal plants in the pond there should be a shelf 9in (225mm) wide at the edge, 9in (225mm) below the surface of the water, in order to accommodate a standard-size planting crate. Preformed rigid and semi-rigid liners will conform to these proportions, which you should also take into account when designing your own concrete or flexible-liner pond.

Positioning the pond

The pond should be sited where it will receive plenty of sunlight, and away from overhanging trees to avoid too much shade and autumn leaves clogging and fouling the water. Sunlight is necessary to encourage the growth of water plants; it also helps to prevent the establishment of algae which may clog the pond with unsightly growth. Installing oxygenating plants and shade-giving floating and marginal plants helps to keep the water reasonably clear, but careful management is required to maintain clear, algae-free water and thus to retain a balance of plants, fish and other pond life.

When planning the pond's location, ensure that digging the basin will not disturb the foundations of nearby outbuildings—or even the house—or dislodge underground drainpipes or electricity cables.

Use a length of string or hosepipe to mark out the shape and size of the pond on the ground, then cut around the outline using a spade or lay a trail of sand as a guide to its shape and size.

Digging the base for a rigid liner

To fit a rigid or semi-rigid pond liner, prop the shell itself in place on bricks, boxes or wooden stakes and mark around its perimeter. Transfer the position of the outer rim of the liner to the ground by standing a spirit level next to it, and push a wooden peg into

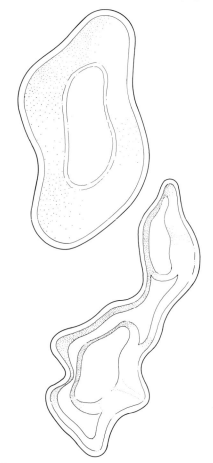

Informal pond shapes fit in best with most garden settings, and there is a range of rigid and semi-rigid preformed types in glass-reinforced plastic and PVC. Most types have moulded marginal shelves and deep centre pools, typically in kidney shapes, crescents and figure-of-eight formats. Alternatively, simply create the required shape with a flexible pond, as described on page 158.

Rigid pool liners 2

the earth at intervals of about 1ft (300mm) as you work around the liner.

Remove the liner and dig a line around the outside of the pegs, about 4in (100mm) away, removing them as you go. Dig away the topsoil to a depth of about 6in (150mm) and reuse this fertile soil elsewhere in the garden.

Excavate the earth further, copying the profile of the underside of the liner as closely as you can, but making it about 6in (150mm) broader all round. Check the depth of the hole by spanning across the top of the excavation with a plank, then use a tape measure to measure to the base.

Remove all sharp stones, thick roots and flatten out any bumps. When you are satisfied that the hole is sufficiently deep, compact the surface by treading, then line the base and any shelves there may be with a 1in (25mm) thick layer of sharp sand.

Fitting the rigid liner

Carefully lower the liner into the hole and shake it to settle it, then press it down firmly on the sand bed. Place a spirit level on a straight-edged length of timber spanning the rim of the liner to ensure that it is horizontal. Check the length and the width, then place

Fitting a rigid liner

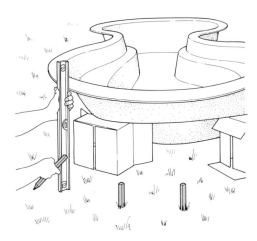

1 Set the rigid liner on supports and mark around its perimeter on the ground, using a spirit level and pegs as a guide.

2 Dig out the hole, following the profile of the liner. Use a plank spanning the pond to determine the depth at the centre.

the spirit level diagonally to ensure the liner is level that way, too. Chock up the liner temporarily until you can backfill it.

Filling the liner

Run a hosepipe to the pond liner and drape it over the edge, then start to fill the liner. While the water level rises, backfill with sand or sifted soil (without any stones, which could damage the walls of the liner). Use a small trowel (or your hands) to feed the backfilling under the marginal shelves, and pack it down firmly. As the liner becomes filled with water it will settle down on its bedding. See page 160 for edging the pond.

Setting the liner in sloping ground

In order to install a rigid pond liner in a naturally sloping site, excavate horizontally into the bank, shoring up the earth at the high side by constructing a small earth-retaining wall of brickwork or natural stone. The choice of material for this wall is basically determined by the style of garden and the shape of the pond itself: bricks will give a formal effect, best suited to an angular pond, while stone or concrete walling blocks create a more natural setting in which an irregular

pond is more suitable.

The low side of the slope may need to be built up slightly, in order to even out the transition from the pond to ground level.

MAKING A FISHPOND COVER

A fishpond in the garden can be a real danger to children, and neighbourhood cats can easily destroy a fish colony. A removable cover can be made from heavy-gauge wire mesh. Cut the mesh with wirecutters roughly to the shape of the pond, but about 12in (300mm) larger all round. Fold over the cut ends of the mesh like a hem on fabric.

Lay a pair of timber battens treated with preservative across the length and width of the pond, resting on the sides, then stretch the mesh over the pond and the battens. Secure the mesh to the ground at 24in (600mm) intervals using metal tent pegs. The battens prevent the mesh from sagging into the water, and provide support should anyone happen to fall in.

3 Set the liner in the hole on a layer of sharp sand. Press it down to bed it firmly, then check the level across the rim.

4 Backfill behind the liner using sand or sifted soil, while a hosepipe fills the liner with water to settle it properly.

Flexible pool liners 1

Planning
Liners are well suited to the creation of curved pools. Use a garden hosepipe to plan the overall shape of the pond on the ground, experimenting with the shape.

Weedkilling
Ground that is badly infested with weeds is best treated before you begin in order to eradicate them. Some weeds have razor-sharp growing points which can soon pierce a liner and cause a leak. Use a weedkiller which will destroy the roots of the weeds to prevent regrowth.

Digging the hole
Dig out the hole for the pond within the guideline formed by the hosepipe. To create a split-level base, excavate the area to about 8 to 12in (200 to 300mm) deep, then, leaving a 9in (225mm) wide shelf around the perimeter of the excavation, dig over the remaining area a further 8 to 12in (200 to 300mm) or to a greater depth if required. Remove any large stones or roots that may puncture the liner.

Do not make the sides of the pond too steep, particularly in light soils, or they are liable to collapse. A gradient of about 4in (100mm) in a depth of 8in (200mm) should guard against collapse, although a shallower gradient may be required depending upon the prevailing soil type.

Dig out any further planting shelves, or deeper areas required, and compact the soil by treading. Take care not to crumble the ledges as you compact the earth.

Using a garden rake, spread about $\frac{1}{2}$in (12mm) of damp building sand over the entire surface as a cushioning layer for the liner.

Underlining
Pond liners normally do not require any form of underlining apart from a cushioning layer of sand, but if the ground is very stony it is advisable to lay a special polyester mat (available from a pond suppliers) over the excavated earth, prior to laying the liner. This will provide an extra cushion against rips.

Installing the liner
A flexible polythene or synthetic rubber liner will mould itself to the shape and size of the

pond. To calculate the dimensions of the sheet, add twice the depth of the pond to its maximum length and width. For example, a pond with an area of 4 × 10ft (1.2 × 3m) and a depth of 24in (600mm) will require a sheet measuring 8 × 14ft (2.4 × 4.2m).

Constructing a flexible liner pond

1 Outline the shape of the pond using a hosepipe, then dig out the base, using pegs for accuracy when gauging the depth at the centre and for the marginal shelves.

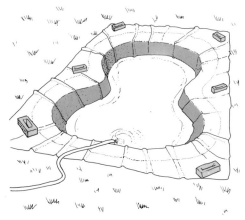

4 Drape the flexible liner across the pond, weighted down with bricks at the edge. Fill the pond with water from a hosepipe: the liner will be stretched into the shape of the hole as it fills.

Drape the liner over the surface of the pond excavation and weight it down at the perimeter with a few bricks. Place a hosepipe into the pond and begin to fill it with water. The liner will be pulled into the contours of the excavation by the weight of the water.

It is important that you maintain equal pressure on the liner as the hole is filling with water. Brush out large creases with a soft broom, but do not worry about minor creasing as this is inevitable. Fill the pond to within about 2in (50mm) of the ground level.

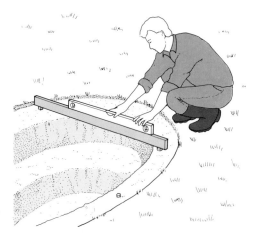

2 Set datum pegs at the edges of the pond and check the level with a plank and a spirit level. The pond must be set horizontal, even if the ground itself is slightly uneven.

3 Spread damp sand over the base and sides of the pond excavation to a depth of about ½in (12mm) as a cushioning bed for the flexible liner.

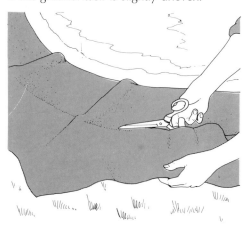

5 Trim off the excess liner from around the perimeter of the pond, using a sharp knife or scissors, leaving an overlap of about 6in (150mm), which will be covered and secured by the edging.

6 Edge the rim of the pond with a row of concrete slabs or natural stones, bedded on mortar. The stones should overhang the pond by about 2in (50mm).

Flexible pool liners 2

Trimming the edge

Pleat the overlap neatly, then trim the edge of the liner with a sharp knife or a large pair of scissors, leaving a margin of about 12in (300mm). Fit the edging around the pond before planting out and introducing fish.

Laying the pond edging

With either rigid or flexible liner ponds, the edge should normally provide a sharp transition between the water and the land. This forms a barrier to discourage roots of trees from penetrating the pool. If the garden is allowed to meet the pool edge, the soil—and the roots of nearby trees such as alder, willow and poplar—would tend to suck out the water. But in some cases, particularly where a log garden is included in the design, the liner can be merged into the edge and covered with soil so that some water overlaps at this point.

A row of irregular-shaped York stone slabs bedded in a mix of one part cement to four parts sand makes an attractive but very expensive edging for a curved pond. A pond that is fairly regular in shape can be edged with ordinary precast paving slabs. To lay these, mix up the bedding material in a bucket with water until it is smooth and fairly stiff,

then spread around the perimeter of the pond, thereby sealing the edge of the liner to the ground. Lay the stones so they overhang the pond by no more than about 2in (50mm): any more than this and there would be a risk of them toppling into the water if anyone stood on the edge.

There are numerous other ways to edge the pond. For example, where the pond slopes gently from the edges, set cobblestones directly on the liner, bedded in sand and cement mortar. Alternatively, set rocks on the marginal shelves, forming sunken walls, then plant the marginals in the recesses behind.

When laying the edging stones, take care not to get any cement in the water as it is toxic to fish and plants. If the water were contaminated, the pond would have to be drained and the liner scrubbed.

Rigid liner ponds can be edged in the same way, using slabs, although some manufacturers supply an edging strip, which slots onto the rim of the liner and forms a ledge on which the slabs can be laid. It is also possible to edge the pond with turf up to this strip—although in that case extra care would be needed when mowing near the edge of the pond.

MAKING A RAISED POND

A raised or partially sunken pond has some practical advantages over a fully sunken type: it is easier to build up the edging around a raised preformed liner rather than to dig a hole, and also garden chemicals which could harm the fish are kept out of the water. A raised or partially raised pond can be a focal point in a garden, especially when a fountain or other ornamental features are added.

To install a fully raised pond, set the liner on a compacted, level base and mark around its perimeter. Construct a wall around the liner using bricks, blocks or stone set on a strip foundation encircling the area of the liner. Build up the walls: no more than nine courses of bricks are necessary for a standard-sized liner.

Reposition the liner on a 1in (25mm) thick cushioning base of sharp sand, add about 6in (150mm) of water to hold the liner steady, then backfill between it and the wall with soil. Bridge the gap between the liner edge and the wall with an edging of paving slabs or other suitable material leaving the appropriate spaces for marginal planting, if required.

For a less formal raised pond, a small rock garden or scree with rocky outcrops may be built as an alternative to the retaining wall. The rock garden should, of course, blend as naturally as possible with its surroundings.

If appropriate, the liner may be partially sunk into the soil and a low wall or rock garden constructed around it.

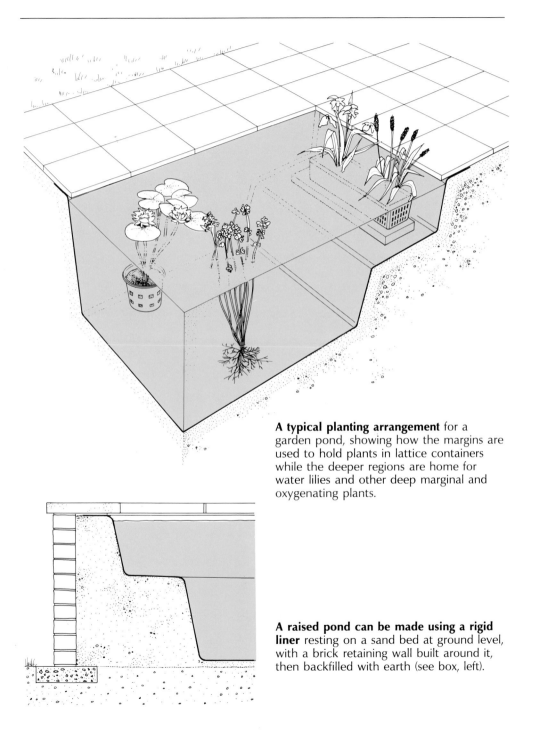

A typical planting arrangement for a garden pond, showing how the margins are used to hold plants in lattice containers while the deeper regions are home for water lilies and other deep marginal and oxygenating plants.

A raised pond can be made using a rigid liner resting on a sand bed at ground level, with a brick retaining wall built around it, then backfilled with earth (see box, left).

Fountains and waterfalls 1

A pool of still, placid water in the garden has considerable charm which can be enhanced by introducing the sight and sound of running water. An electric water pump can power a fountain and even a watercourse that circulates the water to a waterfall.

In addition to providing an attractive focal point, the circulation process will help to oxygenate and clean the water—which is vital for the health and welfare of your plants and fish.

Types of water pump
Two main types of electric water pump are available: submersible or surface-mounted.
Submersible pump This, the cheapest and easiest type of water pump to install, is placed underwater in the centre of the pond. The centrifugal pump, which is powered by a low-voltage transformer (usually 24 volts), has a plastic impeller to draw water inside the unit. A strainer is fitted onto the inlet to prevent

debris from being sucked inside the mechanism, and the outlet delivers either to a jet fixed onto it, or to a remote jet via an extension hose.
Surface-mounted pump Intended for larger fountains, or where it is necessary to run several pond accessories, the surface-mounted pump is usually housed at the side of the pond. It draws water from the pond by suction hose, then delivers it by hose to the sprayhead.

Some pumps are intended only to power a waterfall or a fountain, while other, combination types will serve both at the same time, or one or the other if required.

Power outputs
The power output needed depends on the size of the waterfall, and whether the pump is also intended to run a fountain. The ratings of pumps are usually expressed in watts and in litres or gallons per hour. The flow rate

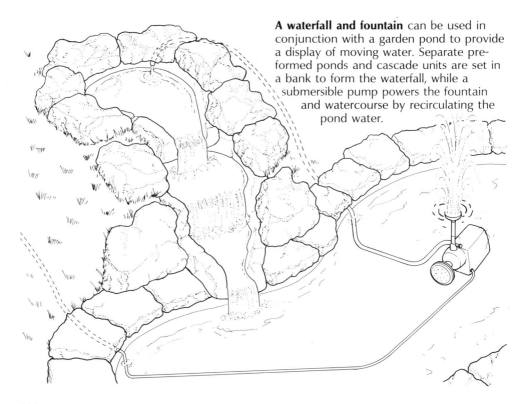

A waterfall and fountain can be used in conjunction with a garden pond to provide a display of moving water. Separate pre-formed ponds and cascade units are set in a bank to form the waterfall, while a submersible pump powers the fountain and watercourse by recirculating the pond water.

depends on the volume of the cascade and the "head", or the vertical height to which the water will have to be raised. This means that a large fall will need a more powerful pump.

Low-voltage pumps do not exceed 70 watts rated power, but their flow rate of about 150 gallons (650 litres) per hour at a head of 5ft (1.5m) is usually enough for most applications.

Most pump suppliers also sell the pre-formed cascades used to make a waterfall, and combinations of pump and cascade are commonly supplied. However, when choosing a pump to power a fountain and a waterfall, ensure that the model will supply the high pressure/low volume necessary for the fountain in addition to the low pressure/high volume required for the waterfall.

Housing the transformer

The low-voltage pump transformer must be housed in dry conditions indoors or in an outbuilding with mains electricity installed, where it can be plugged into a three-pin socket outlet. However, as the low-voltage power supply cables are normally only about 20 to 30ft (6 to 9m) long between pump and transformer, the cable may have to be extended. You must use only a weatherproof cable connector to extend the cable, or else have an outdoor mains supply installed to a remote transformer.

Should you decide to extend the existing low-voltage cable, bear in mind the fact that extensions over about 40ft (12m) may cause the pump output to be reduced, in which case you would need a more powerful pump.

Choosing a fountain

Many types of pond fountain are available. They are differentiated largely by the type of water display they will produce. Fountain-heads can be obtained to give numerous different spray shapes, heights and patterns,

How to make a waterfall

1 Mark the positions of the pool and cascade units on the bank using stringlines and pegs, then dig out the bank. The lip of the higher pool must overlap the edge of the lower pool.

2 Partially fill the cascade pools with water to hold them in place and backfill the excavations to bed them level and firmly on sand. Install the pump and hosepipe.

Fountains and waterfalls 2

and few are more spectacular than those that produce shimmering cascades which rotate slowly as water is sprayed high.

A bubble fountain produces a pattern of bubbles on the surface of the water. Domes of water with diameters of between about 20 and 40in (500mm and 1m) can be produced with a water bell attachment to a standard pump. The bell size can be adjusted and colourful effects created by fitting submersible pond lights beneath to illuminate the dome.

Decorative centrepieces combined with garden ornaments may also be installed. This type of fountain uses a submersible pump near the ornament to feed the sprayhead, which may have a height above the ornament of between 24in (600mm) and 6ft (1.8m), depending upon the capacity of the pump.

Choosing a waterfall

A series of interconnected, small raised ponds linked by waterfalls may be connected to the larger pool, if required. The smaller raised ponds can be made using flexible liners (which must be overlapped to prevent water seeping out), or from concrete castings which have the same disadvantages as main ponds made from this material. Rigid, moulded cascade units can be used to connect the pools. They are moulded from semi-rigid polythene or tougher glass-reinforced plastic, and are simply set on a prepared base in much the same way as full-sized rigid liner ponds. It is much easier to use these units than to construct waterfalls from concrete which, though possible, is very difficult to achieve satisfactorily.

The simplest construction can be just a single, small-lipped pool raised above the main pond, the former discharging its recirculated water directly into the latter. More complex features, however, may consist of three or more linked raised pools, from which

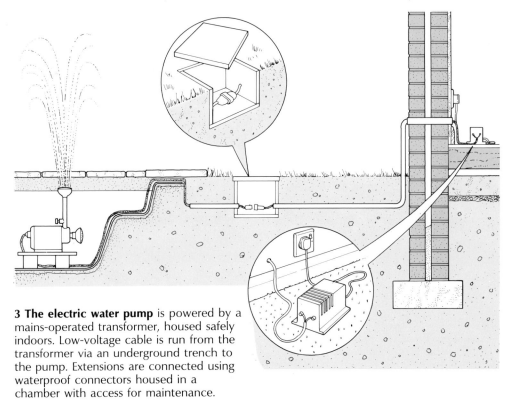

3 The electric water pump is powered by a mains-operated transformer, housed safely indoors. Low-voltage cable is run from the transformer via an underground trench to the pump. Extensions are connected using waterproof connectors housed in a chamber with access for maintenance.

water spills downwards in stages, eventually returning to the large, main pond. A triple rock cascade installed at the top of a rise will spill pump-driven water down the three steps and into the main pond below.

Pool and cascade units will blend in well if surrounded by rocks and softened by plants.

Installing a fountain

To install a submersible low-voltage pump to power a fountain, first assemble the fountain-head. The components of this will probably simply push together, and the fountain jet fit at the top. The power cable will already be attached to the pump, so that no further electrical work is required.

Place a few concrete slabs in the base of the pond, in the middle of the deepest pool, then lower the pump onto this plinth. Ensure that the fountainhead protrudes just above the waterline.

Run the cable out of the pond by the least noticeable route, taking it under the stone or slab edging. Although the low-voltage cable would present no danger from shock if it were cut or broken, it is preferable to place it below ground where it will be safe from damage. Dig a trench at least 20in (500mm) deep in the most direct route to the site of the transformer. Insert the cable in lengths of plastic conduit (or use an old hosepipe) to protect it from damage, lay it in the trench and fill in with earth.

Where it is necessary to extend the cable, use a waterproof connector housed in a loose-brick chamber topped with a slab lid, which can be removed for access.

Lead the cable to the transformer through a hole drilled in a window or door frame, or through the wall. Where the cable is run along a wall, it is best to feed it through a length of conduit, which itself can be screwed to the surface using clips every 3ft (1m).

Connect the cable to the transformer by preparing the ends with wire-strippers. There are only two cores inside the outer PVC sheathing which can be attached to the low-voltage terminals of the transformer any way round. The mains lead of the transformer, which will already be connected to the device, must be fitted with a three-pin plug: brown core to live; blue core to neutral; green/yellow

striped core to earth. Make sure that there is a 3 amp fuse fitted in the plug, insert the plug in the socket outlet and test the fountain.

Constructing a waterfall

Unless there is a natural bank of earth by the side of the main garden pond, you will have to remodel the earth to create a base for the cascade units. Lay firm subsoil, packing it down firmly, then add topsoil to achieve the correct height.

Once the bank has settled and it has been topped up as necessary, lay out the pre-formed cascade units in their approximate positions. Remember that the higher cascade units must overlap the lower ones so that water can spill over the lip without trickling behind the rim.

Use stringlines to mark the outline of the units, with pegs attached to determine their height above the bank. Remove the liners and dig out any turf. Dig out the bank roughly to the shape of the individual units, then try them to see if they fit. Remove large stones and roots, then line the base of the excavations with a $\frac{1}{2}$in (12mm) thick layer of sharp sand as a soft but firm bed.

Bedding in the cascade units

Lay the cascade units in place, starting with the bottom one, the lip of which must overhang the main pond to provide an adequate fall of water. Pack soil under the rims of the cascade units and around the edges, to bed them down firmly. Partially fill the pools with water to weight them down while you bed them into place.

Positioning the water supply hose

The water is circulated from the main pond via the pump and up to the header pool of the waterfall through a length of hosepipe. The hosepipe will simply push onto the nozzle of the pump, and may be secured with a spring clip. Position the pump in the bottom of the pond then run the hose out of the rim, under the lip of the lower cascade, where it will not be visible. Take the hose up to the header pool under the rim of each lower cascade and drape it over the edge of the header. Cover the hosepipe with a stone—but be careful not to crush it.

Swimming pools 1

Modern prefabricated swimming pool kits are both economical to buy and quite straightforward to install yourself, following the manufacturer's detailed instructions—although you might consider it best to have professional help with the heavy excavation work, and the installation of the heating equipment.

There are basically two types of swimming pool to choose from: above-ground or below-ground.

Above-ground pools The cheapest type of swimming pool is the above-ground type, which requires no excavation. It will, of course, be a prominent and perhaps unattractive feature having little relationship to other parts of the garden. Having a depth of anything from about 3 to 10ft (1 to 3m), an above-ground pool can be quite a daunting presence if the garden's prevailing profile is flat.

This type of pool is commonly constructed from galvanized steel panels with a heavy-duty vinyl liner clipped to the top, and surmounted with a plastic trim. It can often be dismantled and stored away during the winter. Access is usually by clip-on stainless steel steps. In any event, assembly should take no longer than one day.

Alternatively, it is feasible to dig a fairly shallow hole and set an above-ground pool in this, so that its dominance as a feature is lessened. With this arrangement, however, a gap must be left around the pool for rainwater to drain away.

Above-ground pools are fairly limited in the shapes available; these are commonly rectangular, circular or oval.

Below-ground pools Despite the fact that they are more costly to purchase and much more complicated to install, below-ground swimming pools offer the best scope for design. Below-ground pools may vary in depth from end to end which above-ground pools cannot—and the overall shape need not be regular. The usual shapes are oval, rectangular or kidney-shaped, and there is a far greater choice of size. Typical pools will measure from about 20 × 12ft (6 × 3.5m) to 35 × 17ft (10.4 × 5.2m).

The walls of a below-ground pool are commonly constructed from interlocking panels of glass fibre, precast concrete, galvanized steel—or even plywood—set on a con-

crete ledge; the base of the hole is screeded before being fitted with a prefabricated vinyl liner to contain the water. However, precise methods of construction differ from manufacturer to manufacturer.

Construction details
The method used to construct a sunken pool will have a bearing on the size, shape and depth possible. To meet specific requirements, it may be necessary to opt for a custom-designed pool rather than a kit.

Kit liner pools Using vinyl liners can limit the choice of sizes and shapes for the pool, because this is dictated by the sizes of available liners. However, you might consider constructing a reinforced concrete pool. The perimeter panels are usually bolted together and reinforced by a steel band which runs around the outside of the wall, and additionally supported by brackets set in the ground.

In other kits the perimeter walls of the pool are constructed from walling blocks or hollow plastic blocks fitted with reinforcing rods and filled with concrete, both built on a cast concrete footing, also called a ring beam. A second ring beam may be laid around the top of the pool to anchor the wall in place.

The vinyl liner is then dropped into place

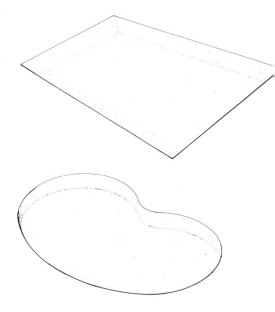

and sealed to a receptor at the top edge.

Custom-built pools A reinforced concrete pool has a cavity wall of concrete blocks (the cavity filled with concrete as reinforcement), lined with concrete if soil conditions demand this extra support, and topped with a waterproof screed. The surface is then tiled or treated with special swimming pool paint.

With both types of below-ground pool the gap behind is backfilled with gravel or soil from the excavation.

Swimming pool shapes

Swimming pools are traditionally rectangular in shape—the best format for swimming true lengths and widths. However, oval ones are also popular. It may also be possible to incorporate a Roman end to your pool. This is a half-rounded, usually stepped end at the shallow end of an otherwise rectangular pool, which allows you to enter the pool gradually, without having to dive or jump in from the side, or climb down a ladder.

Dog-leg, L-shaped and even triangular designs are available, as well as kidney-shaped pools which are softly rounded and can look attractive when the shape echoes existing curves in the garden. Similarly, a teardrop-shaped pool offers a softer shape.

When designing your own pool, it is best to keep the shape as simple as possible, both for practicality and appearance. Size is an important factor too: a useful gauge is to allow 86 to 108sq ft (8 to 10sq m) of pool area for each member of the family: this will also give sufficient space for friends. The minimum practicable size of pool is 24 × 12ft (7.2 × 3.6m).

Pool depth profiles

The shape of the base of the pool in profile is also an important factor. Excavated pools are often of the "hopper" type which has a level, shallow end for children and non-swimmers, with a deep end that is hopper-shaped for diving. The other type of pool, which is more suitable for adults, is one in which the base slopes steadily from the shallow end to the deep end.

Accessories and equipment

The swimming pool will need to be fitted with a number of accessories, some of which are essential to maintain the cleanliness of the water, and others which merely add to the enjoyment.

Circulation pump An electrically operated circulation pump is necessary to carry the

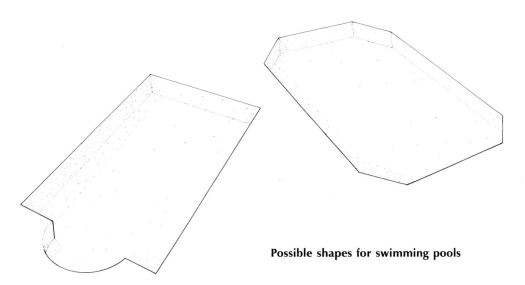

Possible shapes for swimming pools

Swimming pools 2

contents of the swimming pool to the filter unit and back to the pool. Pumps range in size from 0.75 to 1.5 horse power, depending on the size of the pool. Above-ground and below-ground versions are made. They are often incorporated into a filter unit.

Filter unit A filter unit is essential, linked to the pump, to suck water out of the pool, clean it of dust and debris from the surface, then return the water to the pool. There are basically two types: small-capacity cartridge; and high-capacity sand bed.

Cartridge filters are used for pools up to about 11,600 gallons (53,000 litres) capacity, and require regular maintenance to keep clear: when the pressure gauge attached to the unit registers that the flow is being impeded, the cartridge is removed and hosed down, or else replaced.

Sand bed filters, which may be connected to an integral pump, are available in numerous sizes to suit larger pools. Water is forced through this type of filter in the opposite direction to normal flow to flush out impurities: this "backwashing" is carried out once or twice a week.

Skimming weir and drain Set in the side of the pool walls, the skimmer removes any surface debris from the water, while the drain

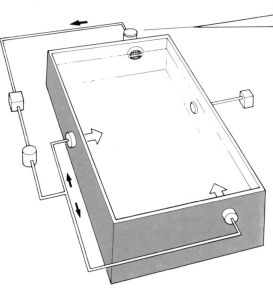

Accessories essential to a swimming pool include a filtration system connected to a pump. The skimmer removes dirt and debris from the surface of the water,

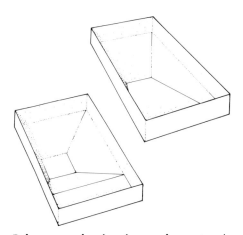

Below-ground swimming pools use tough vinyl liners to cover side walls built from blockwork or preformed panels and braces, with a screeded base.

outlet, set at the base of the pool, collects dirt which has sunk to the bottom. The skimmer and drain are both connected to the filtration system. After filtering away debris, they return the clean water to the pool via the pump.

The skimmer can usually be connected to the pool vacuum, and is used to remove debris from the floor of the pool.

Access ladder Essential for getting in and out of the pool, an access ladder is usually anchored to the concrete casting around the pool's rim.

Underwater illumination Not a vital accessory, but one which is very useful for swimming at night, and which enhances the appearance of the pool. Operating on a 300w rating, the lights usually have a 12-volt supply run from a transformer. They are normally set within a waterproof niche in the wall of the pool.

Heating system For comfortable use in tem-

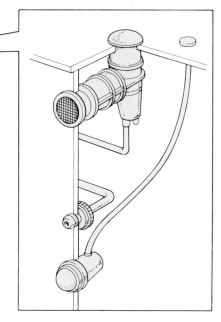

returning it via outlet nozzles set in the pool walls. A pool light is essential for night-time swimming, positioned underwater in the deep end.

perate climates some form of pool heating is vital. There are various options. A heat exchanger may be fitted between the pump and return inlets and connected to an oil- or gas-fired boiler. There may be spare capacity in your domestic central heating boiler. Electric heaters, although expensive to run, are also available.

Heat (or air) pumps may also be used. These work rather like a refrigerator in reverse, by drawing in heat from the surrounding air and ground, compressing it, concentrating its heat, and then transferring the heat to the pool water.

Solar heating is a very economical system for heating swimming pool water. One popu-lar type comprises a grid of heat-gathering black plastic tubes that are plumbed into the filtration circuit of the pool, which draws the water around the network of tubes. The grid can be housed at the poolside or on the roof of the house or changing and pump room.

SITING THE SWIMMING POOL

Trees and shelter Position the pool away from trees so that it will receive ample sunshine in the summer and will not collect dead leaves in autumn. Provide some form of shelter from the prevailing wind so that you can sit comfortably beside the pool.

Lie of the land A level site is generally best so that excavation is easier: on sloping ground it will be necessary to excavate or build up the ground levels. In some soils the considerable weight of water may cause the ground to subside, so ground that is marshy or soft should be avoided.

Existing services The location of existing drainage pipe runs and other underground services such as gas pipes and electricity cables must be determined before the site is finally chosen. If they have to be diverted to make way for the pool it will make the project more expensive.

Changing facilities and services Aim to locate the pool as near to the house as possible so that you can get changed in comfort and there is a ready supply of water for filling and topping up the pool, and an electrical supply to power the pool equipment.

Alternatively, arrange for a separate changing room and a home for the pump and filter units near the pool. There should also be a drain or soakaway nearby for draining the pool.

Poolside requirements There should be sufficient space around the pool to allow free movement for non-bathers. Ideally you should allow an area around the pool that is in total about the same size as the pool itself. Use concrete paving stones, bricks or timber decking. Avoid grass or gravel, as these are easily carried into the water on the feet of bathers.

Landscape the garden around the pool to blend with the surrounding scheme, perhaps using the spoil from the exca-vation to create banking for privacy and shelter. A barbecue unit or seating may be installed nearby.

Swimming pools 3

Pool covers There are two types of cover made for swimming pools. One is merely a winter cover, which is intended to keep wind-blown debris from fouling the water; the other is designed to conserve the heat of the water by acting as an insulating layer. Some types of insulating cover will allow the heat of the sun's rays to penetrate and warm the water while reducing the rate at which the heat escapes again.

Most pool covers can be stored at one end of the pool on a roller, from which they are drawn over the water to conserve the heat when the pool is not in use.

Pool enclosures can be anything from an inflatable plastic dome kept erect by air pressure to a glazed, framed structure rather like a greenhouse.

Setting out a sunken pool
Draw a scale plan of the pool and its relationship to the property and services, and consult your local planning and water authorities (see box, page 173). Set out the site accordingly, using working drawings available from the pool manufacturer. Within and beyond the site for the pool, clear an area of all vegetation, rocks and other obstructions, then drive in a timber datum peg about 6ft 6in (2m) away from the lowest edge of the site to indicate the finished level of the pool.

Roughly level the site if necessary. As a guide, drive more pegs in around the site and set to the same level as the datum peg using a spirit level on a plank of wood.

Working from one side of the proposed pool—the house side is probably best, to give you a reference point for measuring—set up stringlines and pegs to indicate one side of the pool. From these points plot the position of the other side of the pool and fix stringlines and pegs parallel to the first.

Set up more stringlines and pegs about 24in (600mm) outside the first set to allow space for the pool wall panels to be erected, and for the concrete supporting ring beams.

Indicate lines passing through the centre of the pool by setting up stringlines and pegs at right-angles, intersecting at the centre.

Marking curved ends
For a curved-ended pool, first plot out the

shape of a rectangular pool and mark the curves after that. Use an improvised pair of compasses to mark the curve: tie a spiked piece of timber to a piece of string the length of the curve radius (the manufacturer's instructions will give you this) and fix one end to a peg fixed at the pool midpoint. Scribe the arc on the ground, then repeat for the other corners of the pool.

As with the straight sides, mark a line 24in (600mm) from the curves for the wall panels and beams.

Mark out the positions for trenches to take the filtration pipes, electrical cables and other underground services.

Excavating the site
To dig out the pool you will probably need a mechanical digger. Small diggers can be hired by the day, with or without the driver. Make sure that you have a suitable site for

Hire a mechanical digger to excavate the hole for the pool according to pre-set guidelines and datum pegs.

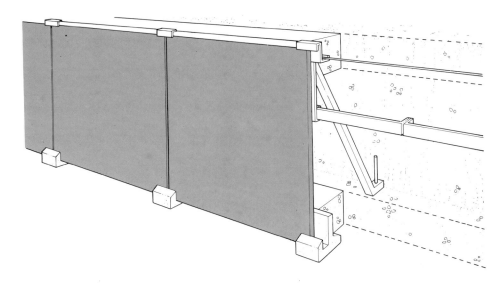

A panelled below-ground swimming pool consists of cast-concrete ring beams which anchor the footing blocks and the top rim, using inclined braces to support the panels. A metal clamping strap, bolted into place, surrounds the pool panel walls.

excavated soil, or arrange for it to be taken to a dump. While the hole is being dug, check that the depth is correct, paying particular attention to the level of the perimeter shelf on which the side walls are erected.

A surveyor's pole and Cowley level can also be hired to check the level of the pool floor against the datum peg driven into the ground: with this equipment you measure the Cowley level's distance above the datum peg, then get a helper to hold the sliding scale in the hole while you adjust the target through the Cowley level's viewfinder: the image must line up. By taking the measurement on the pole and subtracting that from the height of the Cowley level above the datum you can calculate the actual depth of the excavation.

Erecting the wall panels
The exact method of construction for the walls differs from make to make, but most use a similar system, and the following basic guide gives you an idea of what to expect.

Precast footing blocks, channelled to take the wall panels, are first set out around the perimeter of the pool excavation, on the shelf, so they straddle the joints between panels.

Lift the panels and slot them into the blocks, butting their edges tightly together. Special panels are made to house the skimmer, return outlets and any lights that are being installed: make sure these are positioned correctly. The skimmer should be near the deep end on the side facing the prevailing wind; the filter returns should be near the skimmer and on the opposite side, at the shallow end.

Fit the braces to the top of the panels, attached to their brackets, then attach the clamping strap that surrounds the entire pool: this fitting is tightly bolted.

After levelling and aligning the panels, the lower ring beam can be cast, together with iron reinforcing rods set in the trench. The ring beam is cast over the footing blocks. Brackets to support the upper ring beam may now be fitted.

Gun a bead of mastic down each joint between the wall panels, and to seal any accessories that have been fitted into the walls of the swimming pool.

Swimming pools 4

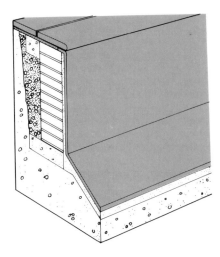
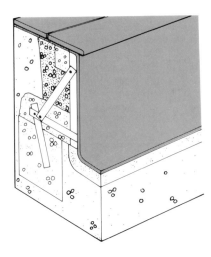

Masonry swimming pools are made by constructing concrete block walls on concrete foundations, with a ring beam at the top. The blocks are rendered, then fitted with a vinyl liner.

Vinyl liners are also used with frame and panel pool constructions, where preformed panels are anchored in concrete; the walls are backfilled with gravel to balance the water pressure.

Masonry wall pool construction

Another popular method of swimming pool construction involves casting a 9in (225mm) thick concrete foundation on which walls of precast concrete blocks are built to form the sides of the pool. A concrete ring beam is installed around the top of the excavation, and the walls are backfilled with gravel to help balance out the pressures of the water on the blockwork. The walls—and the base of the pool—are smooth-rendered, then covered with a waterproof vinyl liner, the top edge of which is firmly locked into a clamp around the rim.

Installing the filtration system

Before the base of the pool can be screeded ready to take the liner, install the filtration equipment and its associated plumbing. Assemble this according to the detailed instructions that come with the kit: this usually involves bolting on the relevant pieces. If there is to be a drain in the deep end of the pool, dig a hole to take this and run a channel under the ring beam to take the drainpipe connection.

Assemble all the associated pipework using the ABS plastic pipe and solvent-welded joints supplied for the underground or outside runs. Connect the polypropylene pipes to the pump using the screw-on connections supplied with the kit.

Install the electrical connections to an underwater light and run the cable back to the transformer in the pump room.

Screeding the floor

The floor of the swimming pool is screeded with a mortar mix consisting of 1 part cement to 6 parts soft sand, mixed in a hired motorized mixing machine (see pages 12 and 16). The mix should have a semi-dry consistency so that it will not run away on the sloping sections of the pool base.

Check that the base of the excavation is level, free from rocks and other obstructions, then shovel on the mortar in the flattest part of the base.

Level the mortar to a depth of 2in (50mm), using wooden pegs driven into the base as a guide. Trowel the mortar level and smooth in easily manageable sections, then leave to set

Screeding the pool Start to screed along the sides, working in easily manageable sections. Form the curved shape evenly to the floor of the pool.

hard before screeding the sides.

Mortar the sides of the pool, working from the deep end to the shallow end. Curve the mortar gently from the floor of the pool and over the footing blocks, tapering off about 2in (50mm) above the bottom edge of the wall panels.

Adding the liner
When the floor screed mortar has cured, take the liner into the pool and unfold it carefully. Working from the deep end, fit the edge of the liner into the receptor fitted along the top of the wall panels. Work towards the shallow end, smoothing out the liner as you go along.

To get rid of creases and bubbles in the liner, set up a vacuum cleaner with its nozzle inserted behind the liner through the skimmer. With the nozzle sealed carefully behind the liner air is sucked out from underneath to ensure a good fit.

Filling and backfilling
The job of filling the pool with water and backfilling behind the pool walls must be carried out concurrently or unequal pressure could cause the walls to warp out of alignment. Run garden hoses to the pool and start to fill with water: it is a job which can take many hours.

Start to fill the gap behind the wall panels so that you keep pace with the level of the water in the pool, and tamp the soil (or pea gravel) to compact it using a stout length of timber.

If you are fitting an underwater light, turn off the flow of water when the level reaches just below the fitting. Fit the outer gasket over the liner to align with that on the other side of the liner. Once this is screwed into place, the liner can be cut from within it and the light unit fitted, before the water flow is restarted. This procedure applies to the other accessories fitted in the wall of the pool, such as the skimmer and return outlets. Cut the flow of water for the final time when the level reaches halfway up the skimmer mouth. The filtration system should then be checked for any leaks.

Casting the top ring beam
To complete the pool installation, a concrete ring beam is cast around the rim of the pool and a pool ladder set in it. Leave an allowance between the beam and the top edge of the pool walls so that you can fit the paving coping stones on top, bedded on a dryish mortar mix.

Play areas/slides

Ideally, if space permits, children should be allocated a separate area in the garden. This should be somewhere you can ensure their safety while at the same time protecting lawns and flower beds from the inevitable rough-and-tumble. When planning, consider the future too, as the play area might progress from a playground to something more like a children's garden as they grow older.

Boundaries

First of all, think about how you can provide some form of demarcation for the children's garden. Use a low barrier, say a simple post-and-rail type such as ranch fencing, to hem them in without their being out of sight from the house or another part of the garden. The fence should be substantial enough to stand up to rough play, but should not have pointed poles or protruding wires which could be dangerous.

As an alternative, a low wall may be built using reconstructed concrete walling blocks, bricks or pierced screen walling blocks. This is less satisfactory as it is a more permanent structure and cannot so easily be removed once there is no further use for the play area.

Provide a gate, fitted with a good latch on the opposite side, if you do not want young children to wander.

Surface materials

Choosing the most suitable surface for the children's garden depends on the age of the children and the use to which the play area will be put. There are various options.

Concrete slabs Although an area paved with slabs or cast concrete will offer the toughest, most hardwearing surface for a play area where bicycles are going to be ridden, it is not a sensible choice where small children will be playing; neither should it be used as a base for a climbing frame, slide or other structure from which they might fall.

In its favour, however, concrete does drain quickly and dry rapidly, which is useful when children want to play outside after it has been raining. Choose the smooth-faced slabs in preference to riven, textured or patterned types, which are more likely to cause grazes.

Gravel Gravel, like concrete, is not the most friendly surface for boisterous games and also tends to create a mess throughout the rest of the garden as the stones are flung everywhere, or dragged along by feet.

Sand Suitable only for small areas such as underneath a climbing frame, at the end of a slide, or beneath a fixed toy, sand will break a fall and prevent a potentially serious accident. On the other hand, it will attract neighbourhood cats (which could give rise to a serious health hazard) and after heavy rainfall it remains wet for some time.

If a sandpit is provided, it is important to ensure that the sand is kept contained, covered when not in use, and clean. Special playpit sand will not stain clothes or skin, and can be obtained pre-bagged from garden centres and DIY stores.

Grass A turfed area soon deteriorates if bicycles are ridden across it and ball games played on it. It is, however, the most suitable surface to use as a play area, and although during spring and summer it will almost certainly become very worn, re-turfing the area in early autumn will allow it to recover and be ready for use again in spring.

Timber A timber decking, although not really practicable for large areas, can be useful as a surface for a play area that contains a climbing frame, where the deck can become part of the frame itself.

Assembling a slide

A slide may be constructed from timber using a framework of 3 × 2in (75 × 50mm) softwood as the main supports. Fix four posts in the ground—using metal fence spikes or setting them in concrete—to form the corner posts of a rectangle, between which you can fix a stepladder for climbing to the top of the slide. The posts, and ultimately the height of the slide's chute, depend on the age of the children, but as an overall guide, a small slide can be about 30in (760mm) high at the top; a large one about 8ft (2.4m).

The ladder, made from lengths of 3 × 1in (75 × 25mm) softwood bolted diagonally between the outer and inner posts, is fitted with 1in (25mm) diameter dowel rungs housed in holes drilled in each stile (the side upright of the ladder). To save having to construct a stepladder from scratch, you could use an

Make a slide by erecting four stout posts as the supports for a ladder bolted diagonally between them. Fit a platform and guard rail between the uprights and attach the chute—a panel of marine plywood—to the top.

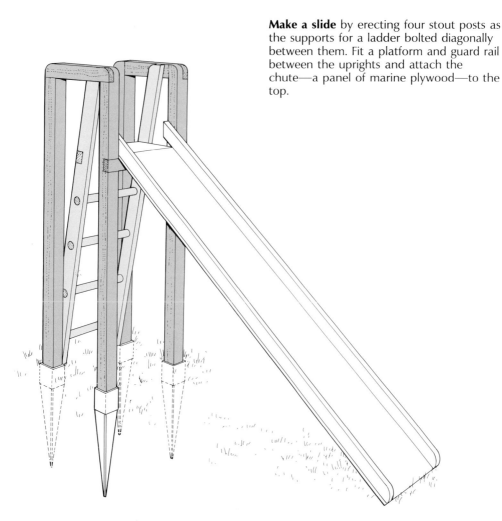

old wooden stepladder, provided it is sound. Bolt the stepladder between the posts, anchoring the stiles in place.

Bolt a crossbar at the top of the main side support posts as a guard rail and stiffening batten. A stout crossbar near the top of the outer posts forms the support for the chute itself and also a platform at the top of the steps. The chute is constructed from a length of marine plywood, stiffened below by a pair of 3 × 2in (75 × 50mm) lengths of timber to which it is screwed, which run the full length of the chute.

A pair of side rails made of 3 × 1in (75 × 25mm) planed softwood is screwed to each side of the chute from beneath. These rails must be sanded absolutely smooth and the top edges rounded off to prevent splinters when the slide is in use. The chute surface itself should also be sanded thoroughly and given several coats of gloss exterior varnish to protect it from the weather. The chute can be made more slippery by applying a wax polish at frequent intervals after varnishing.

Swings and seesaws

A tree swing

If you have a tree in your garden with a suitably strong bough—say, about 6in (150mm) in diameter—at a convenient height of about 6–10ft (1.8–3m) and virtually horizontal, you could attach a swing to it.

Use a strong, thick rope or nylon line to support a wooden (or proprietary plastic) swing seat. To suspend the swing, use a single length of rope attached at each side of the seat and looped at the top. Pass the rope through the holes at the sides of the seat and double-knot it.

Throw the looped end of the rope over the bough, then pass the seat itself through the loop, securing the rope around the bough. Position the swing so it will not collide with the trunk.

A tyre swing

Instead of using a conventional swing seat, string up an old car or tractor tyre. Either use one rope so that the tyre hangs vertically or suspend the tyre horizontally on four evenly spaced ropes.

Constructing a swing

A swing can be constructed from a pair of stout planed timber posts measuring about 4in (100mm) sq, fixed in the ground and encased in concrete or housed in metal fencing spikes. A cross-piece of the same timber, its ends tenoned and housed in a notch cut in the top of each post, forms a rail on which a single swing seat, or a series of swing items such as a trapeze bar, tyre, knotted rope or rope ladder with wooden rungs, can be supported. For a series of swings, space the uprights apart accordingly—but not so that the crossbar is more than about 8ft (2.4m) long unless an additional central upright post is provided to prevent it from sagging. A second crossbar bolted to the first for extra strength will also prevent the frame from twisting.

Support the ropes of the swing on eyebolts

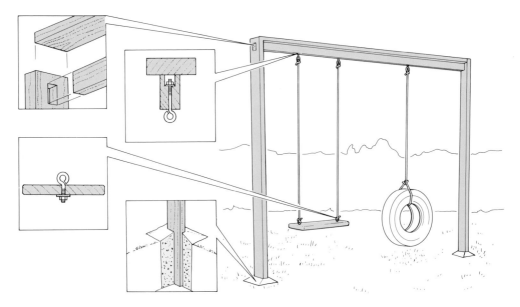

A swing can be made from a pair of upright posts with a horizontal cross-beam notched into the top. A second cross-timber adds extra rigidity, while the swing itself is suspended from eyebolts by nylon cord. Erect the swing on an existing grassed area to afford some measure of protection in case of a fall. The posts should be supported by concrete castings or metal fence post spikes.

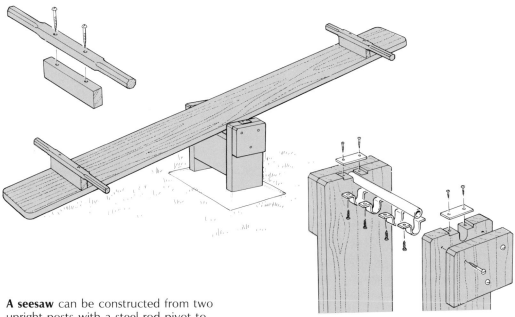

A seesaw can be constructed from two upright posts with a steel rod pivot to which is attached the seesaw plank, strengthened below by a stout timber batten the length of the plank. Handles and buffers complete the construction, which should be set up on a fairly soft ground surface in case of falls.

housed in holes drilled in the crossbar: use a thick nylon twine, securely knotted through the eyebolt, or a stout chain.

Make the swing seat itself from a length of 9 × 1in (225 × 25mm) timber, thoroughly sanded, treated with preservative and varnished to protect it against the weather. Insert eyebolts through the underside of the seat, centrally placed at each side, and attach the rope to this. A simple trapeze bar can be made from a length of 1in (25mm) diameter dowel tied to the ropes at each end.

Making a seesaw

A seesaw can be constructed from timber, using a pair of stout 5 × 4in (125 × 100) upright posts driven into the ground about 12in (300mm) apart, and protruding about 18in (450mm). A notch cut in the top of each post will accept a 1in (25mm) diameter length of steel rod, which forms the pivot of the seesaw. Retain the rod in its notches with a steel bracket screwed over the top.

The seesaw itself is a length of 9 × 1in (225 × 25mm) softwood, planed and sanded, then sealed with varnish. Stiffen the plank further by screwing a length of 3 × 1in (75 × 25mm) softwood along the underside, driving the screws through the top of the plank, and countersinking their heads below the surface.

The plank is attached to the pivot rod by metal brackets screwed over the rod from underneath. A pair of handles is fitted to the seesaw plank, about 18in (450mm) in from each end: these may be lengths of dowel or metal rod fixed with brackets, or else a shaped wooden handle screwed on from underneath. Buffers in the form of thick, replaceable foam rubber wrapped in polythene can be attached to the underside of each seat by pinning overlaps of the polythene to the sides and end of the plank. When worn, the buffers can be renewed.

Climbing frames

The basic framework

A sturdy rectangular or square framework can be erected using 4in (100mm) sq planed softwood as the main supporting uprights, with intermediates of smaller-section 3 × 2in (75 × 50in) timber. The top rail of the climbing frame should be constructed from the smaller-section timber, bolted to the main uprights and screwed to the intermediate posts.

For greater rigidity, cut halving joints at the corners of the surrounding top rail, and notch the intermediate bracing horizontals between the perimeter rails. The arrangement of the intermediate rails depends on the configuration of the climbing frame, and what facilities are to be included. The swing, knotted climbing rope, rope ladder and climbing tyre are strung on eyebolts from the rails.

Lengths of 1½in (35mm) diameter hardwood dowel or steel rods are fixed into holes drilled in the supporting uprights to form climbing rungs and somersault bars, or fitted between the intermediate horizontal rails at the top of the frame to act as the monkey bars.

Building a metal climbing frame

A climbing frame constructed from tough steel tubing and proprietary galvanized metal couplings is easy to erect. The fittings are commonly available, and consist of a range of tee-sockets, single sockets, elbows, straight couplers and end cups, which can be used to design the climbing frame. The structure is also easy to dismantle and move.

The steel tubes are sold either by the manufacturer of the fittings, or at DIY stores builder's merchants or scaffolding suppliers. They come in a choice of six diameters from ⅞in (21mm) to 2⅜in (60mm). To join the tubes, simply slot on the fittings and tighten them using a hexagonal (Allen) key.

Dig holes in the ground for the main supporting tubes, setting them in concrete if the frame is to be permanently sited. If the frame is to be moved, embed tubes of larger diameter into the ground in concrete supports and then slot the frame supports into these: the fit does not need to be precise, as the weight of the completed frame, and its span, will prevent it from wobbling.

Dig holes about 12in (300mm) deep and about the same square, fill with hardcore and

ram down with a stout length of timber. Set the lengths of tubing upright in the holes and pour in the concrete to retain them. Compact the concrete mix around the tubes so that it sets level with the ground.

Once the ground supports have been set, insert the uprights for the climbing frame and

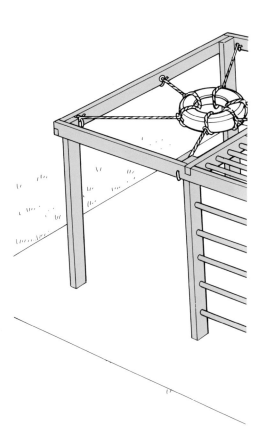

A climbing frame can be built to the shape and size you want. It does not have to be a simple rectangle but perhaps an L-shaped unit; or you could add extensions at each side to form a Z-shaped frame. Set the main uprights in concrete or fence post spikes and connect the horizontal top beam with halving joints. Bolt on all major components, and slot dowel or metal rod

connect them to each other by inserting lengths of tubing into the sockets in the upright; these tubes should be horizontal so the pairs of sockets must be level.

Should you need to cut lengths of the metal tubing to fit, mark the length in pencil, wrap paper around, aligning its ends with the line, and cut with a hacksaw: the paper acts as a guide to cutting squarely. File the cut ends of the tubing to remove burrs.

Build the climbing frame up to the preferred geometric shape, remembering to connect all exposed ends of the tubing to form a series of interlinking square frames.

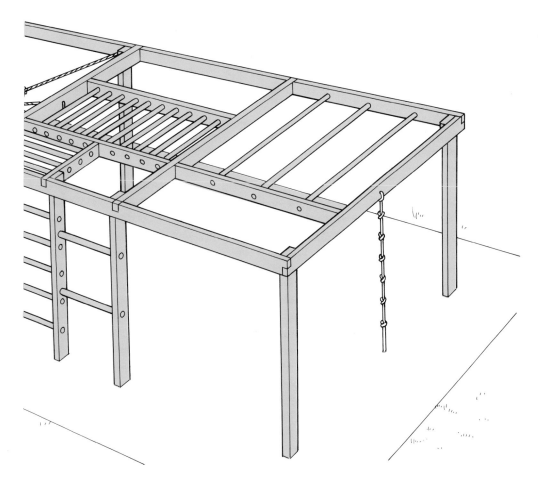

rungs or monkey or somersault bars in the uprights or intermediate horizontals. String ladders, swings or climbing ropes from the frame.

Tree houses

Tree houses

A tree house can be anything from a simple wooden platform inserted between the branches, and reached via a rope ladder, to an elaborate play hut complete with windows, door, roof and sturdy staircase for access aloft.

There are several factors to bear in mind when considering the construction of a tree house, not least of which is the availability of a suitable tree with strong enough trunk, boughs and branches to support the structure. However, safety for the children is the main concern, second only to the welfare of the tree itself. For example, it is imperative that the structure is properly supported, not simply by wedging it in a handy junction of branches and trunk, but by transferring its load to the ground.

Your tree house should, in effect, be accommodated around the tree, rather than being

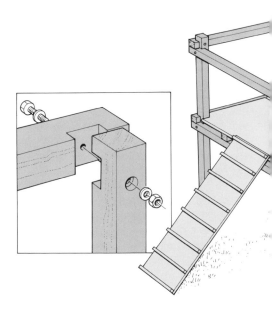

Tree houses and platforms must be constructed securely and safely. Joints should be held firmly together using nuts and bolts with washers. The heads of bolts

permanently attached. It should be unnecessary to make any fixings directly to the tree, and you should avoid cutting branches where possible. Take these points into consideration.

Independent platform The tree itself must have room to grow over the years, without dislodging the play house, and to this end it is best to arrange for the platform base to be independent of the tree itself, using a series of supporting posts, or stilts, that are firmly secured to the ground at the base of the tree. Set the posts—which should be about 3in (75mm) square—in concrete, avoiding damage to the roots of the tree, or else fit them into metal fence post spikes.

Room to grow The small gaps between the base of the house and the branches of the tree will allow the tree to grow unhindered, and you could fill these with a flexible sealant such as foam rubber to keep out draughts.

A sturdy base The walls or surrounding frame-

work of the tree house should be constructed on a sturdy platform base, which will not move when climbed upon, attached to the supporting posts. The base itself may be a solid panel of $\frac{3}{4}$in (20mm) exterior-grade chipboard or plywood, fixed to a rigid framework of joists, themselves attached to an outer horizontal support frame fixed to the posts.

Guard rails and walls The tree house must have, at least, sturdy guard rails or, better still, walls to prevent a fall from the tree. If you extend the support posts beyond the base of the tree house you will be able to attach wall panels or guard rails to the sides, using nuts and bolts for strength. The wall panels themselves can be made from woven or overlapping fence panels (standard-sized or cut-down); you might even be able to assemble a small prefabricated garden shed on the base platform.

Access Access to the tree house can simply be via a rope ladder strung around a stout branch of the tree, although a pair of proprietary wooden ladders firmly attached at the top would provide a more convenient route. You could even construct a permanent flight of steps, or a spiral staircase.

Ideally, you should arrange for the ladder or steps to enter through the base of the tree house, to avoid the danger of a fall from a side entry.

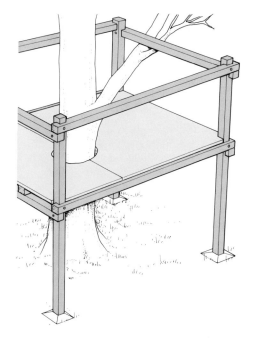

and the nuts should be recessed into the timbers. Ladders must also be well secured, whether they are wooden or of rope.

CLIMBING ROPES AND ROPE LADDERS

Perhaps the simplest type of garden plaything is a climbing rope strung from a high tree branch. Tie the rope firmly around the bough and allow to dangle down to ground level. Knot the rope at 24in (600mm) intervals to give suitable foot and hand holds.

To make a rope ladder, use strong ropes and lengths of timber, 12in × 2in (300mm × 50mm). Drill holes through the timbers, about 1in (25mm) from the ends. Thread a rope through each hole and knot firmly underneath. Continue knotting and threading, spacing the rungs 9in (225mm) apart.

A sandpit-paddling pool 1

A dual sandpit and paddling pool, specially designed so that the water and sand will not mingle, is an attractive addition to a play area.

The basic frame
The design of the sandpit/paddling pool is simple: it consists of a rectangular box made from planks of wood and divided into two halves by a pair of planks, fitted with a slatted wooden seat-cum-lid, under which the children can store buckets, spades and other toys. The sandpit and paddling pool areas are fitted with slatted lift-off covers to keep out animals and debris that would foul the sand and water.

The unit is straightforward to construct using old floorboards or skirting boards, or new planed timber planks measuring about 6 × 1in (150 × 25mm).

Preparing the joints
The corners of the frame are connected using simple halving joints. First cut the boards to length, bearing in mind that they should be about 12in (300mm) longer than the finished size of the box, to allow for the overlapping joints.

Stack the long and short boards together so that they are aligned at one end. Tape them together temporarily while you mark out the joints. With the stacked boards lying flat, measure in from the end a distance of 6in (150mm) and scribe a pencil line across at this point against a try square. Continue the squared line around one edge of the stacked boards and onto the opposite side.

Now measure a distance of 1in (25mm) in from the scribed line and scribe a parallel line around the boards in the same way as before, using the try square: this gives the thickness of the joint, which is equal to the thickness of the timber. It is best to measure the actual thickness of the board, as given dimensions are only nominal, and slight differences may occur.

Measure across the boards from a long edge a distance equal to half the width of a board and scribe a line at this point, connecting the parallel lines at right-angles to them. This gives you the depth of the joint. Release the boards from the tape and continue the

marking lines around onto the opposite face of each individual board. The boards which were central in the stack must be marked according to the parallel lines marked on one edge.

Mark the joints on the opposite end of each board in the same way.

Cutting the halving joints
Cut the halving joints by placing the boards, stacked and taped together again, in a vice or workbench jaws. Saw down the parallel lines from the scribed edge as far as the joint depth lines. Repeat for the joints on the other end of the boards.

Free the boards and chop out the finger of waste from each using a wood chisel.

Assembling the basic box
Slot the halving joints together to form the rectangular box. If necessary, dismantle and make any adjustments to the component parts. Continue to reassemble the box without adhesive until you are confident the pieces will fit, then dismantle the box again and apply PVA woodworking adhesive to the joint faces, then reassemble. Clamp up the joints and set aside until the adhesive has dried.

Fitting the dividers
Measure the distance between the two long sides of the box frame and cut two lengths of board to fit. Mark guidelines on the inside of each side board for positioning the dividers: as a guide, these should be about 24in (600mm) apart. Slot the dividers between the sides of the box and drill clearance holes for screws through the side boards and into their ends. Insert screws and tighten to secure the dividers.

Making the slatted lids
The slatted lids for the paddling pool, sandpit and storage area between the dividers are simply loose-fitting, although the storage box/seat lid with hinges could be attached to one of the dividers.

To make a basic slatted lid, construct a simple butt-jointed frame of $2 \times \frac{1}{2}$in (50 x 12mm) softwood to fit inside the perimeter of the sandpit or paddling pool compartment using nails to connect the pieces.

Now pin a ledge of 1in sq (25mm sq) softwood around the frame, aligned with the top edge.

Make up a slatted square of softwood to fit within the butt-jointed frame as the lid by pinning 2 × $\frac{1}{2}$in (50 × 12mm) slats of softwood at right-angles to formers (battens) of the same timber, spaced near each end of the slats, and one centrally. This assembly slots into the butt-jointed frame, and is nailed to it. The ends of the slats, which should be spaced about $\frac{1}{2}$in (12mm) apart, should overlap the framework so that it finishes flush with the outside edge of the thin ledge fixed

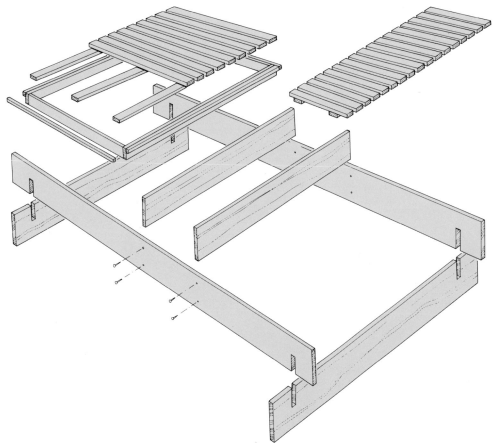

The combined paddling pool and sandpit is made from reclaimed floorboards, connected at the corners with halving joints for strength, and divided into three compartments, with two dividers fixed to form a central compartment. The sandpit and paddling pool are fitted with slatted top lids, while the central compartment for toys has a slatted seat-cum-lid. To make the paddling pool waterproof, a proprietary garden pond liner is used, pinned or stapled to the top edge of the compartment walls.

A sandpit-paddling pool 2

around the butt-jointed section.

Drop the completed slatted top into the compartment of the main box to check the fit. Assemble a matching top for the other compartment.

The slatted top for the divider compartment is of simpler construction: simply pin slats to a pair of formers cut to fit along the inside edges of the dividers.

Finish the unit by applying clear preservative or preservative stain.

Alternatively, substitute the slatted compartment tops with solid tops of exterior-grade plywood, fitted with a central handle for lifting. Plywood tops need to be thoroughly treated with preservative, then coated with exterior-quality varnish to protect the wood from the weather.

Fitting a pool liner

The paddling pool section of the unit must be fitted with a flexible pool liner to make it waterproof. Cut a square of vinyl liner to fit within the compartment, lapping up the sides and just over the edges. Pin the liner to the top edge of the compartment and trim off the excess with a sharp knife. At the corners,

fold over the flap of liner and pin this in place, too.

Emptying the pool is simply a matter of lifting the box frame to pour out the water. As an alternative, drill a hole through the side of the end plank and the liner and fit a plastic tap used for water butts. The vinyl liner must then be sealed to the board at the hole, using waterproof adhesive, to stop the water seeping behind the liner.

Constructing the base

Unless you provide a suitable surface for the paddling pool/sandpit to rest on you will find that the sand will be spread onto the surrounding garden. A hard surface should be provided on a base from which the sand can be swept back into the pit.

Concrete paving slabs make the most practical surface, and should be laid in an area about one slab wider than the box itself all around, with a further slab-wide paved area beyond at a slightly higher level. This is done by sinking the main surface about 4in (100mm) below ground level, with the higher skirt of slabs at ground level. This confines most of the sand to the play area.

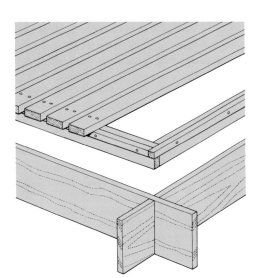

Slatted lids are made from a simple framework which slots into the compartments.

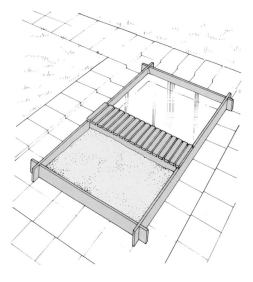

Contain the sand by setting the entire unit in a sunken area lined with slabs, surrounded by a higher skirt of slabs.

Bird accessories

Although birds can be a menace to soft fruit and seedlings, it is still a pleasure to see them in the garden—especially if they can be distracted from causing damage. Bird boxes, baths and feeding tables will bring many species to a garden.

Making a bird box

Use unstained, unplaned softwood, $\frac{3}{4}$in (20mm) thick, cut with a fine-toothed panel saw. To house smaller species, make a box to these dimensions: base, $4\frac{1}{2}$in (115mm) square; front, $6\frac{1}{4} \times 6$in (160 × 150mm); sides, 5in (125mm) wide by $7\frac{1}{4}$in (185mm) at the front and $9\frac{1}{4}$in (235mm) at the back; roof, $7\frac{1}{2} \times 6\frac{1}{2}$in (190 × 165mm), bevelled along one of the shorter edges; back panel, $12 \times 7\frac{1}{4}$in (300 × 185mm); finally, two slats, $6\frac{1}{4}$in long and $\frac{3}{4}$in deep (160 × 15mm). Smooth all the cut edges.

Drill the holes: the entrance hole, $1\frac{1}{4}$in (32mm) in diameter, in the top half of the front, and a $\frac{1}{4}$in (6mm) hole $\frac{1}{2}$in (12mm) beneath this for the perch; two $\frac{1}{4}$in (6mm) drainage holes in the base; small holes, top and bottom, in the back panel for screws.

Assemble the box, without the roof, using glue and panel pins. Insert a 4in (100mm) length of $\frac{1}{4}$in (6mm) dowel into the small hole, half inside and half outside the box, to make the perch. Glue and pin one of the slats between the sides and against the back panel. This will create a space for ventilation. Place the roof on top. This is wedged in place by the second slat that is bevelled and secured to the back piece. Secure the front of the roof with a screw eye. (Remove the roof once a year, when the nest has been vacated, to clean the box with water—but no detergent.)

When the glue has dried, apply wood preservative to the outside of the box; leave to dry before fixing the box.

The size of the entry hole and whether or not there is a perch will influence which species of birds use the box. Never place a box in full sun as too much heat can kill young birds. Keep it out of the reach of predators, from below and above (a box high on a fence can expose birds to a prowling cat).

Birdbaths

A concrete bath can be made using the inside of a dustbin lid as a mould. Place the lid, upside down, in a weighted dustbin and line it with a polythene sheet; this will make it easier to remove the bath. Spread a $\frac{3}{4}$in (20mm) layer of concrete in the mould. Press in a piece of wire mesh for reinforcement, then add a similar layer of concrete on top. Centre the base of a second dustbin in the mould and fill the gap with more concrete. Smooth with a trowel. When the concrete has begun to harden, remove the top dustbin and turn the lid handle-side up onto a flat surface; tap to release the birdbath. Decorative cuts can be made in the concrete at this stage. When dry, wedge the bath onto a tree stump or use a garden urn as a base. Keep it filled with clean water and ice-free; scrub occasionally to remove algae.

Birdtables

A birdtable comprises a flat wooden surface with side pieces that prevent the food from sliding off and provide a perch. The table must be firmly attached to a post sunk well into the ground—a 5ft (1.5m) post needs a 12in (300mm) anchor; or secure the table to a tree or wall. Hooks around the edge of the table can be used to suspend nets of seed and lumps of fat. Cheese and bruised fruit will also attract birds; bread is not very good for them.

A small bird box

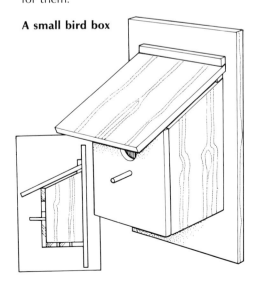

Glossary/Information 1

Aggregate Particles of sand or stone mixed with cement and water to make concrete.

Arris rail Horizontal rail, triangular in section, used in closeboard fencing.

Ballast Sand and gravel mix used in making concrete.

Batten A narrow strip of wood.

Batter The slope of the face of a wall that leans backwards or tapers.

Blocks Building units moulded from concrete, also called breezeblocks. Pierced versions are used for decorative screen walling. Reconstituted blocks are made from natural stone aggregates.

Bolster chisel A chisel with a wide blade, used in conjunction with a club hammer for breaking or cutting masonry.

Brick trowel A trowel used for handling and placing mortar in bricklaying.

Builder's square A large try square, used for checking squareness in building walls or laying foundations.

Cement Fine grey powder, a mix of calcined limestone and clay; used with water and sand to make mortar, or with water, sand and aggregate to make concrete.

Claw hammer Heavyweight general-purpose hammer, with a claw at the back for levering out nails.

Club hammer A heavy hammer used in building work, usually with a chisel.

Cold chisel A long, slim chisel used for cutting or breaking masonry.

Concrete Sand, cement and aggregate, mixed with water to form a hard building material for slabs and foundations.

Coping Bevelled wooden strips or cast concrete pieces used to deflect rainwater from the face of a fence or wall.

Closeboard A type of fence consisting of vertical overlapping feather-edged boards attached to arris rails between posts.

Creosote Oil- and tar-based preservative.

Datum A wooden peg set at a particular position, forming the point from which measurements are taken during, say, the laying of slabs or concrete.

Fall A downward slope for rainwater drainage.

Feather-edge The edge of a wooden board in closeboard fencing, which is narrower at one side than the other.

Float A wooden tool used for applying and smoothing cement renderings and concrete with a fine texture.

Footing Narrow concrete foundation for a wall, or the base of garden steps.

Frog The angled depression in one or two faces of some bricks.

Galvanized A protective coating of zinc to prevent nails, screws and other materials from rusting.

Gravel boards Horizontal lengths of timber at the base of a fence to protect the cladding from rising damp.

Handsaw Saw with a flexible, unsupported blade used for cutting solid timber and man-made boards.

Hardcore Broken bricks, concrete or stones used as a sub-base beneath foundations and paving.

Hardwood Timber cut from deciduous trees (not necessarily hard in a literal sense).

Joist A horizontal wood beam used to support a floor, deck or wall.

Mastic A non-setting flexible compound used to seal joints.

Mitre A joint formed between two pieces of wood by cutting bevels of equal angles at the ends of each piece.

Mortise A rectangular recess cut in timber which receives a matching tongue or tenon.

Nosing The front edge of a step, often protruding from the riser.

Panel In fencing, any prefabricated section, usually made of woven larch strips in a thin frame.

Pavers Small-scale blocks or bricks used in path and patio laying.

Picket (or palisade) A post-and-rail fence with thin, usually pointed, vertical pales attached to the rails.

Pilaster A hollow channelled block used to construct piers in screen block walling.

Pilot hole A small-diameter hole drilled prior to the insertion of a woodscrew, as a guide for the thread.

Planter An enclosed, usually raised, container for soil used as a planting bed.

Post-and-rail Any type of fence that comprises vertical posts with horizontal rails between.

Render A thin layer of cement mortar spread on exterior walls to give a smooth, protective finish.

Riser The vertical part of a step.

Rustic poles Poles, used for fences and arches, which are irregular in shape, and which sometimes have bark attached.

Screed A thin layer of mortar applied to give a smooth surface on which to build brick or block walls, or as a finish for concrete.

Seasoned Describes timber which has matured to reduce sap and moisture content, making it easier to work, with greater resistance to rot.

Slabs Moulded concrete units in various sizes used as paving.

Soakaway A pit filled with rubble, into which water drains and percolates to earth.

Softwood Timber cut from coniferous (cone-bearing) trees.

Spike A metal preformed spike with a collar at the top used in fixing fence posts and other vertical timbers to the ground.

Spirit level A tool with a bubble vial used for checking horizontal levels; some types have a vertical vial and angle-finder.

Tamp To pack down firmly with repeated blows, as in casting concrete.

Tenon A projecting tongue on the end of a piece of wood which fits into a corresponding mortise.

Tread The horizonal part of a step.

Try square A tool for checking right-angles.

Wallplate A horizontal timber beam placed along a wall to support joists or rafters, spreading their load.

Wall tie A strip of metal or bent wire used to connect sections of new masonry together, or to strengthen existing masonry.

Warps Twists in lengths of timber; such timber should be rejected.

Weep hole A small hole at the base of a wall to allow absorbed water to drain away.

Although this book deals with construction projects in some detail, no one book can contain all the information you are likely to need. The keen garden-maker will find a wealth of helpful books and magazines available nationwide, which will give more detail about specific points than is possible in this volume.

Where modern techniques, materials and equipment can be used, these have been mentioned where relevant in *Garden Structures*, but by keeping in touch with the monthly developments listed in popular journals it is often possible to discover further shortcuts and less expensive options—in addition to keeping abreast of current trends, new products and the advice of other experts in the field.

Listed below, with a selection of helpful books, are some of the monthly magazines currently available. These regularly feature articles which are relevant to the subjects described in this book.

Monthly magazines

The Gardener, Home & Law Publishing Ltd, Greater London House, Hampstead Road, London NW1 7QQ.

Practical Gardening, EMAP National Publications, Bushfield House, Orton Centre, Peterborough PE2 0UW.

Practical Householder, Home & Law Publishing Ltd, Greater London House, Hampstead Road, London NW1 7QQ.

Do It Yourself, Link House Magazines Ltd, Link House, Dingwall Avenue, Croydon CR9 2TA.

DIY Week, Benn Publications Ltd, Sovereign Way, Tonbridge, Kent TN9 1RW.

Books

Collins Complete Do It Yourself Manual, Albert Jackson & David Day, William Collins Sons & Co, 1986.

Information 2

The Complete Home Improvement Manual, Consultant Editor Richard Wiles, Dragon's World Ltd, 1986.

The Outside Handyman, John McGowan & Roger DuBern, Swallow Publishing Ltd, 1984.

The Garden Handyman, Richard Wiles, Marshall Cavendish Ltd, 1985.

The Small Garden Book, John Brookes, Marshall Cavendish Editions, 1978.

Creative Garden Projects, Richard Wiles, Salamander Books Ltd, 1985.

Directories of suppliers
Benn's Guide, Benn Business Information Services Ltd, 1989.
This lists do-it-yourself/home improvement/building products and suppliers; garden and leisure products and other associated materials and equipment.

Building materials and services
Builders Merchants Federation, 15 Soho Square, London W1V 5FB.

Brick Development Association, Woodside House, Winkfield, Windsor, Berkshire SL4 2DX.

Rules and regulations
Certain aspects of garden construction described in this volume will require you to consult your local authority's Building Control Department for permission under the planning rules, which govern the appearance of developments and their effect on the environment. Other aspects are covered by the Building Regulations, which deal with the safety of structures— particularly those which front a boundary with a highway.

On the question of Planning Permission, the following points should be noted:

Sheds and greenhouses
You will not need planning permission for a shed or a greenhouse provided that:
● A shed or greenhouse does not cover more than half the area of the garden, not including the area occupied by the house.
● It is not more than 3m (10ft) high, or 4m with a ridged roof.
● No part projects beyond any wall of the house that faces a road.

Swimming pools
A swimming pool is generally exempt from planning permission, unless you live in a conservation area, although the Water Authorities must be notified: water rates will usually rise on installation of a swimming pool.

Gates, walls, fences and hedges
Gates, walls and fences are permitted under the Planning Rules provided that:
● They are not more than 2m (6ft 6in) high.
● They are no more than 1m (3ft 3in) high if they adjoin a highway.
Hedges can be any height in any location in the garden.

Index 1

Index 2

Index 3/acknowledgements

Acknowledgments
Artists: Stan North, Rick Blakely, Steve Cross.

The publishers have made every effort to ensure that all instructions given in this book are accurate and safe, but they cannot accept liability for any resulting injury, damage or loss to either person or property whether direct or consequential and howsoever arising. The author and publishers will be grateful for any information which will assist them in keeping future editions up to date.

Typesetting by Lasertext Ltd, Manchester
Origination by M&E Reproductions, North Fambridge, Essex
Produced by Mandarin Offset. Printed and bound in Hong Kong.

THE R.H.S. ENCYCLOPEDIA OF PRACTICAL GARDENING

EDITOR-IN-CHIEF: CHRISTOPHER BRICKELL

Mitchell Beazley and the Royal Horticultural Society have joined forces to produce this practical, clear and fully comprehensive library of gardening.

"hard to fault" *Stephen Lacey*

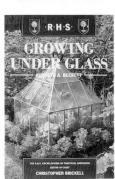

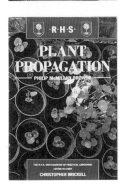

Also available: **GARDENING TECHNIQUES** by Alan Titchmarsh

Forthcoming titles include:

ORGANIC GARDENING by Roy Lacey, **WATER GARDENING** by Philip Swindells

MITCHELL BEAZLEY